OUR
LIFE
OUR
WAY

A Memoir of Active Faith, Profound Love and Courageous Disability Rights

William L. Rush and Christine F. Robinson

ISBN 978-1-64515-926-1 (paperback)
ISBN 978-1-64515-927-8 (digital)

Christian Faith Publishing, Inc.
832 Park Avenue
Meadville, PA 16335
www.christianfaithpublishing.com

Printed in the United States of America

Acknowledgements

What began as a labour of love to complete this book for Bill became an unexpected spiritual journey of drawing closer to God. For over 14 years, through seasons of silence and also much activity, the Holy Spirit has worked in and with me, to bring this work to fruition.

Throughout my writing journey, God, in His faithfulness to complete the work that He had begun in Bill, brought many individuals to provide an endless (and unique) array of talents and gifts to both encourage and to guide me. I will not begin to list all of you. You know who you are. Please know I am deeply and eternally grateful for each and every one of you.

Christine Robinson

RUSH'S RULE

"MY PLACE

MY BODY

MY LIFE

MY WAY"

I AM NOT A CLIENT.
I AM NOT A RESIDENT.
I AM NOT A PATIENT.

I AM A PERSON.
I AM A CITIZEN.

I AM AN INDIVIDUAL; I have
value and worth - recognize this.

Photo of Rush's Rule Framed and Displayed in William
Rush's apartment and later in the Rush Robinson home.

Preface

Rush's Rule

"My Place
My Body
My Life
My Way"

"Rush's Rule" was created by Bill in response to an incident when at attendant would not listen to him.

"One night an Aide tried to take off my wheelchair tray and I said "NO" because I was not ready for the tray to come off. The Aide threatened to leave me three times. I would not be threatened or blackmailed by my aides. So I said, LEAVE. The next day I asked my mom to make a framed copy of Rush's Rule for me. I needed to display it in my home to remind both the aides and myself that I am in charge of my life and not them."

Rush's Rule, as shown below was displayed prominently, first on the walls of Bill's apartment and then in the house that Bill and Chris built together.

The title, *Our Life Our Way A Memoir of Active Faith, Profound Love and Courageous Disability Rights*, is an adaptation of Rush's rule, expanding Rush's rule to include Chris into the equation. Rush's Rule remained a constant central theme throughout their life together.

CHAPTER 1

(Bill's Voice)

The Perfect Rescue

T he sun burned the back of my neck on this hot Nebraska day in July of 1988.

Restlessly I moved around in my power wheelchair, my eyes scanning the crowd gathered in front of the state capitol building. People around me held protest signs. I was looking for a woman I knew, the one who had invited me to this rally to protest wearing motorcycle helmets.

She hadn't come.

"(So here I sat)…surrounded by a group of people I didn't like and didn't want to be associated with. I didn't even agree with the signs raised high all around me."[1]

Continuing my visual search for the woman who was supposed to be here with me, I happened to glance at a church on the other side of the street.

"(While looking at the church) a voice inside me said, "You don't belong here with these people. There's where you belong." [2]

"I had a strong faith in God." [3] In fact, I had become a Christian at age eight, while watching Mr. Graham on TV. Then I asked my mom to help me write for all the material from the Billy Graham Evangelistic Association and I had read everything that they sent me.

My mom had taken me to our local church as a child. But I never felt accepted there for who I was. I was told to keep quiet and not to sing because when I tried to sing I could only holler, making what I called my "joyful noise" unto the Lord.

"(And later, when) I heard that people were trying to drive the pastor out the church... I figured that all church-attending Christians were hypocrites and that I (would be better off worshipping) God by myself." [4]

I also had a bad experience while attending journalism school at the University of Nebraska at Lincoln. A 'Christian' told me outright that I was not able-bodied because I didn't have enough faith to be healed! He continued to harass me day after day.

The student's insistence that I was not who God wanted me to be began to wear me down. I began to question my belief that God's plan for my life *included* me having a significant disability.

Finally I went to get help from one of the campus pastors to get him to leave me alone. She spoke to the guy to get him to stop bothering me, and assured me that my disability was not because of a lack of faith.

This dreadful experience furthered my belief that God and I would do our thing away from organized Christianity. I was fearful that another one of these healing freaks would be ready and waiting for me at any church that I tried to attend.

And, for over a decade "I had been asking God for someone I could love who would love me. God didn't answer as fast as I wanted and expected. (So), I had cut the telephone lines and had turned my back on Him. (With)...my mother praying for me, (I figured that) I didn't have to talk with God."[5]

Besides, churches I saw in the neighborhood where I lived were either inaccessible or only offered side or back door entry to people with disabilities. These churches were saying to me that since I was imperfect physically, I would have to go through an inconspicuous door. And I would not budge when it came to front door accessibility as a chief requirement for my attendance.

However, God and my mom continued to hound me. They both said that I needed to find a church home.

To appease both the "Hound of Heaven"[6] and my mom, I had made a deal with God. I told God that if He would give me a front door accessible church, in rolling distance from my apartment, I would at least try to attend.

God had met my challenge and won. Now here I sat in amazement, looking at the front door accessible First Baptist Church, probably the only one in downtown Lincoln.

"OK, Uncle!" I cried to God, realizing that I had been checkmated. He had planned the perfect rescue to call me back into the fold.

Smiling to myself, I left the protest rally where I didn't belong and rolled across the street to read the sign in front of the church where I did. The sign said, "Wednesday Evening Bible Study 7 pm, Sunday Worship Service 10:30 am. All welcome."

The following Wednesday evening I rolled the several blocks from my apartment over to First Baptist Church. I followed a small group of people toward the alley doorway at the back of the church where they were entering the building. Feeling frustrated that they were not using the accessible front door, I found myself sitting in the alley at the bottom of the stairs looking at the rear entrance of the church.

A tall kind looking man at the door smiled at me.

"Can we help you?" the gentleman said.

"The sign outside said that you have Bible Study every Wednesday night. I want to join if I may," I said, (using my new and first-ever-for-me, portable voice-output communication system, the TouchTalker™).[7]

This new device that I had been using for only five months, was giving me the capacity to speak out loud anywhere in clear understandable English, using a male sounding voice.

"We'd love to have you, (but our Bible study is not accessible," the broadly smiling man responded).

(He continued), "We do have an accessible Sunday morning worship service that you are welcome to come to. (My name is

Howard Keeley. I'm the Senior Pastor here at First Baptist. What's your name?)"

("Bill, my name is Bill Rush." I said with my Touch Talker™ and looked up to see that he had waited to hear my response). I noticed his intense pale blue eyes. They gave me the impression that he really cared about me.[8]

"Bill, I look forward to having you with us on Sunday." Howard responded with a smile.

I nodded and returned home.

I gladly accepted Pastor Howard's invitation to attend worship service on the next Sunday morning. "I desperately needed somewhere that I could feel I belonged and I needed a church home. I needed accessibility, acceptance, and I needed God."[9]

As I rolled through the accessible front door, "people greeted me with a mixture of trepidation and good will. "Good morning!" many said as they walked past me. I understood their apprehension and appreciated their brief words of welcome."[10]

I nodded and smiled. It felt good to be welcomed and treated as a person.

Motivated by their desire to include me in their church community and to show me the love of Christ, these people were miles ahead of many other Christians I had met and also many people in the larger community who were not able or willing to treat me like a person of worth.

Most people don't know how to interact with me, and in their discomfort, they ignore me. When people look at me, all they can see is my large power wheelchair, my large wheelchair tray, my communication device and my welder's helmet liner that I wear on my head to hold my headstick. I need all this technology to be able to move around by myself and to talk because I have quadriplegic cerebral palsy.

It takes time for people to find me behind all of my bionic stuff. After people realize that I am a person, they then have to learn how to communicate with me. Because I am unable to speak using my vocal cords, I need a computer to speak for me.

One of the biggest differences when communicating with me is the speed of conversation. My fastest communication is at eight words per minute using my TouchTalker™ that says the words for me, while most people talk at a rate of about 120 words a minute.

Then there's the matter of my needing to look away from the other person to program my TouchTalker™ to speak. When this happens I have to lose eye contact. People often interpret this loss of eye contact as being finished with the conversation. Then they leave while I am trying to respond.

Some of the people at First Baptist took the time to figure out how to communicate with me.

After worshipping with them several times I found myself wishing I could become more involved within the church. They announced an upcoming committee meeting to decide how better to serve the community...

I attended and made my case for putting in an elevator to the lower level where the Wednesday night Bible studies were being held.[11]

As a disability rights advocate, I was accustomed to my role of pointing out unequal access and demanding change using logical arguments.

"I reminded the congregation that the aging members who were having trouble climbing the church's stairs could take advantage of it. And I pointed out that as more people with disabilities were beginning to live in the community, they were going to need churches that were fully accessible. Even though accessibility laws would not be legally applied to the church, I pointed out that God's house should be accessible to all, not because it was mandated by federal or state law but because God mandates it.

"I see your point. We'll seriously see about putting in an elevator," the chair of the committee said.

I was skeptical. I didn't think that one small plea would have an impact. As a disability activist, I was used to having to start boycotts and set up picket lines outside inaccessible buildings to make the public aware of their discrimination.

(But, surprisingly, and in contrast to my experience in the community), this congregation's attitude toward me was inclusive instead of being exclusive. They moved the Bible study to the sanctuary so that I could join them. I was surprised that they would do this for me. (And I was delighted and grateful.)[12]

Attending the now accessible Bible study, I found out that people also shared some of their personal struggles and supported each other with prayer and encouragement.

A middle-aged woman who was nearing the end after a long battle with cancer said, "Why doesn't God heal me? I'm going to die, and I have prayed, and prayed for healing, but it hasn't come. Why won't God heal me?"

Our Bible study leader didn't know what to say.

With my (TouchTalker™.) I finally said, "There are many ways that God can heal people."

"What do you mean by that?" the leader asked.

"There is spiritual healing and emotional healing…" I continued.

"…And when we die, we're going to heaven where there is no sickness," the leader said.

"Not only that but I believe that God has given me the gift to accept my disability, and I believe that He will give you the peace to accept your death," I said.

"I never thought of it that way, but you are right. Thank you for sharing that with me," the woman said with tears in her eyes.

When I was leaving that night, the leader said, "Do you know that God sent you here tonight? What a great job you did of ministering to us. I'm so happy that God brought you to our community. Good night, my friend."

That night during the fellowship my own healing had begun. Some of my pain of not being accepted in the larger world was beginning to vanish. [13]

However, like the woman I met at the Bible study, I had also been asking God for a miracle. My miracle would be to find a woman who would have a significant relationship with me. I wanted this more than anything else. I had asked God to fulfill this desire or take it away. Thus far, He had not taken it away from me. So I continued to ask, day after day and year after year.

Photo of First Baptist Church Lincoln,
Nebraska. Taken by Christine Robinson.

Endnotes

1. Bill Rush, "A Personal Spiritual Journey Testimony," *First Baptist Church Tower* (Volume 3, Issue 26, 1996). Reprinted by permission of Church Life Council, First Baptist Church, Lincoln NE.

2. Ibid.

3. William L Rush, "A Model to the Community," *Christian Single*, (November 1992). Reprinted by permission of the publisher.

4. Rush, "Personal Spiritual Journey."

5. Ibid.

6. Francis Thompson, "The Hound of Heaven" in *The Works of Francis Thompson*. (Ann Arbor: University Press, 1913).

7. Rush, "Model."

8. Ibid.

9. Ibid.

10. Ibid.

11. Ibid.

12. Ibid.

13. Ibid.

CHAPTER 2

(Bill's Voice)

Field Testing My Way to California

"Hi Bill," I heard Cathy's now familiar and friendly voice speaking to me over my speaker phone.

She continued, "Would you like to take an all-expense paid trip to the International Society of Augmentative and Alternative Communication Conference in California in October?"

"Who wants me to go and why?" I responded using my Touch Talker.

"Bruce Baker (Semantic Compaction Corporation) and Barry Romich (Prentke Romich Company) would like you to go and talk with your Touch Talker™ to show others how you were able to make this communication device your own." Cathy said.

"Sure. I'll go." I replied, thinking that it might be fun to fly to California for a few days. Besides, as a member of the Disability Rights Movement, it was my responsibility to show my community that if I could learn to use the Touch Talker™, others could do it too.

My mind turned back to my first telephone conversation with Cathy, eight months earlier, when she had called to ask me to begin to field test the Touch Talker™.

"I'm a speech language pathologist with Prentke Romich Company, a new company creating voice synthesizers for people who cannot speak." Cathy had said. "When I was speaking with Bruce, he mentioned that you were brought in to a brainstorming session on the east coast of the US a year or so ago to help him to development a new linguistic system for a voice synthesizer. He really appreciated all your ideas and support."

"Bruce is now recommending that we have you try his new creation, the Minspeak™ linguistic system which we have integrated into our latest communication device, the Touch Talker™. Minspeak™ is highly innovative. It will allow you to speak your own novel thoughts faster than your current rate of communicating by spelling every word, because now you will be able to use preprogrammed words to minimize the number of key strokes needed to type each word. As you well know, this is currently not available in any voice synthesizer."

"We'd really like you to be a field tester for the Touch Talker™. We need someone with your intelligence to try it and give us some feedback. Are you interested?" Cathy had asked.

"OK." I had responded, thinking that I had nothing to lose by trying it, purposely squelching my growing excitement until I had at least worked with the device.

On the other hand, I was still holding out hope that one day I would have a portable voice synthesizer that would meet my needs, allowing me to speak both out loud and also faster than communicating just with my alphabet board. When I spelled to someone, I was at the mercy of the patience of my communication partner, to follow my pointing to letters on my alphabet board, and be able to combine the letters into words and remember the sequence long enough to understand my thoughts. If someone could create a fast voice synthesizer, then I could be in charge of when I spoke my thoughts out loud. I relished the thought of that possibility.

I first developed a reputation for being a test pilot while at the University of Nebraska in the late 70's and early 80's. There, the wonderful world of electronic adaptive and assistive devices had opened up to me and I eagerly tried anything that anyone wanted to share with me. I was stubborn enough to stay with any new device until I figured it out. I was mouthy enough to tell the designers what I didn't like about their creations. But I was diplomatic enough to remember that I was talking about their babies.

By trying out new assistive technology devices that people were creating for persons with disabilities, I learned that I could live on my own without walking or talking or using my hands. Contrary to my childhood experience with years of rehabilitative therapy that tried to fix me, at UNL I was accepted for who I was, and assistive technologies were provided to accommodate for my disabilities. Surrounded by people with this disability-friendly assistive technology philosophy, I found myself adopting it at an astonishing rate, until it became my own philosophy.

If I didn't walk, I was still OK. They gave me a power wheelchair that was customized for my needs. If I couldn't use my hands to turn on and off my electrical appliances, engineers modified my dorm room with an environmental control unit that I could operate with my headstick. If I couldn't talk, rehabilitation specialists contacted someone to create a desktop voice synthesizer for me.

At home in my apartment, I continued to use this first desktop voice synthesizer that I had field tested for my friend Mark Dahmke, who created it for me in 1979. Mark's voice synthesizer was ahead of its time, so much so that it was featured in a *Life* magazine article, titled "The Expanding World of Bill Rush", written by Anne Fadiman in 1980. Mark had faithfully maintained this first system for nine years, updating it with new software and voice synthesizers as they became available. It was reliable, but it wasn't portable.

The second voice synthesizer that I field tested was created in 1984 by Jim Mosenfelder to work with the Epson HX 20 portable computer. Jim had created a way for this portable computer to speak or print out what I carefully typed into it. It also had some preprogrammed speech options that were created to help me increase my rate of speaking. However, the preprogrammed options were too limited and I found myself reverting back to carefully and slowly spelling every word on the device. But eventually I realized that my alphabet board was still faster, because my pointing skills did not have to be as accurate when using it. After giving it a good try, I discontinued using the Epson HX20. I wondered if the Touch Talker™ that Cathy was now describing might have the portability and preprogrammed options I was looking for.

"Would it be OK if I come over and show it to you sometime?" Cathy had asked.

"OK. Can you come sometime tomorrow?" I had replied, becoming more eager to lay my eyes on this new device and start to think about how I could modify it.

"Yes Bill I can come at 2pm. Will that work for you?"

"OK. Thank you. Goodbye." I had responded before hanging up.

Thinking about my friend Mark and the desktop system he had developed for me, I was concerned about offending him by using something else. So I decided to call him and get his thoughts about trying the Touch Talker.

"Hi" Mark had said.

I told him how Bruce and Barry had worked together and now had a new portable voice synthesizer ready for me try.

"Sure." Mark replied. "Bill you don't have to worry about being loyal to me. I don't think that I'm ever going to ever get around to building a portable voice synthesizer for you. It's time to move on to the next generation," he concluded.

With Mark on my side, I was ready to at least think about making the switch to a different language system that might allow me to talk easily and also have portability. Spelling was still my current language. The Minspeak™ language system sounded like a lot of symbols that I was going to have to memorize in order to speak words out loud faster. I was very apprehensive about having to learn a new language at 34 years of age.

I first met Cathy the next day when she arrived with my Touch Talker™. When she took it out of the box, I saw a computer keyboard with a lot of pictures on it and thought to myself, *Oh no! Here come the hieroglyphics!* There were 3000 combinations of picture symbols that I would need to memorize in this Minspeak™ language.

Right from the beginning, I decided that if Minspeak™ was going to be my new language, it would have to make sense to me. I spent hours debating the logic of each symbol and combination of symbols with Cathy. She patiently worked with me day after day, explaining the logic and supporting me when I wanted to delete symbols or make changes. After eight months of intensive drilling and customization to make the Touch Talker™ with the Minspeak™ language my own, I was able to begin to integrate it into my life. I thought that my progress had been slow. Cathy thought it had been very short and quite remarkable.

A very interesting thing happened when I started to use this Touch Talker™ instead of my alphabet board with my attendants. One attendant training another at my place said, "Yeah Bill has a new voice synthesizer. This machine makes Bill more real."

My first impulse was to tell that attendant that I was probably more real than he was. However, I started to think about what he had said.

I first thought that my aide meant that I was imaginary, fictional or pretend- that I was not an actual, authentic, or genuine person without my Touch Talker™. But when I looked up real in the dictionary, I found out that the fifth meaning of real was "serious, not to be taken lightly". If this was what the aide meant, then I agreed with him that I am 'more real' with my new voice output device.

Other people began to take me more seriously as well because talking with me became easier and quicker and also I think that people associate intellect with speech. The gift of speech output proved to greatly enhance my quality of life, both in my profession as a journalist and my social life. I was now able to interview people by pre-programming questions into the device and I toasted one of my little brothers at his wedding.

What I didn't know was that the most significant reason for my needing the capacity for speech from a voice synthesizer was just around the corner.

I was brought back to the current conversation with Cathy on my telephone when I heard her ask me a question. "Bill, can you get yourself an attendant to go along with you to California? Someone will call you about plane tickets."

"One never knows what can happen in California," she added and laughed.

Yeah, I thought. *One never knows what might happen in California.*

CHAPTER 3

(Chris' voice)

A Chance Meeting

"Bill, this is my colleague Christine," Shelly, my speech language pathologist colleague said, introducing me to him.

I was at the International Society for Augmentative and Alternative Communication Conference (ISAAC) in Anaheim, California to do a presentation with my colleague Shelley from Hamilton, Ontario, Canada.

I was the youngest and least experienced on a work team of four professionals from the Children's Developmental and Rehabilitation Centre, at McMaster Hospital, and part of the Hamilton Health Sciences, and one of several Ontario Treatment Centres, created to provide rehabilitation services to children with disabilities. Shelley, the speech language pathologist on our team had submitted an abstract for our team to present our work with teenagers at the California conference and she wanted a co-presenter to go along.

Being the junior occupational therapist member on the team, I had assumed that either one of my two senior colleagues, Rita, a social worker, or Sandi, my occupational therapist supervisor, would be making the trip stateside with Shelley. However, both of my senior colleagues had personal things going on such that they both declined the offer and this amazing opportunity landed in my lap. Seizing it, I had worked hard to prepare my part of the presentation for this big league conference.

I really enjoyed talking about how we supported our teenagers to get physical access to their communication device." Shelley and I had presented "Speak Out: A Group for Adolescents Who Use Augmentative and Alternative Communication".

"Hi Bill." I said in a friendly assured tone. I was confident and comfortable when meeting someone like Bill, someone with a significant disability and without natural speech. After all, I had been working with teenagers who were unable to speak for several years. I was familiar and comfortable with the process of communicating with someone who used a voice synthesizer or a low technology (low tech) alphabet board or symbol system.

But I was not comfortable introducing myself to him. So I had asked Shelley, who had met Bill when he came to Canada as a paid speaker after *Journey Out of Silence* had been published, to do the introduction for me.

We had been sharing Bill's humorous and informative writings about living on his own in an apartment in Lincoln, Nebraska, with the teenagers we worked with back in Canada, because they had requested that we find some role models of non-verbal adults, who had significant disabilities like theirs. They were anxious about what it would be like to live as adults and Bill was of much encouragement to them. I was curious to meet him but not bold enough to do it myself. Shelley had obliged me.

She discretely slipped away, leaving me standing in front of Bill, in the middle of a crowd of people on a dance floor, many able-bodied and some using wheelchairs, waiting for the music to begin again.

Bill looked me in the eye, smiled and nodded his head as if to say, "Hello."

I quickly realized that Bill was sitting in his wheelchair without his communication device.

"I see you don't have your Touch Talker™ (voice synthesizer)." I said, acknowledging what was obvious, that Bill could not communicate with me beyond his head nods, gestures and facial expressions. But I wasn't afraid or deterred by the situation. This was familiar territory for me. I was merely finding my way to be able to communicate with him.

Bill turned to look toward the top of a half dozen stairs where his power wheelchair, wheelchair tray and Touch Talker™ sat, awaiting his return from the inaccessible dance floor.

After following his eyes I verbalized what I assumed were his thoughts, "Oh I get it! You had to move to this manual chair to get down to the dance floor and so your communication device is not with you. It's up there." I said and pointed to what I thought were his technological things.

He smiled a stunningly handsome smile and nodded yes, clearly delighted that I was able to follow his gaze and communicate his thoughts out loud for him, in the absence of his Touch Talker™.

"Hungry Eyes" from the movie "Dirty Dancing" started to play through the sound system. Bill looked at me, and smiled while beginning to stand up and sit down in his wheelchair, doing what I assumed was his way of dancing. I could see that his ankles were strapped to the footrests but that the rest of his body was free to move. I started to dance, enjoying what felt like a very comfortable and friendly connection with him.

Suddenly and seemingly out of nowhere, three women who were speaking a language I thought might be Swedish interrupted our dancing together and pulled Bill away from me. As they turned his manual wheelchair to push him away, Bill turned his body to look back at me. A playfully pleading expression on his face said, "Save me from these women!"

I laughed at his expression. Inside I was angry that these women would just take him away from me. It felt bizarre and rude.

But Bill was being playful about it. So I followed his lead and tried to keep it playful.

I let the group of women dance around Bill for a few minutes. He continued to look around to find me, looking visibly relieved when he found me and caught my eye. His facial expression continued to beckon me to come and get him.

So I did.

Looking relieved and nodding at me as if to say, "Thank you for saving me from those do-gooders!" We continued to enjoy our time of dancing together, with the occasional interruption from the small group of women who came to steal him a couple more times.

We both laughed with delight every time I would steal him back.

The DJ announced that the last dance was about to happen.

Out of nowhere Bill's attendant Don suddenly appeared to help him.

Two days later, back in Hamilton Ontario, exhausted from my four-day, whirlwind Disneyland trip that included a chance meeting of some guy named Bill Rush, I was still buzzing with energy and bounced into my supervisor Sandi's office to tell her about my trip.

"You know Bill Rush, the guy whose stuff we were reading to the teenagers in our group?" I said, trying to sound nonchalant.

"Looks like you didn't just meet him" Sandi, the ever-astute one said, "Looks like lots more has happened than that!"

"Yeah", I responded. "Lots more happened than just meeting him." I said out loud, admitting my intense attraction to and curiosity about a guy with a significant disability in the USA.

Sandi continued her silly grin, while I rambled on about Nebraska and Bill's obvious and significant disability. "He lives in Nebraska of all places. Where is Nebraska anyway? One of those western states isn't it?" I pondered out loud. "All I know about Nebraska is Omaha from Mutual of Omaha's Wild Kingdom TV show that I watched as a kid. I think he lives in Lincoln, the state capital. It's all corn fields out there isn't it?" I continued my chattering at break neck speed. "Bill is very disabled. He's physically very much like the teenagers we work with, except that he is a lot more independent." I said. Then I added, "He has a university education, works as a journalist and a disability rights advocate, is very funny, and very good-looking".

Sandi just continued staring at me with an incredulous and also playful expression that I tried very hard to ignore. I was pretty excited and needed to talk about what had happened.

I was feeling very exhausted from the intense emotions of the last four days; both the anxiety and excitement from presenting my work material and performing in a fun talent show contest with Shelley at the conference had taken its toll. Meeting Bill Rush had been intense emotionally and cognitively conflicting.

I continued telling Sandi about the conference. ""How did your talent show thing go? Did you win?" Sandi asked playfully. I had played The Rose on the piano and sang it while Shelley performed it beautifully –in choreographed American Sign Language. To add some Canadian disability-related content, we also performed St Elmo's Fire, a theme song created by David Foster for Rick Hansen, the Canadian who wheeled through thirty-four countries to complete his famous Man In Motion World Tour. Rick raised awareness about spinal cord injuries and the need for research and accessibility for persons with disabilities. As proud Canadians, we had draped a Canadian flag over the piano while we performed.

"The playing and singing were fun." I said, "Shelley's sign language was beautiful to watch. And no. We didn't win… Bill Rush did!"

"And what was Bill Rush's talent, might I ask?" Sandi continued her teasing.

"He programmed Frank Sinatra's My Way into his communication device. So in his own way he sang it." I said.

"That's pretty impressive. What an overachiever!" Sandi responded. "How did he do that?"

"I have no idea." I responded honestly.

I then began to talk about what had happened at the dance after the talent contest. "Lots of people -including Bill- had to be carried down the stairs to the dance floor in their wheelchairs. Bill was in his manual chair without his communication device."

"The day before the talent show, I saw a tall, handsome guy zipping around Disneyland in his power wheelchair. I remembered seeing Bill's picture in his book that we have at work and thought, "That's him!"

"That good-looking, eh?" Sandi continued with more interest.
"Yeah. That good-looking," I admitted.

I continued, "Maybe I'm old-fashioned or just shy, but I wasn't comfortable introducing myself to him, even though I really wanted to meet him."

"Sounds like you managed to get that done," Sandi continued, in her interested and teasing tone.

I kept to my story. "I remembered that Shelley had met Bill when he came to Toronto last year, so at the dance I asked her to introduce me to him. You know Shelley. She's pretty laid back. Without hesitating, she said, "Sure", takes me over to him and introduces me. And then I suddenly realized that Shelley had disappeared, leaving me alone with him," I said.

"Bill and I started to dance. He was jumping around in his wheelchair and I was dancing with him. I loved watching his dark, expressive eyes, playfully looking at me while he so naturally moved his wiggly body around. His eyes were telling me that he was having fun, even if he couldn't use words to tell me. I'm sure my eyes were saying the same thing back to him." I reminisced.

"Sounds like you had a good time with Bill?" Sandi asked with her incredulous look. I wondered if she was asking herself why I would want to dance with this guy who couldn't talk with me and couldn't be up on his feet dancing. But I couldn't worry about her response. I had my own to figure out.

I went on, "Then all of a sudden, some well-meaning Swedish ladies took Bill from me and started to spin his wheelchair in circles. They must have been really blind to not see that Bill and I were having a good time with just each other. I think they thought that they had to give Bill a 'good time'."

Sandi was silent and serious now as I recounted the rest of the story. The look on her face made me realize that my intense feelings for Bill in Disneyland had come home with me to Canada.

"So these ladies are spinning Bill and he was looking for me with an expression of "Please come rescue me from these ladies" on his face. It was a playful look but it was also very serious on another level. He wanted to be with me and I wanted to be with him and yet the ladies kept taking him from me."

Sandi had stopped the teasing and was now just listening.

"The DJ said he was going to play a slow song and Bill's attendant, Don, came out of nowhere and asked Bill if he wanted to stand on his feet with me helping him balance to dance, and then he asked me if I would be OK with that. I knew that I could help move our teenagers with ease, by helping them to stand to transfer them in and out of their wheelchairs. The teenagers we work with are about five feet tall and I'm pretty strong so I said "sure"."

"So then what happened?" Sandi asked, with genuine curiosity.

"Don helped Bill to stand and I quickly figured out that he is much taller and stronger than the teens. He's over six feet tall and can push through his legs to stand to support himself with an incredible strength in his legs." I said. "But of course he has no balance so his body is like a weaving, wiggling rod that I had to hold still, so that he wouldn't fall over." I said.

Now Sandi was really smiling and back to the teasing mode that I ignored again. "Yeah", she said. "You had to hold him close. Sure. And then what happened?" she quizzed.

"I'm holding the weaving, wiggling Bill and he starts to kiss my neck and I was so surprised that I just froze."

"What??" Sandi retorted. "You've got to be kidding me!"

"Nope, no kidding!" I said. I'm wondering if Sandi is thinking that I have really gone off the deep end -- by holding some guy I don't know, close enough to let him kiss my neck.

"He wasn't hurting me. He was gentle." I said, feeling some need to clarify this. "But I'm saying to myself, "This is weird because I haven't heard him speak and he is kissing my neck" and "I really need to stop him"".

"So what did you do?" Sandi asked with real interest.

"I said, trying to be firm but not angry, "Mr. Rush. Please stop. I haven't heard you speak and you are kissing my neck.""

"Oh boy! This is juicy!" Sandi teased again.

"Yeah, I guess my neck was juicy to him." I laughed.

"And while he is doing this, I could hear my hotel roommates, the Toronto Speech Pathologist friends of Shelley's, saying from the side of the dance floor, "Get this woman her green card!" It was crazy!"

"Meanwhile, hearing me tell him to stop, Bill physically jerked back into reality with his entire body wiggling involuntarily, because of his Cerebral Palsy. I'm trying to keep him- and me- from falling over. Then, out of nowhere Don appeared. How did that guy know just when to show up? Bill's eyes were fixed on mine in absolute horror. He begged me with his eyes not to leave him."

"I was right. It *is* about a guy." Sandi continued seriously.

"Don started to drag Bill up the stairs off the dance floor in his manual chair to get him up to his power chair and his communication device. He knew what Bill needed. And Bill is looking at me, pleading with me with his eyes, not to leave."

"Bet he was," Sandi murmured.

"I kept saying, "I'll wait", but Bill kept his beautiful dark eyes glued on mine the whole time while Don got him back into his power chair, where he could talk to me with his computer. Bill looked so upset, ashamed and afraid. Meanwhile I'm feeling a wonderful connection to him and I wanted to be with him. I wasn't angry or upset. I just wanted to talk with him."

"Yeah! Then what?" Sandi continued.

"The first thing Bill says to me is, "Temporary Insanity" and then he added, "Sorry. I'm socially retarded.""

"I told Bill that I didn't think he was socially retarded. I really didn't. What he did was inappropriate. But, it wasn't a big deal." I said.

"Wow! This is quite the story." Sandi said more seriously. And then she added, "Something serious happened with Bill, didn't it."

"Yes, I think so," I said with some trepidation. After all Bill was American, and had a significant disability.

Getting on with my work, throughout that day, I continued to have flashbacks to pictures of Bill and the interaction I had with him on the last day that I was in California.

I remembered seeing Bill eating breakfast at the hotel's restaurant early on that last morning at the hotel. With his headstick removed, I could see his disheveled, beautiful black hair and eyes looking away while he chewed with concentration and deliberation.

When he finished his bite, Bill would look to his attendant, Don, to request another bite of food. I would find out later that somehow he had found out that I was going to leave that morning and he was trying to eat quickly so as to make his way to the florist shop to get me a red rose in addition to a copy of his book, before I left.

I remembered how Bill had paged me at the Disneyland hotel on the last morning of the conference. I had gathered my things to leave and found Bill sitting at the front desk with a rose and a copy of his book, *Journey Out of Silence* [1], resting on his wheelchair tray.

Bill was so casual about what must have been a huge effort for him to go and get that red rose. I knew that he would have had to find a florist shop, get help to get inside the shop, and then get someone to interact with him to buy me a red rose. And he had done it all by himself! I was surprised and delighted by his forwardness and effort.

"I'll be in touch," I had casually responded and then wondered why I was feeling both so casual and so certain.

After taking the book and the red rose off of his tray, I walked away as Bill sat there looking at me, with a big pleased smile on his face. Giving me a red rose rather than a yellow one had been bold, but I liked it. It went along with his confident self.

Endnotes

[1] William Rush. *Journey Out of Silence*. 2nd Edition, (Lulu.com, 2008).

CHAPTER 4

(Bill's Voice)

Sharing Brings Healing

"Bill I am going to set aside entire afternoons to come over and visit with you." Pastor Howard said with his now characteristic caring smile.

"Thank you." I responded. I wanted to talk with Pastor Howard but the speed of my communication, even with my new voice synthesizer, was still very slow.

"I'm feeling intimidated Bill. I don't know how we can communicate with each other but I am willing to try." Pastor Howard continued. "You will have to teach me how to communicate with you."

True to his word, Pastor Howard set aside a couple of Wednesday afternoons a month and started visiting with me at my place. He seemed to settle into the slow pace of our conversation, waiting until I was finished before responding, so that the conversation was easier for both of us to follow.

Pastor Howard was more than willing to listen to whatever I needed to talk about. On this day, I needed to share my frustration and anger towards God. I had both unrighteous anger at God and some righteous anger at a discriminatory society to work through with my Pastor.

"I'm angry at God because I've had to work so hard to get this far, and yet there is still so much to do to create a life for myself. I'm so tired of the endless fight to live a normal life. That's all I want. I don't want to be a "Super Crip", I said, using a derogatory disability term. "At UNL I had to fight to prove that someone with a significant disability could get a university degree. I had to do it really well, graduating with distinction, to prove my many naysayers wrong." I continued.

I continued my venting to my caring pastor and friend. "When I left UNL, the able-bodied world was not ready for me to live in the community and outside of an institution. I've been fighting alongside of other Americans with disabilities to break down barriers to be able to live outside of institutions. And I'm tired. State regulations, education, and transportation that segregate and discriminate against people with disabilities are slowly being changed to support people with disabilities to live in the community. I was the first person without speech to live on my own, at least in Nebraska, if not the USA. It's good to be moving things forward for myself and for others. But, being a pioneer is isolating and exhausting. It can also be dangerous. I have so few housing options because I need accessible low-income housing. This apartment is not the safest but its' all there is - so far…"

"What has happened to you?" Howard asked, quickly and with great concern, picking up on the dangerousness of my situation.

"Many things including a drunk man getting inside my apartment." I said, anxious to share one of my stories with my Pastor friend.

"Oh no Bill!" Pastor Howard exclaimed with genuine empathy.

I had written about this "drunk guy incident" but hadn't published it yet, because I was afraid that it might scare off others with disabilities from living on their own. I found my story and printed it for Pastor Howard to read, so as to help with the speed of communication. This is what I gave him to read:

> *About 3 months after I moved in, I had paged my night aide. I heard a knock and thinking it was him, I opened my electronic door. It wasn't my assistant. It was a man and he was swaying. I could see he was very drunk as he wove his way into my apartment.*

"He said, "Mr. can I use your phone? Gotta call my wife. My ex-wife.""" My unwanted visitor said.

This guy didn't have both oars in the water.

I began to panic because my phone was not the same as this guy's phone. He would not know how to use my computer phone. I had it set up for medical, smoke and burglar alarms but not for drunk men to dial.

I went over to my desk and pushed the dial button on my computer phone, with my headstick. My phone said out loud, "Enter a number to dial." The guy, hearing the instruction from my computer phone, gave me a number and I entered it for him.

A woman's voice answered, 'Yes who is this?" Deadly silence from the drunk man. Click. She hung up.

I pushed the repeat button, and the phone redialed the number. Again, the woman said, "Yes? Who is this?" Again, the drunk guy sat on my bed and did nothing. Again there was a click. This time she slammed the phone down with a hard click. The click said, "Don't bother me anymore."

Suddenly, I realized that I would have to get the drunk man out of my apartment by myself.

"You stupid idiot," I thought, "Why don't you say something to your wife? One more time."

I hit the repeat again. This time the woman didn't answer. I guess she had too many annoying calls that evening.

The drunk seemed to be sleeping.

I decided to call the cops. I pushed the dial button and my phone said, "Enter a number to dial," which revived the drunk.

"Gotta reach my wife and can't. Your fault," he said. He then moved toward me in my tiny apartment and slapped me before I could move away,

knocking my headstick off. In that one slap he had effectively bound and gagged me.

I knew I was in trouble. Alarm turned to panic. Without my headstick I was at the drunk guy's mercy. And He didn't look too merciful.

He had tan skin, brown hair, a mustache, and mean-looking hazel eyes. He reminded me of Cheech as in Cheech and Chong. Under different circumstances I might have liked him, but I doubted it.

"Now you slap me and we'll be even," he said. "Go on. Slap me."

I shook my head no and backed away from him. If I tried to hit him, he could hit me back again. I doubted if I could have hit him, let alone knocked him out in one punch. With cerebral palsy, my arm movements were not controlled. The joke in my family was that, when upset, my arms moved rapidly, like I was doing the "Flight of the Bumble Bee." My only chance would be to wait him out.

And where was my assistant?!

In my panic I backed my wheelchair into a corner. Somehow I felt safer with my back against the wall. At least he couldn't attack me from behind. I couldn't get away from him either.

Cheech leaned on my desk, which was at the other end of my efficiency apartment. We were about eight feet apart. Far too close for comfort.

He looked at me and said, "You're a mess, ain't you? I'm a mess, too. But you're a bigger mess than me. I had a wife, but she divorced me and took my kid away. God, I'm tired. But I'll clean up this mess. Someone has to do it."

I wondered what mess he was talking about. My apartment wasn't that dirty. I was looking at the floor to avoid looking at him. I didn't want him to see the fear in my eyes.

"That's right. Look down because that's where you're going. Straight to hell. I'll cut you in the heart," he said.

*Panic turned into terror. He meant **I** was the mess. He was going to clean **me** up by killing me. I didn't want to be that tidy.*

Where was my assistant? If he didn't come soon, he'd be out of a job.

I resented being called a mess. I resented it even more coming from the drunk guy. He looked my age -- maybe a little older. But while I was trying to write for a living, he had turned to drinking to run away from his problems. How dare he call me a mess! If I got out of this, I would make sure he got sensitivity training from the local independent living center- The League of Human Dignity. Surely they offered a class on the proper way to threaten people with disabilities, I thought with sarcasm.

But, in a way he was symptomatic of how society views people with disabilities. I thought about how I'm not so much a victim of my disability as I am a victim of the attitude of society -- a society in which we have been told in many subtle ways that I'm not worthwhile. Buildings that are inaccessible or partly accessible tell me that I am neither expected nor wanted inside, and TV shows tell me that I should be incredibly brave, incredibly bitter, or incredibly nonexistent.

I thought about my parents. They would mourn, but they would know that I died doing something that I had to do.

I was more worried about the Independent Living Center. My death would make my adviser fill out endless forms and would probably set Lincoln, Nebraska's independent living program back ten years. Some impact.

"Where's a knife," the drunk muttered with glazed eyes, "Might as well get this over with."

Well, at least he wasn't a procrastinator, I thought to myself.

I began to mentally recite the Twenty-third Psalm:

"The Lord is my shepherd; I shall not want..."

But I did want. I wanted to live. A close friend had a four-month-old baby. I wanted to go to her college graduation. I wanted to continue to be a writer. I wanted to get married and have a family. I wanted to die 40 or 50 years from now.

I saw the drunk. He was staring off into space. He acted like he was in the Twilight Zone. I hoped he was having a nice chat with old Rod.

"Where's a knife?" he asked.

I wasn't telling. I looked at my smoke detector. A friend had suggested, "Get one to make sure you don't burn up in your own house." We tried to cover all the bases. But now I would be killed by some scum of a drunk guy with my own steak knife. Embarrassing.

I let my mind wander. I tried to think of anything to take my mind off my predicament. I mentally recited the Pledge of Allegiance, the Cub Scout Oath and the Boy Scout Oath.

I thought about my friends.

I saw a housefly buzzing around me and wondered where they went in the winter. If they died, where did their bodies go? Did they just disintegrate or did they become a part of the earth or my apartment?

Who decided April 15 as tax day?

It wasn't working. I could still see Cheech sitting on my desk.

He didn't go get my steak knife and he didn't leave, so I went back to the Twenty-third Psalm.

Reciting it made me feel close to God, so I kept repeating it over and over again.

And then, I heard a thud and saw the drunk sprawled on my carpet. My cup runneth over. Thank you God. Goodnight, not so sweet prince.

I slowly made my left hand push my forward button on my wheelchair and slowly drove to the phone. I didn't want to wake "Sleeping Beauty."

I looked at my phone clock. 11:30 p.m. I tried to push the help button on my phone with my left hand. It took five tries, but on the fifth try the phone said in its computerized voice, "Help On... I am calling for help now... Phone on... Calling..."

My morning assistant answered sleepily, "Hello?"

The phone said, "This is an automatic call. There's an emergency at..."

I yelled to let her know this wasn't a false alarm. She said she would be right over.

I slowly turned around to face Cheech. He was still sleeping. Good boy: sleeping is good for you. I opened my door and waited for help.

Finally, my night assistant with the beeper came. "Bill, I got tired waiting for you to call... What the... Who's he? Why is your headstick on the floor?"

He put my headstick on me. I spelled out on my letter board, "CALL THE COPS HE WAS GOING TO KILL ME"

Cheech moved and groaned.

I started to run over him with my wheelchair. Terror had turned into anger.

"Don't!" my assistant hollered to me, "He could file a lawsuit." Then, my assistant said to Cheech, "Move, and I'll shove your head where the sun don't shine."

I wondered why my assistant could shove the drunk's head where the sun doesn't shine but I couldn't put a few tire tracks on him. After all, it was my life that he'd threatened.

Before my assistant could call a cop, there was a knock on the door.

"Bill, I got your call... I brought the police just in case... What the... Who's he?" my petite morning assistant asked. "Are you all right?"

I nodded, "yes" even as I didn't feel OK.

"What happened?" the cop asked.

"He tried to kill Bill," my assistant said.

"How did he get in?" the cop asked.

"I HEARD A KNOCK AT MY DOOR" I spelled out on my letter board with my headstick, "I FIGURED IT WAS MY AIDE I HAD CALLED HIS PAGER AT TEN BUT I LET IN THE DRUNK GUY"

"I never got your call," my assistant said. He looked at his pager. "Off..." He looked physically ill. "Bill, I'm so sorry."

The cop had to steady him.

"I turned the damn switch off to save batteries. I was almost shot by a cop because... I didn't turn off the alarm in the store I was cleaning.

"Now, you almost get killed because I didn't have another switch on. I'm sorry, Bill."

"I don't see any weapon on the suspect," the cop said. "How was he going to kill you?"

My assistant with the beeper walked swiftly to my kitchen, flung open my cupboard and showed him my steak knife. "With this."

The knife shook in my assistant's hand.

The cop, convinced that I had been in mortal danger, booked the drunk guy on making death threats and criminal trespass. My male assistant helped the cop get the drunk guy into the squad car.

My other assistant gave me a drink and rubbed my neck to settle my nerves. She said, "Glad you're okay."

My male assistant came back in, "You'll never guess where that idiot lives… "my assistant said, "Here… In the apartment next to yours. Apparently, he was so drunk that the jerk knocked on your door by mistake and thought this apartment was his."

"DO YOU MEAN THAT HE IS MY NEIGHBOR?" I spelled out.

"Yeah," my assistant said.

Suddenly I cried hysterically. It was the only release I had.

A few days later, the landlord knocked at my door. "That guy is out of here. He's evicted." He said.

"Are you sure?" I asked.

"Absolutely." he exclaimed.

When the drunk was arraigned I went to the City/County building. I needed to see him being taken into custody.

The District Attorney called me to say that he would do whatever I wanted him to do. If I wanted him to go to prison, he'd petition the judge to put him there. If I wanted him to go to a rehabilitation center, he was confident that the judge would do agree.

It was ironic that I would have some say in the destiny of someone who thought that I was a mess. A part of me wanted my neighbor to rot in a dark, damp dreary dungeon, where rats would gnaw at his flesh. But, another part of me knew that everybody had a right to be rehabilitated. I said that I wanted him to be sent to a drug rehab center. I felt relief when I was told that he would be sent to a drug rehab facility, ninety miles away from me in Lincoln.[1]

I watched Pastor Howard's expression of concern as he poured over my story. He finished reading and looked at me with horror.

"Oh Bill, I am so sorry!" he exclaimed. "I thank you for sharing this with me. I now understand so much more about your life. I will be praying for God to put a hedge of protection around you. You are welcome and safe at First B, you know Bill. It is your church home and we are here to help you in any way you need."

"Thank you for listening and for reading my story," I replied.

My frustration and anger at God for having to go through so many difficult experiences, while doing what I thought that He wanted me to do, that is create a life for myself outside of an institution, lessened by sharing this and other stories with Pastor Howard.

His fatherly support reminded me of my own dad, who always said, "Call if you need anything, Bill." But, because my dad lived an hour and a half away from my home, I appreciated Pastor Howard's more local offer of support.

At a future visit I planned to talk with him about being fully dunked in the baptismal tank to become a real Baptist, as my next step in repairing my relationship with God.

Endnotes

[1.] William Rush, "Drunk Guy Incident" (unpublished manuscript 1987), Word File.

CHAPTER 5

(Chris' Voice)

Making the Call

"It's complicated," I said to the woman speaker during some discussion time at a women's ministry evening held at my church in Hamilton, Ontario. She had asked me if I had a boyfriend.

"Well there is a guy. He's not my boyfriend. He lives in the USA and has a significant disability. There are so many obstacles but there's really something amazing about this relationship. I never believed in love at first sight, but something tells me that's what happened to me." I said.

I was well aware of all the things that my able-bodied family and friends in Canada who knew me, must have been thinking about my relationship with an American guy who had obvious significant disabilities. "Why was I attracted to such a guy?" "Would I have to care for him?" "Could this person make me happy? "Could a relationship with this person give me all that life could offer?"

I knew full well that my able-bodied Canadian world didn't want this for me.

I didn't feel the same way because I already had one foot in the world of people with disabilities. "Was God just moving the other foot over as well?" I questioned. All my work with individuals with disabilities taught me that disability is a natural part of life, not something to be avoided or feared.

"This is going to be OK, whether it works out with Bill or not," the deep down part of my soul said to me.

"About the international part, it wouldn't be the first time," the presenter continued, "And if it is in God's will for this relationship to develop, there will be a way, even around the disability," she continued. "Maybe you should just let God guide you through this to see if it could work. After all, nothing is impossible with God," she concluded. This might have been a platitude that she offered to all of the women that she met with their life's complications. But it landed with me.

The presenter's confidence in a God who works all things for good, matched what I believed deep in my spirit.

It was early November 1988, a couple of weeks since I returned from California and I had not yet called Bill. I needed to call him because I said that I would be in touch after I finished reading his book, *Journey Out of Silence.* [1]

I could have written to him but I was far more used to calling people if I wanted to chat. Dismissing my thought that it was definitely outside of my comfort zone to call a guy in the USA, I found his number by calling directory assistance, took a deep breath and made the call.

"Hello, this is Bill Rush's place," the personal attendant said, when I called Bill's number in Nebraska.

"Hi. I'm Chris," I said. "Could I please talk with Bill?" I asked, trying to sound calm, like I called guys- let alone guys in other countries- every day.

"Sure. Just a minute. Bill just has to get set up here", said the helpful personal care attendant. "Is this the Chris that you met in California?" I could hear the attendant talking to Bill. Then it was silent for a moment, and I imagined that Bill was nodding his head. "I'll do some paperwork while you talk," the pleasant sounding woman said.

"Ah-ha! Bill has a speakerphone. That's how he can talk on the phone," I thought to myself, impressed by his technology without even having seen it, hearing the clang of Bill's legs moving his footrests as he got physically set up to talk to me, presumably at a desk.

"Hello, this is Bill Rush," his computerized voice said. The calmness of the computerized voice was in stark contrast to the excited sounds that I heard Bill and his chair make as I pictured his body jumping up and down in the chair with excitement.

I would find out later that Bill was dumfounded that I had actually called him. It was the first time that a woman had ever called him to chit chat about anything. He was thinking, "This is costing Chris money so I'd better say what I want to say and get off the phone."

"I wanted to tell you that I finished the book and I really enjoyed it. It *was* better than the inflight magazines. You were right. It was a good way to get to know you." I said, as matter-of-factly as I could.

"Glad you liked it, Christine," Bill responded.

"Please call me Chris. That's what all my friends and family call me." I said.

"OK. Chris. How is your work with the teenagers going?" Bill asked.

"It's going really well. The teenagers really want to meet you now that I have met you. We are starting to read your book to them," I responded, delighted and feeling very comfortable now that he was addressing me as Chris.

"What are you working on?" I asked, interested in what Bill did when he wasn't wheeling around Disneyland.

"I'm always working on something," he said. "I'm doing some work on the Board of the League of Human Dignity. And I've been working with my church on installing an elevator so that everyone can get down to the fellowship hall," Bill replied. (Bill would later write a letter of support to the congregants at First Baptist Church in 1990.) [2]

"Glad to hear that your church is getting an elevator. But I have no idea what you mean by the League of Human Dignity," I responded.

"I'll write and tell you about the League and my chur/
offered.

"That would really help," I responded. "By the way, where did
you fly from?" I quickly added.

"Eppley Airfield in Omaha," Bill responded. "Why?"

"I was just wondering. It's getting late. I'd better go. Bye." I said
and hung up, beginning to worry about the cost of the call.

I had not realized how stressful it would be to talk with Bill
over the phone, with his fastest capacity for speech being 8 words
a minute and the meter running on an international, long distance
call. As calm as I might have sounded, I was quickly realizing that if
I was going to get to know Bill, it was going to be hard to do over
the phone.

Bill had been right when he said that we would need to write to
each other to get to know one another.

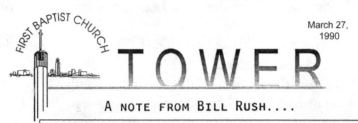

FIRST BAPTIST CHURCH

March 27, 1990

TOWER

A NOTE FROM BILL RUSH....

I attended the business meeting Sunday. I was proud of the congregation for voting to spend extra on the elevator. It showed me a caring that is rare. Thank you.

But, I feel an obligation to tell you that spending $200,000 for just one person isn't frugal. Listening to the moderator made me feel that the new elevator was solely for me. While its true that I plan to become more actively involved in fellowship when the elevator is in, I'm not worth $200,000. But having an fully accessible church is.

A friend who doesn't have a disability is trying to have her church put in an elevator. She is becoming frustrated because the congregation is saying that they don't have anyone who has a disability, so the church doesn't need one. This attitude is very disturbing to me. If I should die before the elevator is complete, would that mean our elevator will become cancelled? I hope not. The church needs an elevator not only because of me but also because people acquire disabilities. Statistics say that one in four people will experience a disability before dying.

So, this is why the First Baptist Church should be prepared to continue to offer any member fellowship in Fellowship Hall, even after they have a disability. I think that by tearing down barriers within the building, the congregation has chosen to assure people who will acquire disabilities, that the thing that makes them people is not in their unconventional muscle movements, nor in their wounded nervous systems, nor in their difficulties in moving, but in the God-given self which no disability can confine.

--Bill Rush

Figure Bill's letter to First Baptist Lincoln supporting installation of the elevator. Reprinted by Permission of Church Life Council, First Baptist Church, Lincoln. NE.

Endnotes

1. William Rush, Journey Out of Silence 2nd Edition, (Lulu.com, 2008).

2. Bill Rush. "A Note from Bill Rush…" *First Baptist Church Tower,* (March 27 1990).

CHAPTER 6

(Chris' Voice)

The World of Bill Rush

True to his word in our phone call, Bill wrote to me to tell me the "League" or "LHD", his affectionate names for The League of Human Dignity, Lincoln Nebraska's Independent Living Center. If I was going to begin to understand Bill's life, this was a very good place to start. He wrote:

> *Dear Chris,*
>
> *It was nice to have your warm Canadian accent filling my apartment when you called the other night. I'm happy that you liked my book. I always say that it can cure insomnia, if nothing else. Ha!*
>
> *I want you to know how about the League and how they supported me to live in my own place. Maybe it will help you to understand my life a little better.*
>
> *When I entered my last semester at UNL in 1981, I was very sick of living in the dorm. I was growing increasingly tired of freshman pranks year after year. My dorm mates didn't understand me. Most hadn't seen anyone with a significant disability (By the way, we in the disability rights movement*

prefer significant over severe because significant reflects better the impact of my disability on my life, neutral, positive and negative verses severe that has a connotation of being negative only.)

The farm boys in my dorm all reacted differently towards me. Some were mature and tried to get to know me. Some ignored me. Some obnoxious ones left signs in the restroom and on my door harassing me. One sign had a cartoon of a head in a wheelchair holding a can of pencils. That really hurt.

The final straw happened in the middle of the night. My phone rang, and my answering machine recorded and played the message, "Isn't making love to a quad like necrophilia, you know, making love to a dead person?" I knew it was time for me to leave. This prank continues to haunt me.

I didn't know anyone with the same degree of disability having their own abode. But, on the other hand, I didn't know of anyone who had the same extent of disability going to college then. To the best of my knowledge, I was rolling blindly where no one had ever been before. Sorry about the pun Captain Kirk. Ha!

Moving into my own apartment wasn't the most ideal option. It had risks no one could imagine. But it was the only choice I could live with. I didn't have any reservations. Anxieties, yes. Fears, yes. But reservations, no. An apartment was the next link in my evolution of independence. Besides, my two other choices, living in an institution or at my parent's home would have left me safe but not sound of mind.

I didn't know that the economic benefits of independent living outside of an institution for people with disabilities had already been proven. I just knew that I need to get out of the dorm and that I didn't want to go back home to live with my parents. But after some research I learned that the cost was estimated to be twenty-five percent (or even less) than the cost of institutionalization.

This is when the League of Human Dignity came into the story. Chris, it's what we call an independent living center. There are more than a hundred of these across the United States. The center is a community-based non-profit, non-residential coordinating office. It provides professional, lay, and volunteer personnel to work with clients who have any type or degree of disability. They have many resources that I access when I think that I need them: housing assistance, peer sharing, financial and legal advocacy, attendant referral and a barrier-removal program.

At the League I have an independent living adviser, someone philosophically aligned with the disability rights movement and familiar with all available community resources to assist me with working toward my own goals. In the disability rights movement we are working for integration of people with disabilities into the fullness of society. The advisor makes suggestions but ultimately support my decisions.

When I wanted to move into my own place, my advisor suggested that I wait to move until the League had established its own transitional living program, a housing facility with a residential supervisor who would offer to teach independent living skills to people with disabilities at their request. I rejected the suggestion because the program wasn't ready and I was.

I applied for a rent subsidy. My adviser explained that under the Federal Community and Housing Act of 1974, the Lincoln City Housing

Authority, could sign a one-year lease for apartment and then rent them to low-income people with disabilities. I would be responsible for a maximum of a quarter of my income going towards the cost of rent. Another federal government program Housing and Urban development would pay the rest. The unfortunate thing was that there was a long waiting list for subsidies and the available accessible housing options were few and often in low-income and higher crime environments. But I wanted it badly enough to go for it anyway.

While we waited for my subsidy to be approved, my adviser made sure that I knew what to eat, how to balance a check book, and how to deal with the problems that would most certainly arise when living on my own. College didn't have a course that adequately covered these matters. If it did and I had taken it, I probably would have failed.

Meanwhile several people told me that they didn't think that I could live on my own. These people mentioned several problems of living alone with a significant disability.

At UNL my professor of independent living ironically said, "There's no way that you can live by yourself. There are too many variables and no way to control them. What if your aide doesn't show up? What if someone robs you? What if? I was astounded by how negative she was until I learned that she was playing devil's advocate to make me think.

I guess that I didn't realize how frightening my position seemed to others. I knew that I wouldn't be able to rely on my own body to do things. I would be dependent on machines to do things for me and machines will break down. I would have to contend with my power wheelchair breaking down in the middle of traffic, and driving in the street when curb cuts are not available. (This will change when we get The Americans with Disabilities Act passed that will require accessibility including curb cuts.) I would have to deal with rolling around town in zero degree weather to do my work because of an inadequate para transit system (Yes! Lincoln like Canada can get really cold!). I suppose another person in my position would not have tried to move into his own place. But I had to.

Other things influenced my decision to live on my own. From my studies of the Disability Rights movement I have learned about institutional care, my only other option. For years people with disabilities were kept in institutions that are usually on the edge of town. In these institutions people were taken care of by caring people. So went the comfortable myth. The fact is many people are abused inside these institutions.

When they aren't being abused, people in institutions don't have any risk or responsibility. They are cared for. But they exist to exist. They are kept safe, but is that life? Not for me.

Back to the League, they helped me with many things, including access to needed technology and a barrier-removal grant. They taught me to learn to think in terms of teamwork to solve any problems that would arise.

The League also helped me to get to field test a device called the Ability Phone by Basic telecommunications Corporation. The device could ask for help with the press of a button. It helps me to control my lights.

I found out that there was a proposed city ordinance that, if passed, would ban automatic phone devices from calling the Lincoln Emergency Center. The supporters of the ordinance felt that too many of these systems were creating false alarms and costing the city lots of money. I reported the ordinance to the League and they helped to work out a compromise. I was given a different number to call instead of 9-1-1. That way, I would still have access to emergency services without bothering the central dispatcher. I had another problem to solve. How would I pay my bills? I couldn't write checks because of my disability and sending money through the mail would be foolish. I was able to find tele-banking services. With a touch-tone phone I am able to pay my bills.

My housing subsidy was approved in 1982. The League helped me to find and efficiency or bachelor apartment. It was in a lower-income neighborhood. It needed some modifications which were provided by my family, the League and the state's vocational rehab program. The apartment is not totally accessible but it is the best I could do to get out on my own. We put an electronic door opener on my door. One of my brothers built a desk for me.

To save money on costly modifications to my tiny bathroom, such as removing the tub and putting in a roll-in shower, I opted to just have bed baths. I do miss tub baths and showers but I couldn't see spending thousands of dollars on it. No tub baths or showers are the price I pay for being a pioneer. I could have pushed for it but, unlike my door opener, it was not absolutely necessary. So I didn't. I pick my battles. Also we didn't modify my kitchen. I can't cook and if I could I would have no way to get the food to my mouth.

And lastly, the League helps me to find attendants. I use a combination of people I hire privately and people that the League recommends. I prefer to call them "personal service assistants". I prefer assistant over attendant because according to the

American Heritage Dictionary, the word attendant means, "One who attends or waits for another," or "One who is present." I don't need someone to wait on me, but I need someone to do more for me than to be simply present. According to the dictionary, aide means" A naval or military officer acting as secretary and confidential assistant to a superior officer of general or flag rank. "I'm not an officer. And assistant means, "One that assists, giving auxiliary aid." This is the type of help I need. Unfortunately, only a few people share this perspective.

Chris, I hope that I have not overwhelmed you with all of this. I do want you to know how I am able to live on my own and how the League has supported me.

Affectionately,
Bill. (Bill Rush, pers. Comm.)

I finished reading Bill's letter, totally impressed both by the community supports Bill had in place to allow him to live on his own and his sheer determination to create his own life, outside of an institution. Wow! There was a lot going on in Lincoln Nebraska (of all places!) to support people with significant disabilities ("Not severe Bill, I hear you.") to live outside of institutions. Bill was one strong guy. He had clearly faced incredible barriers and discrimination at UNL and had succeeded, even graduating with distinction. (Two things that are also nothing short of amazing!) Then he took it one step further and ventured out on his own, when many in a similar position would have retreated. The more I learned about his life, the more I realized that this was one incredibly determined and resourceful person.

Bill was also wise. He knew that writing to me about his life experience was necessary to help me to understand his life before I could consider becoming more than friends with him.

CHAPTER 7

(Bill's Voice)

Welcoming Chris to Nebraska

After Chris called me in November 1988, we started to single-handedly support two national postal systems and at times two telephone companies. At least twice a week I rolled over to the post office to mail another letter to Chris. I was determined to not let this one get away.

My track record with women had been terrible. My family and friends in Nebraska were telling me that pursuing this relationship with Chris was not wise. They were worried that both Chris and I would get hurt. I heard their heartfelt concerns but then dismissed them.

I had proven a lot of naysayers wrong by achieving the impossible already twice in my life, first when I completed my college degree and now by living on my own. Perhaps I could also achieve having a serious relationship with Chris. I wanted it badly enough to fight for it with all I had.

Chris had enough naysayers in Canada. She didn't need to know that there were well-meaning equal opportunity naysayers in Nebraska. So I didn't tell her.

I tried to understand Chris' life while she learned about mine. She really enjoyed her work and loved her life in Canada. Her letters also told me that she was growing in her already deep understanding of people with disabilities. Her heart told me that she knew that people with disabilities are "normal", whatever that is. However, her experience with people with disabilities, primarily in segregated environments, had not given her an opportunity to really experience them as normal. Because I consistently challenged people's assumptions about people with disabilities, I had forced many to grow to see me as no more and no less than them, but rather simply human. Therefore, I was not surprised when Chris wrote:

> *"Bill you seem so normal. I must be crazy because when I think about you, I hear you talk to me in what I think is your own voice. It's not your computer voice that I hear but rather it's what my mind hears as your own voice."*[1]

With absolute delight I responded:

> *"Chris, I have that effect on people. After people spend some time with me, they forget that I have a pretty significant disability. I tend to force people to see me for who I am. And you have done that through our letters. Wow! Welcome to the world of disability cool! Disability is just another way of living. I embrace it and hope that you will too."*[2]

I heard her concern that she did not know an adult with a significant disability who lived outside of an institution in Canada and could see the concerned looks in the faces of family and friends about this relationship she had with me. I suggested that she might need to come and see me and my world.

Chris grabbed the offer. She said that she was coming in December.

She had innocently booked her flight to Omaha because I had told her that I had flown out of Omaha when I went to Anaheim CA. I used Omaha to travel to Anaheim because I couldn't get connecting flights out of Lincoln.

When I told her that Omaha and Lincoln were about 60 miles apart and that Lincoln had its own airport, she said that she would take a bus to Lincoln.

I considered. It would be less work for me, but she was my friend traveling 1000 miles to see me. The least I could do was to meet her at the airport. I thought about how I could get to Omaha. There was an airport transportation service to take people from Lincoln back and forth to Omaha's airport. However that service was not accessible. My options were limited to hitching a ride with a good friend.

So I asked my chess playing buddy, Tom, for a ride. We would have to put me, my manual wheelchair, my wheelchair tray, my Touch Talker and my headstick all into his compact car. I knew that Tom was able and willing to do this because we had done it before when we went together to chess tournaments in Omaha and Lincoln. Tom and I had always had fun together, so I asked him to help me out.

"She must be special for you to want to go to Omaha," he said, "Sure, I will. You have told me so much about her that I'm anxious to meet her. I just hope that my car's heater pumps out enough heat for you two, given that it's pretty cold out."

On December 7, 1988, unlike December 7, 1941, a famous date in American history, Chris came to Lincoln, Nebraska, for the first time to spend a few days with me. Both of us didn't know where our relationship would lead. We only knew that we had to see where it would go. If we didn't, we would always wonder.

Perhaps it was an omen. When I was getting ready to go to Omaha, I heard that Roy Orbison had died. I wasn't that big of a fan, but I could empathize with Orbison when he sang "Pretty Woman" because women had never wanted to have any romance with me. My pain had been easier to bear because someone like him had sung about it. Now that a beautiful woman, namely Chris, was interested in me, Orbison could rest in peace.

Tom and I drove the 60 miles from Lincoln to the Omaha airport. Tom filled the time with chitchat about his latest escapades at a chess tournament. The weather was crisp and cold. I was thankful that Eppley Airport had underground parking.

We waited for what seemed like an interminable amount of time for Chris to appear. The devil tried to put thoughts into my mind. Maybe she wasn't coming. Maybe Chris had missed her flight. Maybe this had been all an elaborate ruse by AT&T to get me to spend all my money on long distance phone calls. I laughed at myself for these thoughts.

Then I thought about how much I had been trusting in God, when it came to difficult aspects of my life lately. My time with Pastor Howard and with my fellow congregants at First Baptist were helping me to rebuild my faith and trust in a God who loved and wanted the best for me.

While we waited for Chris' arrival, I intentionally reminded myself of how God had been in our relationship so far. He had set up our "chance" meeting in California that was a divine appointment.

He had allowed for us to be able to communicate easily, right from the beginning. This was something that happened with very few people. Most people got the timing of communicating with me all messed up and we spent our time trying to fill in the pieces that were mixed up. Chris was naturally good at reading my non-verbal signals and patient with my Touch Talker™. God had prepared her, by having her work with teenagers with significant disabilities.

And He had given us our national postal systems and telephone companies and also airlines to help us to stay connected.

He had brought us this far. He would not abandon us now.

Then, suddenly Chris appeared and said, "Hi, it's good to see you again! Who's your friend?"

"Hi I'm Tom," Tom said, "I had the honor of being Bill's first opponent in his first game of his first chess tournament."

"And, he is the first person to whip me in a tournament," I said.

"You aren't supposed to say that," Tom said.

I wanted to say it. I didn't want to have any misconceptions between Chris and me. I enjoyed chess but I wasn't a really good chess player. I saw no need in pretending that I was. I wanted to have a good, honest relationship with Chris. I didn't want to play games with her.

I had asked another friend Connie if she would host Chris to stay with her at her home for the time that she was visiting with me. Connie gladly said yes. She lived across town but for a few days was more than willing to give Chris rides to and from my place so that Chris could spend lots of time visiting with me.

I wanted Chris' experience of my world in Lincoln, NE to be positive. So I put my best wheel forward. I took her to the League of Human Dignity to meet the people who supported me to live on my own. Chris was very impressed by how the staff at the League embodied self-determination in their conversations with us. She became a member of the League and I smiled. I was creating a Canadian disability rights advocate and I relished that idea.

I became a tour guide to downtown Lincoln. My world was limited to twenty square blocks, the distance that I could roll in my power wheelchair on one battery charge. Downtown Lincoln is an entertainment district, so I would have no difficulty finding things for us to do. We enjoyed spending time together at a movie, roaming around the UNL campus showing Chris where I went to school, checking out the Sheldon Museum to show her that we had cultured things in Lincoln and hanging at my place. I took Chris out to eat once so that she could begin to experience eating with me in public.

I loved having Chris with me in my world, hanging with me, talking with me and seeing where I lived. She seemed to enjoy letting me take her out to explore the downtown and clearly enjoyed being with me. But there was one thing that she didn't like and she was honest enough to tell me.

"Bill. Why do you have a Marilyn poster?" she asked.

"It's like a travel poster to me. Some place that I thought that I would never get to visit. The land of women," I answered with a nervous laugh.

"I don't like it. It's soft porn." Chris responded.

"OK It's gone." I replied. She was right. It was soft porn. Not God honoring and not woman honoring either.

As soon as the next assistant arrived to help me, I asked him to take down the poster and to destroy it. I'd happily put my tire tracks all over it, if Chris wanted me to do it.

I was concerned and worked hard to protect Chris from anything do to with my need for personal care assistance. She was not my assistant. She was my friend. I told her that I had rules about friends not doing my personal care because I was afraid that they would feel used. I would not risk losing her friendship (or whatever this was) because of my ongoing care needs.

When my assistants arrived I introduced them to Chris. "This is Chris, my friend. She is not my assistant. You are. Thank you for continuing to assist me the same as always, while Chris is here."

Our visit was so short that I didn't get to take Chris to First Baptist church with me. But that was OK for this trip, I decided.

People at church were just beginning to get comfortable with me. And I wasn't sure how they would react to Chris being with me. I didn't want her to have to answer people's questions or make her have to deal with the stares of curious people. I wanted to keep her as comfortable as possible in my environment on this first trip.

The time with Chris went by far too quickly. Before I knew it Tom and I were taking her back to the Omaha airport for her return trip to Canada.

God did not let me down. He had helped me to make this trip a success for both of us.

Tom went for a walk to give us some time alone when we got to the airport. Chris gave me a hug as we sat waiting for her plane to board. She looked happy.

"I feel much better Bill, now that I have been here. This trip had really helped me to see how you live in Lincoln. You have many supports Bill. I like your friends. We were able to do so many things together. Thank you for organizing all of it. I really enjoyed being here with you."

"Your welcome. Thank you for coming," was all I could say, as she walked away to board the plane.

I was feeling very happy that she had come and very sad that she was leaving. I sat in the window of the gatehouse, watching her plane back away from the Jet Way, thanking God for helping me to pull off this visit without a hitch. God had helped me to keep Chris protected from problems that I faced when living in the community, at least during this first pleasant trip. And I was so grateful.

I began pleading with Him to help me to get her back here again. He knew I needed this wonderful woman in my life and I desperately needed His help to make it happen.

Only God could pull off this relationship. I knew it now. I couldn't do it without Him.

Endnotes

1.   Christine Robinson, Personal Communications 1989.
1.   William Rush, Personal Communications 1989.

CHAPTER 8

(Chris' Voice)

Disability Rights Movement
Creates Servant Leader

Back in Canada after my visit to Nebraska, I was feeling more comfortable about my developing relationship with Bill. Seeing how Bill was able to live independently and control his own life had done much to assure me that Bill was more than capable of being in whatever kind of relationship we would work out.

I was especially delighted to find that Bill put my needs first when I was with him, careful to make sure that I was comfortable and happy. I needed someone equally dedicated and attentive in a relationship with me or it wouldn't work. Bill was my match in this.

The able-bodied Canadian men I had known did not measure up to Bill in capacity for demonstrating caring. These men did nice things for me to show affection, such as taking me to dinner and giving me flowers on Valentine's Day. However, ironically, these able-bodied men with intact neurological systems did not work nearly as diligently and consistently as Bill did to make sure that my every need was met when I was with him. I continued to think about this interesting contrast as the New Year approached.

Early in January 1989 I called Bill to wish him "Happy New Year."

"Happy New Year Bill!" I exclaimed. "What's happening in your world?"

"I'm going to Washington for a few days." Bill said.

"What are you doing in Washington?" I asked, curious about Bill's travel plans.

"I've been asked to go and open my big American mouth," Bill joked.

"What do you mean?" I asked, becoming even more curious.

"Chris, you really don't know who I am, do you," Bill responded.

"No I guess I don't." I answered honestly.

"I'm going to brainstorm with some others with disabilities for a government agency." Bill explained.

"Wow!" I responded, amazed. I really didn't know who Bill was to his nation. I only knew how he lived and what he did in Lincoln Nebraska. There was clearly much about Bill's life and work that I had yet to learn.

"It's not that exciting." Bill responded. "I would like to get to see DC but I don't think I will get to. I'll call you when I get back. Gotta go."

"OK. Have a good trip." I said still feeling a little stunned to hear that Bill had been summoned to the US capital.

Bill called after his trip to Washington.

"I was in a hotel working for two days and didn't get to see any of the sights." Bill said. "I wanted to see the Lincoln Memorial and the closest I got was flying over it." he lamented to me.

He moved on to talk about other more urgent things. I wanted to know what he had been doing in Washington but I didn't press him.

Much later I would learn a little about Bill's first "Washington" trip and a lot about Bill. He was one of 60 people with unusual viewpoints, invited to meet at a National Conference on Self-Determination, to give recommendations to the Office of Special Education and Rehabilitation Services on directions they should take. According to an OSERS official, nothing like this had ever been done before.

Bill was in one of five planning groups. Twenty-nine recommendations were given to policy makers from the branches of the

US Department of Education. The disability rights movement philosophy of self-determination was well embedded in the work completed at the conference. The first recommendation summarized the tone of the conference, "The enabling of people with disabilities to determine their own futures shall be seen as the top priority in all government policymaking functions."

Learning about this conference and Bill's response to it helped me to begin to understand the inner workings of the disability rights movement and how it had contributed to shaping Bill's character into something I liked and admired. Bill's lack of desire to promote his role at this national conference to me was symptomatic of the members of the disability rights movement.

Leadership was expected but not glorified. Everyone in the disability rights movement was required to do what they could on behalf of all persons with disabilities, without drawing attention to themselves. The movement, although with definite leaders such as Bill, focused its energy on defining a common future rather than promoting its leaders. Bill's endless work of caring for all people with disabilities, demonstrated by his unwavering dedication to speak out on behalf of all, without requiring that he be recognized, had been a great training ground for him to learn to put his own interests and ego aside and concentrate on caring for others.

Learning about Bill's trip helped me to figure out why he, with his significantly impaired nervous system was much more capable of caring for me in practical ways that the able-bodied Canadian men I had known.

Servant leadership in the disability rights movement had been Bill's training ground. Servant leadership of any kind had not been required in the lives of the able-bodied Canadian men I had known. And it showed.

CHAPTER 9

(Bill's Voice)

Bill's Baptism

"Bill, do you want me to give you communion?" Arch, the stern retired Lieutenant Colonel asked, coming toward me with the trays of grape juice and the small crackers. I was sitting at the back of the church in the aisle, so as not to be in the way during the worship service.

Amazed that Arch would do this, I quickly nodded "yes", tipped my head back so he could toss a cracker piece into my mouth and he did. He waited for me to munch on the cracker. When I was done, I looked to him to indicate that I was ready for the grape juice. I tilted my head again and he poured the grape juice into my mouth, while firmly but gently holding a clean handkerchief under my chin to catch any drips. When I had finished swallowing and brought my head down, Arch was still there. He nodded to me as if to say, "Mission accomplished."

The colonel had my back. I was surprised and delighted and emotionally moved by his action. Arch was brave enough to show his love for me in a tangible way in front of the rest of congregation. My caring friend was helping me to eat at the Communion Table to remember what Jesus had done for me.

Meanwhile Pastor Howard and I continued to meet for a couple of afternoons a month at my place. There were many things I wanted to share and discuss with him, including my growing relationship with Chris and my desire to be baptized. I told him that I was growing very close to Chris, a woman from Canada who had come to visit me once.

"I'm worried about Chris," I continued. "I want and need her in my life but I don't know if it is fair to ask her to be with me in a life that is barely created. She would experience so much discrimination herself. The state system is archaic, and so are our communities. Society is just beginning to be ready for me to live in community by myself, but is not anywhere near ready to accept that I could have a wife. The state is not yet set up to handle me having a family. Current state regulations would take away funding for my personal assistant services if I get married and then we would be destitute." I shared.

"Regardless of the financial situation with the state, Chris has the right to explore this relationship with you. You don't have the right to take that away. Enjoy it. That's what I would do." Howard retorted.

"Furthermore, you are working on all of these things Bill. And God is with you." Howard continued. "Let God show both of you the way forward Bill. Don't get in His way."

It was the encouragement that I needed. Maybe God really was working around and through me to give me the miracle that I had prayed for.

I pondered Howard's response. Yes. He was correct. It was Chris' right. But I was still worried for her.

I had been praying about sharing the current state of the state regulations with Chris. It seemed a bit premature to tell her such weighty details when she didn't even live in the same country. However, she did have the right to know the barriers that existed for me to get married. I just didn't know if and when to share these things with her.

"Tell me the Baptist position on baptism." I continued, with my thoughts back in the conversation with Howard. "I was baptized as a baby but want to understand why Baptists dunk adults."

"Baptists practice Believer's baptism, Bill. In the Anabaptist tradition, a person is baptized on the basis of his or her profession of faith in Jesus Christ and as admission into a local community of faith. In the Book of Acts we see many examples of individuals becoming Believers, receiving Christ as their personal Savior to save them from their sins and then being baptized."

Pastor Howard continued, "Water baptism is a picture of what happens when you placed your faith and trust in the death, burial, and resurrection of Jesus Christ to save you from your sins. Spiritual baptism is the Christian's identification with Christ. This is why we, as Baptists, follow this tradition."

I was taking all of this in. It made sense to me to proclaim my faith in Jesus as an adult. I was grateful for Jesus paying the ultimate price for my sin, by dying on a cross for me, securing my eternal home in Heaven. In my repaired relationship with God, I was learning to rely on His strength to deal with the daily struggles involved in living out my life's calling as a disability rights advocate.

Pastor Howard then added, "My position is that there should be freedom of choice in the setting and the amount of water that is used for the baptism. If conditions are such that sprinkling water on one's head is more convenient, then so be it."

"Does that answer your questions Bill?" Pastor Howard concluded.

"Yes. I want to be immersed." I said without hesitation.

"Bill, it is not necessary for you to be immersed. We have lots of freedom around this issue." Pastor Howard said once again.

"I understand that but I like the symbolism. I don't want sprinkling." I insisted.

"OK. Fine. Then we will find four strong men to get you into the baptismal pool." Pastor Howard said confidently.

He had no idea what he was getting himself into, I thought to myself.

Thinking this through out loud, I added, "I think that would work. I could sit in my manual chair and you could dunk me forward into the water." I offered. "If I'm strapped into the chair, then I won't slide into the water. It could get really crazy if I fall in." I laughed.

"Bill, I appreciate that you want to participate in the completeness of the meaning and symbolism of baptism by immersion. I haven't lost anyone yet in the baptismal pool. I'm not going to lose you. We'll have lots of help." Pastor Howard concluded with total confidence.

In late January 1989 I was baptized by immersion to publicly declare my faith in Jesus Christ as my personal Savior and Lord. Four strong men, including the Colonel, gladly helped me down the stairs into the baptismal pool. The process was flawless; the strong men easily carried me and my chair down into the pool. I even survived having my head dunked forward into the water.

Pastor Howard explained to the church that I had requested that I be immersed to demonstrate the symbolism of my dying with Christ to then be resurrected to new life in Him. I was delighted that the men had been willing to help me to demonstrate my faith through Baptism by immersion.

Pastor Howard's wife Hazel saw me after the dunking and before I had moved back into my power wheelchair. Seeing me for the first time without my headstick she remarked, "What a handsome man you are!" As I beamed, I thought to myself, "Ah-ha! So Chris isn't the only one who thinks I'm handsome, after all."

After the baptism Pastor Howard told me, "This time next year we should have an elevator put in this building."

I nodded with appreciation, knowing that it was going to take a lot of work and money to get the elevator installed.

Neither of us knew at that point that there would be some significant barriers to getting the elevator up and running.

CHAPTER 10

(Bill's Voice)

Eulogy for a Disability Rights Advocate Friend

In late March 1989 I decided to treat myself to Oliver Stone's Born on the Fourth of July. After all, I had heard Siskel and Ebert had given it two thumbs up.

Unfortunately, they would have given my wheelchair battery two thumbs down. When I rolled into the theater, the batteries were almost dead. I was hoping that the batteries would have recharged themselves during the movie. No such luck. When the movie was over, the batteries were still dead. I slowly crept out into the movie theater's lobby where I asked the theater manager to call the wheelchair accessible taxi van.

He did. He said that the taxi company told him that it had discontinued the wheelchair accessible van. No one had been riding it because the city of Lincoln wouldn't subsidize it.

Then, I suggested he call my adviser. She would know what to do. He dialed the number that I had given him.

He said that no one answered. Then, he said that he would call the police because he had to close the theater.

The police were just as baffled, bothered and bewildered as the theater manager. But they had a four-wheel drive vehicle. They tried calling the (UN)Handi-Van. They were told that it didn't run on Sunday nights.

Then, they tried calling my adviser. Still no answer. Where was she?

Then, they called my home health care agency. The on call nurse sent a personal service assistant to the movie theater to see what he could do to help. When he arrived, he said, "I was beginning to worry about you."

A frustrated cop asked, "Can you transport him in your vehicle?"

"No, I can't," the personal service assistant said, "I'm not authorized to transport him, and therefore, I'm not covered by insurance."

"Okay, can you help us get him into our vehicle?" the officer asked.

"Yeah, I can," the personal service assistant said.

"Great. Here's what we are going to do. We will load him into our vehicle and leave the wheelchair here. Someone will have to pick it up tomorrow," the officer said.

I wondered how many others he had casually ordered to leave their legs behind.

My personal service assistant helped me to get into the police four-wheel drive vehicle. Next, he took my apartment key to get my manual wheelchair ready for me and said, "See you in a couple."

I wondered if they were going to let me run the lights and siren. They didn't. Disappointed.

When I got home, there was a message from Chris on my telephone answering machine, "I wanted to know if you had figured out that Mrs. Columbo hadn't died before they told us."

I had forgotten that I was going to watch the Sunday night Columbo Mystery movie with her. Of course, she was going to watch it in Hamilton, Ontario, and I was going to watch it in Lincoln, Nebraska. In a way, I had stood her up. I hoped she would forgive me when she found out.

When I got to sleep, I had a fitful dream that Chris was standing on the shore of a lake patiently calling for me to come join her. I couldn't because my wheelchair's batteries were dead.

The next morning someone from the League of Human Dignity called to cancel my standing appointment with my adviser. The woman said, "Last night she had a heart attack. She is in intensive care now. Knowing her, she will be up around very soon."

I agreed with her and thanked her for calling.

Then, I called my wheelchair repair guy and asked him if he would mind getting my wheelchair at the movie theater. We joked about me being so drunk that I couldn't drive home. He said that they would have the wheelchair back to me by noon. I thanked him.

I did some writing. I had a hard time concentrating. I kept thinking about my adviser. There was a knock at my door. It was the wheelchair technician with my dead wheelchair. He said I should let it have a good charge before I went anywhere. I suppressed the urge to say, "No kidding" to him.

I was remembering once, when I was visiting with Eileen at the League and one of my footrests had broken. The League of Human Dignity's wheelchair mechanic didn't have time to fix it. And I had to get back to my place in time for my supper aide.

Eileen had tried to call the unHandi-van to ask if I could get a ride home. (The Handi-van is Lincoln Nebraska's Para transit system that I humorously call the Unhandi-van.). They had said that I had to wait for two hours. She had said, "No thank you." Then, to me she said, "Honestly, Bill, you'd think they would have an emergency service for a time like this."

I had agreed with her.

"Do you think you can make it home with your footrest like that?" Eileen had asked me.

The pin that held the footrest in place had broken, so every so often the footrest would swing out, making me do a modified version of the splits. "I DONT KNOW. I DONT LIKE HAVING TO DRIVE LIKE THIS BUT I DONT HAVE MUCH OF A CHOICE." I had spelled out to her on my language board.

"I don't like it either, my adviser had agreed, and added, "So why don't I follow you back in my car? I know that there is dignity in risk, but I don't want to worry about you."

I remembered feeling uneasy about having her follow me home. I knew if I had a problem, my adviser would have to stop her car, get her own wheelchair out of her back seat, get in the wheelchair, wheel herself over to me, help me, wheel herself back over to her car, transfer herself back into her car and put her wheelchair back into her back seat of her car. It seemed like too much work for her.

But God had been kind to us that night. I got home without my footrest deciding to leave my wheelchair.

I prayed that God would be equally as good to my adviser today. Unfortunately, I couldn't follow her to the hospital, as she had followed me to ensure my safety.

So, I tried to busy myself. I watched the Columbo movie that I had recorded the night before. I wanted to be able to talk about it with Chris.

Around noon I called the League of Human Dignity again, to ask about my adviser. The word was not encouraging. She had had another heart attack. They were waiting.

Around suppertime I had an uneasy feeling. After we got me some dinner, I asked my 18-year-old personal service assistant to call the hospital to ask about my adviser.

A nurse at the hospital asked my personal service assistant if she was related to my adviser. In a twinkling of an eye and a telling of a lie, my adviser got a new 18-year-old granddaughter. The hospital nurse paused and said, "Perhaps you should call your family."

We didn't have to call, because we could read between the lines. But we did anyway. A sniffling woman told us that my adviser had died.

My personal service assistant said, "I'm sorry about your friend, Bill. Are you okay because I have to go to another client, but I want to make sure you are all right?"

I thanked her for making the calls. I said that she could leave and that I would be all right. She left.

I called the League of Human Dignity to make sure that someone there knew the latest on my adviser. Once a journalist, always a journalist.

The executive director answered the telephone. After I told him the bad news, he sighed deeply and said, "We'll miss her. I appreciate you calling. Good-bye."

I hung up. I missed Eileen and her courage and confidence in the Disability Rights movement already. She had been my adviser, mentor and confidante.

I remembered a recent conversation when I had complained to Eileen about where I was living. The visit from my drunken neighbor and other bizarre incidents had upset me terribly and I had wanted to move but didn't know of any other apartments where I could live.

Always resourceful, Eileen had let me know about an old furniture warehouse building being renovated into an apartment building near the post office in the downtown Haymarket district.

Suddenly, I wanted to go see the building. It would be a way to remember her.

On the way to the apartment building I reflected on the day's events.

Why wasn't I crying? My Adviser was a dear friend and encourager to me. She had died but I hadn't shed a tear. Was I learning how to suppress my emotions so well that I was losing them? Had there been so many people coming into and out of my life that someone dying had become just another person leaving? Even Chris had commented that there was an emotional wall around me.

I also remembered that Dr. Irving K. Zola, Ph.D., the noted disabilities studies sociologist, wrote: "Thus, with virtually no acceptable avenues for expression, those with a chronic disability are forced either to turn their anger in on themselves or to blunt it. To the degree that we succeed in the latter we become increasingly unfeeling, and often so distanced from ourselves that virtually nothing can touch us. In this way we provide the basis for the stereotype in the professional literature, which describes us as "difficult to reach." [1]

The renovated warehouse was very accessible and looked like a good place to live. It was a six-story building that had two security doors. But, I thought about how hard it would be to move all my computer equipment and inwardly I shuddered. I didn't want to deal with the hassles of moving now. Plus asking my family and friends to move me would be like asking them to move the space shuttle, again.

That evening I called Chris and was greeted with, "Hello, how was your day today? How long did it take you to figure out that Colombo's wife didn't die?"

I told her, "The past 24 hours has been the worst of my life." I told her everything that had happened.

"Oh dear. You have had a bad day today. I wish I was down there to give you a big hug," Chris said.

"So do I. So do I," I said.

I hung up the phone. I remembered how happy my adviser was about Chris. Once I had confided to my adviser, "I have a relationship with Chris. It's scaring me to death. My track record with women stinks, and I haven't had a lot of dating experience. Add to this that she lives in Canada…"

"Chris is obviously interested in you and wants to have a relationship with you. So what is the problem?"

"In the past I have made a mess out of every friendship I had with a woman because I had unrealistic expectations of those women," I said.

"I disagree with that. Those women led you on, and when you responded like any other man would have, they ran," my adviser said.

"Chris doesn't do that to me. She is the most honest and honorable person I have ever met," I said.

"Good! You're due for that kind of woman in your life. Enjoy her," she said.

My adviser always did give good advice.

The morning after I told Chris about my adviser's death I saw a FTD delivery truck pulled up outside my apartment. The delivery person came up the apartment's sidewalk and knocked on my door. He was carrying a bouquet of beautiful springtime flowers in a brass vase.

I figured he wanted to know where someone lived in the apartment building. He asked if I was Bill Rush.

I nodded, and he said, "These are for you. Can I put them on the desk for you? Do you want me to open the card for you?"

I nodded. He opened it and left.

I read, "Hope you have a better day. Love, Chris."

The tears came. Finally.

The next day I was rolling past the League of Human Dignity and went in. My adviser's supervisor greeted me somberly with, "Hi, I can't believe she's gone. There is a real void here. Her daughter called and asked me to ask you if you would write a eulogy for her."

I said I would be more than happy to do it. I was grateful to my adviser's daughter for asking me to write a eulogy. I had lost other friends without knowing about their dying. When I found out about their death, I grieved twice as much. Not only did I grieve because they were dead but I also grieved because I didn't have the chance to say "Good-bye," to them.

The League of Human Dignity arranged for the (Un)handi-van to take all her friends who needed accessible transportation to the funeral home for her Rosary. While I was grateful for the chance to say good-bye to my adviser and friend, I couldn't help thinking what would have happened if she weren't a part of the League of Human Dignity.

Would her friends with disabilities still get a chance to publicly mourn her? The (Un)handi-van was used primarily for priority medical visits. Regular buses were not accessible. If the League had not negotiated with the management for the UnHandi-van to get some buses for this occasion, it would have been impossible for people with disabilities to get to the funeral.

The League made sure that everyone who wanted a ride got one. I went. Chris had knitted a sweater for me and I wore it. It was the closest I could get to have her arms around me.

The funeral almost came off without a hitch. Before the funeral I was told that I was to come forward when a person started to read my eulogy. When it came time for my tribute, the center aisle was blocked with the casket in front and with people in wheelchairs in back. I was trapped in the middle.

I tried signaling for help, but no one saw me or was able to understand that my waving arms were an attempt to communicate rather than some involuntary movement.

Slowly, I tried to get around the casket but it was too wide. I ran into it on my way by it.

I wanted the church floor to open and swallow me. It didn't.

So I went to the front where a woman whom I didn't know was reading my tribute to my adviser.

She tearfully read:

> *Once Eileen called me the great communicator. I got mad at her because that was Ronald Reagan's nickname, and I voted for Kermit the frog. So Mary, Eileen's daughter, asked me to introduce myself. I'm Bill Rush, Eileen's friend.*
>
> *Eileen entered my life as an independent living adviser, but she exits as a valued friend. It was a standing joke that when she met me, she didn't have any gray hair, but that after a week of working with me, she was totally gray.*
>
> *We worked together for nearly seven years. During this time Eileen let me know that she was available at any time. I'm sure that her family got tired of my calling in the middle of the night saying that I had fired my night aide and needed someone to help me into bed.*
>
> *Probably the biggest help she gave me was her attitude towards her disability. Many people have told me that I should take pride in my disability. She showed me how. She had polio, but I dare anyone to say that she is better off without it. To her having polio was like having blue eyes. What bothered she was others' attitudes towards her just because she was in a wheelchair. Her life was dedicated to quietly fighting inaccessibility. In fact, Eileen is probably trying to get St. Peter to put in an elevator by his golden stairway.*
>
> *If you are thinking of a suitable memorial to this lady, you might call your Congressional*

representatives and urge the passage of a strong Americans with Disabilities Act. If passed, this bill would end legal discrimination towards people with disabilities.

I ended my eulogy with, "Eileen, you will be missed terribly but remembered lovingly. Good-bye." [2]

The priest said that my adviser was an invalid. I cringed. I half expected my adviser to open up her coffin and to sit up in it and say, "Honestly, I strongly object to that as person with a disability!!"

After the service my adviser's daughter thanked me for my testimony.

I quickly apologized for bumping into the casket on my way to the front for my eulogy.

"You know, Bill, Mom used to tell me about how you two had to maneuver around in her small office and how you two were always bumping into one another. She would say you were playing bumper wheelchairs rather than bumper cars."

I nodded, remembering these movements and our shared laughter.

"So it's fitting that you bump into Mom one last time," she said and hugged me.

Two weeks after the funeral the League of Human Dignity held an open house to dedicate its new large downtown facility.

The powers that be decided that the new digs would be dedicated to my adviser and friend, Eileen.

It was a time of healing.

Endnotes

1.   Irving Kenneth Zola, *Missing Pieces: A Chronicle of Living with a Disability.* (Philadelphia: Temple, 1982)

2.   Bill Rush. Personal Communications. (March 1989)

CHAPTER 11

(Chris' Voice)

American Independent Living Role Model Comes to Canada

"Hey Bill. Why don't you live here in Canada where they keep people like you locked away far from the city? You could live out here with the cows." Don, Bill's assistant joked as we rolled along country roads away from the city of Hamilton Ontario travelling towards Participation House, the 250-bed institution for adults who experience physical disabilities, renowned in Canada for it's exemplary care of adults with disabilities.

It was the 31st of March 1989 and we were on our way to a conference entitled "Moving Towards Independent Living", hosted by the Hamilton-Wentworth Communication Collective. Bill had been asked to be one of the speakers to talk about his experience of hiring and firing his own personal care assistants to an audience of adults and adolescents from the Hamilton area who experience a physical disability, their families, professionals and support staff.

The Hamilton-Wentworth Communication Collective consisted of parents and professionals working to support the lives of individuals who require augmentative and alternative communication. Some parents of the teens with whom I worked were actively lobbying government and local organizations to create a community based living arrangement for their teenagers when they were finished with high school. In Hamilton where personal attendant services were in their infantile stage, the only options for individuals who needed assistant services were to live in a few supervised independent living apartments or in the large institution.

The Collective decided to have a conference about independent living to increase awareness of the need for independent living options. They invited some Ontario government officials, local agencies, and the parents' group to speak of their plans for a community-based home and Bill, the outsider, to speak about his experience of doing what no one in Hamilton was doing at the time -- living on his own.

Feeling proud to have Bill coming to speak about what people in Hamilton could only dream of and very excited to have a chance to spend a little time together, I offered to coordinate Bill's travel plans and accommodation. Bill had shown that he was able to host me in his community. I wanted to return the favor.

I was able to borrow the accessible van from my work's pre-school program to transport Bill and Don from and to Toronto's Pearson International Airport, to Participation House, and out and around the city for some fun. There was one small step to my apartment door. I knew that Don and I could easily lift Bill's manual chair over the one step into my place. Bill's power chair would stay in the van. I was feeling proud that I, like Bill could problem-solve.

I didn't live day to day with disability in the real world like Bill did, but I was getting better at this sort of thing. A Chinese-Canadian colleague at my work had kindly offered her place to me for a couple of hours that evening so that Bill and I could have some time alone, while letting Don have some time to himself at my place. I told Bill and Don about the plans for the evening on the way out to the conference.

"Here comes the big-mouthed American. Rescue me if they try to trap me inside Chris." Bill joked with me, using his Touch Talker™, as we got him onto the lift in his power wheelchair, when we had arrived. With a look that said to me that he wanted to run far, far away from this institution, but was determined to do what he was here to do anyway, Bill rolled into the institution to share what he could about his own life, with people, who could only dream of such possibilities for their lives.

Bill was first to speak at the conference. He spoke about the realities of hiring and firing his own assistants and his work to change the system to better suit his and other's needs in Nebraska. He had carefully prepared and saved his speech into his Touch Talker™.

This is what he wrote for the conference:

> "*It's hard to paint a picture of my first couple of months of independent living without discouraging people who want to try it. Martin Luther King Jr. once said, "If a man hasn't discovered something that he will die for, he isn't fit to live.' I wouldn't die, but institutional living was a fate worse than death to me. So, a commitment to living on my own became my something to die for as well as my something to live for.*
>
> *Often I would get up in the morning, hear that my bedtime assistant couldn't come that night and spend the day searching for someone to put me to bed. Or, an assistant would just not show up. Or give me two weeks' notice. Emerson once said, "Life is a series of surprises, and would not be worth taking or keeping if it were not."*
>
> *I thought, "I have to be on the right track because my life is one surprise after the other."*
>
> *When I lived in a college dorm, I had relied solely on college students. I had found, trained and sometimes fired them. Social services of Nebraska paid them minimum wage. Almost every assistant I had lived within a stone's throw of my dorm room. So I was able to make it work while I lived at the U.*
>
> *But when I moved off campus, I would learn that most college students would find it inconvenient to drive, walk or pedal 20 blocks to my place for minimum wage.*

I learned to manage my assistants by trial and error. It was a trial caused by several errors. For instance one night a new assistant left me on the bedpan for two and a half hours—due to circumstances beyond his control.

Normally an assistant put a stainless steel bedpan in my manual wheelchair, tied my ankles and thighs, and middle with surgical ties and left me alone in my apartment's living room for half an hour because of inaccessible bathroom. Two and a half hours later I was still on the bedpan. My eyes were getting bags under them and my rear was getting a ring around it. There was finally a knock at my door. I opened it via the remote control that was on my lap tray.

It was the police saying to me, sitting naked in my living room, "We have arrested your assistant for having outstanding parking tickets. We have called another assistant for you and he'll be over soon. Good night."

I was wondering if there was an ordinance against having a bowel movement in your living room.

The next day the sorry assistant called to say the he couldn't come over that night to put me to bed.

"You're fired." I typed into my voice synthesizer.

When it came to assistants I had a revolving door on my apartment. Part of this is because I am an exacting person. But the other part was because the bureaucrats in charge couldn't have designed a more self-defeating system if they tried. The state of Nebraska requires copious amounts of complicated paperwork to be submitted by the assistant. The work pays so poorly that good help gets tired of it and leaves. Very few of my assistants are able to see the situation through the eyes of the welfare office, which has regulations that it must follow.

Finding and managing four assistants every day to meet my personal care needs really took its toll on me. After four years of doing this, I was relieved to hear my local independent living center adviser suggest that we begin to look into getting a better source of assistants. She was concerned that nobody could handle the stress that I was under.

We debated the pros and cons of having private providers like I had been doing, verses using an agency. If I had an agency, I would have a built in back-up system. I would also be removed from the hassles of the billing process. If the assistant made a mistake on the form they were not paid. This caused stress between me and my assistants. In California, for example, the person who needs the assistance is given so much money to pay their assistants each month, and this eliminates this hassle with paper work. Unfortunately Nebraska likes its paperwork.

My adviser suggested an agency that some others were using. However, she said that the state would claim that I was doing fine without it. I would have to make a case for needing an agency because an agency would cost the state more per visit for my care.

I had some misgivings about using an agency. I had once used an agency for my chore and attendant care service. I had gotten the impression that the agency had resented me for needing services after their office hours and on the weekends. Something I had thought that they wanted me to dry up on the weekends and hydrate on Mondays.

They had tried without success to get me to do things their way. They said that they couldn't serve me outside my home, which meant that I couldn't eat out like every other American. They said that I had to eat at certain times or I would have to miss my meal. Of course I always fought with them. I told them that they had to feed me where and when I wanted to eat. I was eventually dropped.

I met with my adviser and the head of Nebraska's Department of Social Services. Might as well go to the top with this problem we thought. I wasn't getting much writing done anyway. I was spending my days lining up assistants. The head of welfare seemed open to suggestions and sympathetic to my problem. My adviser explained the difficulty of keeping good assistants. The job offered minimum wage, no travel expenses, no chance of a raise and no benefits. My adviser also pointed out that even with an agency, the state would be paying less than they would should I decide to move to a nursing home.

The head didn't say yes, but didn't say no either. She said she wanted to study the situation before she made her decision. She said to let her know if I had any problems with my assistants.

So I did. The next time an assistant couldn't show up, I called the head and asked her what I could do. She helped me by authorizing an agency for an emergency visit since neither she nor I could find a private provider.

I kept doing this for about two weeks. Five assistants called me and canceled. Each time that a cancellation happened, I let her know so that she could have a taste of the type of stress that I was living under. She had to agree that being so dependent on people and not having a good back up system in place was too stressful for anyone.

Some people in Nice Nebraska would say that I harassed the head, but I prefer to say that I ori-

ented her to the reality of Independent Living in the state.

My adviser at the league asserted that I changed the state's welfare attitude. She said that before our meeting the state welfare people didn't take the efforts of the independent living center seriously. When the head saw what I was able to do with the help of the center, she was impressed. Somehow it legitimized the cause of independent living to her.

To conclude, I think that everyone has the right to move toward independent living should you choose to want to have it. However, supports need to be in place for you to be successful and your government agencies need to be responsive to your needs for personal assistant services. [1]

Bill finished his presentation, carefully rolled his wheelchair over and sat beside me. His facial expression and body told me that he was relieved to be done, but he was still uncomfortable with being in this institutional setting.

I could also feel the looks of the teenagers with disabilities, staring at me with jealousy because I was sitting with Bill and they weren't. They wanted to get close to Bill, to sit by him and touch him, an adult who had achieved the impossible dream, of creating his own life outside of an institution.

After all the speakers were finished, I gathered the teenagers so that they could sit close to Bill. They tried to lean into him, and literally drooled on him because they were so excited to get to be with him. Bill looked at me and smiled, pleased to be able to be with the teens, affirming them for who they were with his confident presence.

Bill told me later, "I would have given my arms to have an older me to be around when I was their age. I had no role models. Everyone needs role models."

I was so proud of Bill and his desire to make himself available to the teenagers who really needed him.

Bill looked at me with a flirting grin and typed, "Chinese Checkers later" into his Touch Talker™. It was code for "I want to get some time with you later at your Chinese co-workers place."

"Sure" I responded, smiling with delight that we could speak in a flirting code. "Chinese checkers this evening." If I had CP like the teenagers and Bill had, I would have been drooling over him too. He was caring and very cute.

The teenagers wanted to take Bill out for supper so that they could have more time with him. Without any hesitation, Bill said, "Sure, let's go". So off we went to find an Italian place that the teens had picked.

Not only the teens, but also their parents appeared to really enjoy spending time with Bill. I noticed how comfortable they were with him. I thought it must have been wonderful for them to meet such a competent adult who was physically like their teenagers. It was great fun for me to look at the pleasure on both the teens and parents faces as they talked with Bill and genuinely enjoyed hanging out with him.

Finally, when everyone had had their time with Bill, and we got Don settled with some beer and the TV at my place, we were able to have some time alone. We headed over to the co-workers apartment. I was able to get Bill out of his manual chair onto the couch and we collapsed together there for a couple of hours. No Chinese checkers. Just some much needed time together without the wheelchair in the way.

Soon we had to head back to my place to get some sleep before the next day, when more people would need to see and speak with Bill.

The following day, a Sunday morning was a set apart time for the parents, teachers, and therapists of younger children, who experience physical disabilities, to come and have a discussion time with Bill about topics of therapy, education, and family living and parenting to create positive attitudes. Participants had submitted their comments and questions for a discussion time that was led by staff at my workplace. Many people again wanted to hear what Bill's experience as a child had been, related to all of the issues that were being discussed.

One child in particular wanted to visit with Bill. Christopher kept saying, "Bill' when Bill was talking. Christopher's speech was difficult to understand but it was clear that Christopher also wanted his own time with Bill. Bill spent his break time with Christopher and his mom, listening to her concerns and speaking positive thoughts to Christopher, affirming who he was and how his mother was working to support him.

Time passed by so quickly, and all too soon it was time to take Bill and Don to the airport for their return flight to Nebraska.

Don and I managed to get Bill and his many bags of luggage, including his large power wheelchair, to the airline ticket counter in Toronto. With some time to kill before the flight, we went to a restaurant to get something to eat.

"Bill you are an oddity here!" Don said, as we noticed people turning to look him, a guy in a wheelchair, with a strange thing on his head.

"Guess they don't let people out of institutions much here in Canada." Don continued with a laugh.

"Wow! People are really staring at you Bill!" I commented, with frustration that my fellow Canadian citizens were being so obviously rude. I felt sad and embarrassed.

This was so very different from my experience with Bill in Lincoln. There, when we travelled around town, people just got on with their business. But here people were clearly uncomfortable and curious.

"Curiosity and discomfort with something new are part of the human condition, Chris" Bill responded with understanding. "They have never seen anyone like me. That's all."

I tried to see the people who were staring at Bill through his eyes. But I was finding it hard to be as merciful as he was.

Bill and Don were ready to go through security to wait for their flight in the boarding area. I gave Bill a hug and a kiss and sent them on their way toward the guys with the scanners.

Exhausted from the busy couple of days, and tearful that Bill was leaving me, I watched with amazement as I saw him clearly telling an agent at security something with his Touch Talker™. Then I watched the agent scan his body while he lifted himself in his wheelchair.

I found out later that Bill had said to the security agent, "Don't assume because I am in a wheelchair that I couldn't be carrying a bomb. People in wheelchairs can do terrible things like anyone else. Please scan me."

My friend Bill; a man who never missed an opportunity to teach about disability was doing it, even here, at the security checkpoint at Toronto's Pearson International Airport. He was truly amazing.

The following day, I was shown an article from my local newspaper, *The Hamilton Spectator*, written by Suzanne Morrison, titled "Meeting of the Minds", describing Bill's participation as Keynote Speaker at the Independent Living Conference and his interactions with one of the teen's Jason Masters and his mother. The article is included at the end of this chapter. [2]

What I did not know until sometime later, was that when Bill got back to his apartment in Lincoln, he found out that he had a new neighbor – the local Grand Dragon of the Ku Klux Klan.

Meeting of minds

Hamiltonian Jason Masters, left, and his hero, Bill Rush, both have cerebral palsy. Through electronic methods they conveyed a need for independence.

John Rennison, The Spectator

A strong voice for independent living

By SUZANNE MORRISON
The Spectator

JASON MASTERS and his hero, American journalist Bill Rush, both have cerebral palsy and yesterday the speakers with no voice shared the limelight at Participation House.

While the 19-year-old Hamilton student dreams of living independently in a young adult townhouse, Mr. Rush, 33, knows what it can be like to depend on attendants for personal care.

"During my seven years of living in an efficiency apartment, I have been left on the bedpan because the police arrested my aide for having outstanding parking tickets, had an emotionally unstable aide who eventually checked herself into a mental hospital, had a home cleaning service which resented that I didn't conform to their schedule, and had attendants who liked to gossip. Doesn't this beat watching soap operas?" Mr. Rush said.

He was the keynote speaker at a workshop on independent living sponsored by the Hamilton-Wentworth Communication Collective, an

Handicapped men just want a chance to go it on their own

advocacy group dedicated to supporting children, teenagers and adults who lack functional speech.

Mr. Rush can't use his arms, legs or voice.

He communicates by pointing with a headstick to letters on an alphabet board placed across the arms of his wheelchair. A computer assembles the letters into a synthesized voice by which Mr. Rush "talks."

A native of Lincoln, Neb., he holds a degree in journalism, is pursuing another advanced degree, and has published his autobiography, Journey Out Of Silence, in which he documents his personal struggle for an identity as a human being.

A strong advocate for disabled rights, Mr. Rush has been asked to serve on a federal task force on self-advocacy and self-determination.

In his home town, he succeeded in getting a taxi company to make a van available to the disabled.

His organization of a boycott against a local theatre that was showing the Oscar-winning movie Rain Man — but had no wheelchair access — is so successful the theatre owner flew into Lincoln from another state yesterday to try and resolve the dispute.

Mr. Rush's message to the 95 people attending the workshop — which included 60 men and women in wheelchairs who came from the Toronto-Niagara area — was that they, along with their families and friends, must "start demanding better training, high pay, and higher status for attendants."

In spite of the problems that can be encountered, "people should be allowed to try to live independently," Mr. Rush said.

"I will not lie to you and tell you it's a bed of roses. But independent living beats being in an institution," he said.

Jason, who made his own presentation with the help of his mother

Judy and an overhead projector, said he wants to live independently from his family.

He would like to live in an apartment close to a mall with a couple of his friends from Sherwood School, he said.

Mrs. Masters said Jason was turned down for existing independent living projects because he can't conveniently activate an alarm on his own.

A $130,000 proposal for an independent living project presented to the Ministry of Community and Social Services two years ago "hasn't gone anywhere," Mrs. Masters said.

She said the plan is to use an existing house, townhouse or apartment and have the help of an on-call person such as a senior, university student or young mother with children.

"A young mother at home with children who lives nearby could pop in and feed them or a high school student could gain a credit by helping at night. There are all kinds of creative options we can use in the community," she said.

Mr. Rush urged Mrs. Masters to "put the pressure on and keep it on."

Source: The Hamilton Spectator, Hamilton, Ontario.
April 1, 1989.

Reprinted with Permission of The Hamilton
Spectator, Hamilton Ontario.

Endnotes

1. Bill Rush. Personal Communications (March 1989)
2. Suzanne Morrison. "Meeting of The Minds." *The Hamilton Spectator* Hamilton, Ontario (April 1, 1989). Reprinted with permission.

CHAPTER 12

(Bill's Voice)

Interference by the KKK Neighbor

"Let me know if anyone bothers you. I have a gun collection, and maybe I could scare them off for you." the man said. He was the new neighbor I met when I returned to Lincoln from visiting Chris in Canada and I felt an obligation to welcome him into my neighborhood. After all, I could remember when I had been the new kid on the block.

["Before I was handicapped], I used to be a mercenary in Africa, so I have a lot of guns. I also have a ham radio you know I'm a licensed amateur radio operator- so I even could call for help." he said.[1]

I wanted to laugh because he didn't have any legs, and he was legally blind, while I could see and I had legs. But remembering that I don't liked to be laughed at, I didn't laugh at him. I decided to follow the Golden Rule. After all he was my brother in disability, or so I thought.

"In fact,' he continued, "let me give you my number, and if anybody bothers you, I can come out and scare them away. "I was a police officer before I became handicapped. Hey I heard you wrote a book. I'm going to get it from the library for the blind. Do you think they would have it?"

I nodded. Something was wrong. I couldn't put my headstick (or finger) on it. There was something about his demeanor. I wondered why he thought that I needed his help. [2]

The day after I met the legally blind legless tin soldier, I started to hear voices while I was alone in my apartment. Hearing voices bothered me until my aide heard them too.

"Do you have ghosts?" my assistant asked.

I shook my head no, and laughed. I figured that the voices were from a kid's Walkie Talkie and that they would stop when the kid tired of his new toy.

One morning my neighbor stopped by my apartment wearing his camouflage outfit. He said to my morning aide, "Tell Bill that I sure did like his book. I sure did like his book."

"Why didn't he talk to me directly?" I thought. I was sitting in the room.

The voices didn't stop. I found out who the kid was. It was my new neighbor with his ham radio.

So I politely told my neighbor, "Your ham radio is interfering with my computer. I'm hearing voices over it. What can be done about it? I feel like I'm losing my fifty-second card every time I hear your voice."

"I don't understand." My neighbor said in bewilderment.

"A full deck is 52 cards. If you don't have 52 cards, you're not playing with a full deck, right?"

"Oh yeah. I get it. Cute. [About the problem, I could stop broadcasting until after ten- thirty." He offered.] [3]

I sensed that didn't seem fair to him, and I wondered if he would keep his word.

I was right. One night when Chris called to talk about something important, my neighbor kept breaking in with an obscene sexual request.

"What did you say?" Chris said startled by what she heard. "Did you just ask me to...?"

"No" I protested adamantly. I quickly explained about my neighbor's ham radio interfering with my computer.

The obscenity continued. "That is really gross Bill. It's hard enough to understand what you are saying with the voice synthesizer. I don't want to have to listen to that to. I'm going ok?" Chris said.

I agreed and hung up. I was angry. "I didn't mind my neighbor having a hobby, but I minded him using obscene language that revolted my girlfriend." [4] Chris was right. My voice synthesizer is hard to understand. It's a tedious, frustrating, way to have a conversation, under the best of circumstances. To have to compete with vulgar interference on top of using this tedious method of communicating to talk with Chris angered me and exhausted my patience.

I did a foolish and un-Christian thing. I lost my temper. I went to my neighbor's door and yelled at him. As a rule, I try not to lose my temper. Thanks to cerebral palsy, when I am experiencing any intense emotion, adrenalin pumps my muscles into an overdrive of uncoordinated movements. I can't stop the movements, no matter how hard I try, until the emotion subsides. So when I wheeled into my neighbor's apartment, I looked like I was directing a hundred piece orchestra playing the Flight of the Bumblebee because my limbs were flying everywhere. Most people, even when enraged, can yell something that someone can understand. Since no one can understand what I am saying when I am yelling, I have to get my body settled down to be able to use my communication device and this is very difficult when I am angry. Plus it takes time.

"Calm down," my neighbor said. "What's wrong?"

"Your damn radio" I finally got out. "I was on long distance to Canada. You broke in with $%^%&^#$%, ^%$#^% %^&" I said and I left.

The next night I tried to mend fences. I wasn't sorry for losing my temper, but I was hoping that we at least could co-exist. I was also hoping that we could find out why my computer was picking up his transmissions and stop it. I saw him with his friends, trying to set up his ham radio antenna.

"Here he comes," one of his friends said.

"Look at him, "my neighbor said. "Look at how his mouth hangs open. You can't tell me that he's not retarded. Why don't he reply when you talk to him if he's not retarded? You can't tell me that there's nothing wrong with him upstairs." [5]

I mentally counted to 10. I hated having my mentality questioned by anyone. My mouth hangs open because my muscles are unable to get the message from my brain to keep it shut. I tried to respond but my TouchTalker™ had a dead battery.

"Why don't you talk to us instead of throwing a fit?" my neighbor asked as my body started to fly around again because I was getting increasingly angry.

I started counting to 100. I tried to remember that what happens around me is largely outside of my control but that the way I choose to react to it is inside my control.

"Maybe he would like information on the Klan," one of his friends said.

"That's right. I'm the head of it. I might put some literature on your door. Maybe it will get you to change your mind about that Martin Luther Coon." he said. [6]

I remembered that four months before the city of Lincoln had a brouhaha over an ad that had appeared in the local paper. It offered prospective members information on the Klan. When I heard about it, I thought it was a joke. After all, the KKK had been a secret society organized in 1866, in the South after the Civil War. The KKK disbanded 1869-71. Then in the 1920's it had rallied again and had reached its zenith when it's members wore white sheets to pass themselves off as ghosts of Confederate soldiers to terrorize blacks. The KKK had copied the terrorism tactics of some slave owners who sought to prevent their slaves from fleeing or meeting. Both groups took advantage of the long held African belief that ghosts brought disease and death, when they covered themselves with white sheets, creeping around at night, posing as spirits to threaten or kill Blacks. I thought that the KKK was a relic of a dead era. Apparently I was wrong.

Suddenly, I felt uncomfortable. I didn't want to mend fences with a bigot.

"Maybe you have too much power going to your transmitter," I said, mustering the voltage to get my voice synthesizer to work and the control to keep my body from starting to fly around again because of my growing anger and anxiety. A friend who is a computer expert suggested that might be the problem."

"Go back and play with your damn computer," he said. "You don't know anything about this. So shut up retard. You had no right to barge into my place and act like an idiot. No right at all."

"Your radio was interfering with a long distance phone call from my girlfriend in Canada," I said rambling and getting anxious.

One of my white supremacist neighbor's friends saw a picture of Chris that was on my tray and made a sexual innuendo about her.

I was viscerally sickened by the guy's actions towards Chris' picture. I was quickly realizing that for my safety I needed to get away. So I went back to my place and used my door opener to make sure my door was shut after I entered.

I felt disgusted at myself that I didn't stand my ground against the racism, sexism and ableism that was spewing from my KKK neighbor who was blind and didn't have legs, and his scary friends. But I knew full well that they were all too far gone for logical arguments.

Endnotes

1. Kathryn Watterson, *Not By The Sword* (New York: Simon and Schuster, 1995), 128. Reprinted with permission.
2. Ibid.
3. Kathryn Watterson, *Not By The Sword* (New York: Simon and Schuster, 1995), 129
4. Kathryn Watterson, *Not By The Sword* (new York: Simon Schuster, 1995), 130
5. Ibid
6. Ibid.

CHAPTER 13

(Bill's Voice)

Adding Insult to Injury

I considered my options to deal with my white supremacist neighbor. I couldn't ignore him. I had tried. I couldn't kill him. I hadn't tried. I just wanted to get him off my back.

I wanted to see what the city attorney could do before I initiated the intimidating, overwhelming and daunting process of moving. I didn't want to bother my family and computer friend Mark by asking them to move me again.

Maybe I could get a restraining order against my neighbor talking to me. I thought about getting a restraining order against him breathing and then realized how un-Christian that thought was.

On a sunny May afternoon I went to the Lincoln City-County Building where the city attorney was. I explained the problems that I had been having and asked if I could get a restraining order. He said that he would look into it and be in touch.

I left his office in a hurry because I was late for my supper attendant, meeting me at my home. I'd spent 15 minutes playing roulette with the building's bank of six elevators: I would press the button using my headstick and then guess which elevator would open, positioning my wheelchair in front of it. I always guessed wrong. Finally a Good Samaritan helped me get into one of the cars and downstairs. My helper left me in the lobby. [1]

When I got out of the building and onto its portico, I put my wheelchair in high gear to make up for lost time. I thought I knew where the ramp was located.

I remember seeing my front wheel go down one step and thinking, "Darn, this is the wrong exit…" I had taken the stairs instead of the ramp on the north side of the building.

"I landed on my left side, head first." [2] I saw blood on the concrete. I lay there for five minutes. My TouchTalker™ fell out of my lap tray. The fall had cracked my tray.

I glanced at my watch. It said twenty minutes after five. Good old Timex. Takes a licking and still keeps on ticking. I prayed that I'd still feel like ticking after this licking.

"I'd better call the ambulance," someone said.

"Don't worry. Help is on the way," another person said.

Don't worry?!? I was lying on the ground and bits and pieces of my electronic shell were scattered all around me. I felt like Humpty Dumpty. [3]

I couldn't talk. And this person was telling me not to worry. It seemed like a good time to worry.

When the ambulance arrived, the Emergency Medical Technicians rushed over and then just stood there for several seconds, staring down at me. Clearly their training hadn't prepared them for anything like me. [4]

"We better get him upright," one EMT said.

That sounded like a good plan to me. I had a cut on the back of my head, a little headache and a skinned-up left arm.

When they put me vertical, they found a cut on my head they said needed stitches, as well as a badly skinned arm. After they'd wrapped my head wound in gauze, I reached for my [Touch Talker] voice synthesizer so I could tell them whom to call.

"No," another EMT said, "We need to keep your neck immobile until they check your spine out."

[Then, he] put a neck brace on me. [5]

"Uh-oh, I'm in big trouble," I thought.

I was being deprived of my primary way of communicating. Slowly, I realized that I was among strangers and was out of control of my life. I couldn't tell these people whom to call. I couldn't even tell them my name. I couldn't tell them that I was late for supper. I couldn't tell them that I had a full bladder.

I felt helpless. I needed to use my TouchTalker™. I remembered a line from the poem that I had wanted to use in Eileen's eulogy. I needed to become the master of my fate and the captain of my soul again.

Then they took me out of my chair, and loaded me into the ambulance. My TouchTalker™ was with my chair at the City-County Building. All my identification was in my wallet that was also with my wheelchair.

I made noises, hoping that the EMTs' would take the hint and play 20 questions with me. [They wouldn't]. They just told me to lie still. I gathered that I was being taken to [Lincoln General Hospital, which was] a Level II Trauma Center. I knew that a Level II Trauma Center had immediate access to the most sophisticated medical technology available. I wished that it had an alphabet board. [6]

When we got to the hospital, the head EMT told the admittance desk about my condition. "He has a cut on the back of his head and his left arm is skinned up pretty bad." Then the attendant disappeared.

In the confusion the nurse at the admittance desk forgot to tell the doctor about the cut on the back of my head. I was lying on the wound with my neck braced and couldn't tell the doctor about it. He ordered x-rays of my neck. I tried to tell him that my head was bleeding.

Why wouldn't they try to find out what I was trying to say? Weren't they trained to handle unusual situations?

Their brochure said that a top priority is the human aspect of their care—the needs and emotions of their patients. My biggest need was to establish a way to be perceived as a capable person, and it went unnoticed. [7]

"I know that you're trying to talk to me, but we need to check out your neck," the doctor said, "Do you experience any pain in your neck now?" [8]

I wanted to say that this whole situation was a pain in the neck. Instead, I tried to shake my head "No", but the neck collar was doing an excellent job.

"There still may be damage, so we will need to X-ray your neck" the doctor said.

They prepared to take me down to x-ray with my head still bleeding. I looked at the hospital clock. It was ten minutes after six. Thirty minutes had passed since I had had my accident. It seemed like an eternity to me. I kept making noises hoping that someone would talk to and with me instead of at and about me and learn that my head was still bleeding.

They loaded me onto a gurney and took me to x-ray. No one asked for my consent, although I was alert and responsive. I felt like a foreigner in my own community. No, it was worse than that. People in foreign countries can gesture to make them understood. I couldn't even do that. [9]

I deserved to have some control over my life.

I remembered that when I was a child and had to have surgery, I had stayed in the hospital just one day after the operation because the nurses, professionals in health care, had been scared to treat me. They had asked my mom to stay with me throughout the night because they hadn't known how to talk with me.

Now that I was an adult I was facing the same problem. No one would take the time to figure out a way to talk to me. Only now Mom wasn't available to help them.

I needed to contact my home health care agency to tell them why I missed supper. I felt alone, isolated and afraid.

It was ironic. Here I was, a trained journalist who was trained in the fine art of communication of complex ideas to large numbers of readers, and [Now] I couldn't even tell one person my name. [Embarrassing and terrifying]. [10]

Then the technicians put me on a cold hard table and told me to lie still. I did my best to follow their instructions. They took lots of x-rays.

I wondered if I should order a couple of five-by-sevens for Chris. I wished Chris was here. I had known her for almost two years and I felt safe with her. I thought about Chris to take my mind off of my predicament. She had wanted to find a way to talk with me without my headstick and had done so. But, for the hospital personnel, communicating with me wasn't a priority.

They found out that my neck wasn't broken. Frustrated about not being able to communicate, that news didn't have that profound of an impact on me.

As they lifted me back onto the gurney I saw blood where my head had been and felt nauseous.

They took off the neck brace. Martin Luther King's words, "Free at last Free at last Thank God Almighty I'm free at last," ran through my mind for some reason.

Then, an intern asked if I was all right. I turned my head so she could see my head wound. [11]

"Oh, you're bleeding," she said.

"Didn't I tell you about that?" the admitting nurse asked.

"No, you didn't," the intern said, as she prepared to stitch up my head wound. There was a touch of irritation in her voice.

The emergency room didn't know whom to call.

"So, I lay there with a headache and a full bladder." [12] I felt like a piece of meat lying on a slab waiting for others to pull my strings. I felt like a hostage. I didn't belong here. I needed someone to help me to communicate.

I thought about others besides Chris who could communicate with me when I didn't have my headstick. My dad had also recited the alphabet to me. When he said the right letter, I would nod. Then, he would go back to the beginning of the alphabet and recite it again until I nodded. This was tedious, but at least I could talk to people. I prayed that someone would become inspired to use this alphabet method.

One woman knew what church I went to and thought she could call my pastor. I shook my head no. It was a good idea, but my pastor didn't know how to talk with me either. Only those who are closest to me knew how to use the alphabet method. The relationship between my pastor and me hadn't gotten that intimate yet.

The woman's comment reminded me that I hadn't called on God to help me out of this mess. I wasn't supposed to be the captain of my fate nor the master of my soul. God was supposed to be. So I gave the situation over to God.

Suddenly I felt at peace. I knew whatever would happen was in God's hands.

Then, the on-duty nurse from my home health care agency came into the emergency room and said, "There you are. I've been looking and calling all over for you. Your supper aide is turning this city upside-down looking for you. Bet you need the urinal bad, huh?"

I nodded. She got me a urinal and helped me use it. Ah!

"Your wheelchair is totaled—worse than you are," she said.

"I'm going to see about getting you a ride home in an ambulance. I'm glad it wasn't more serious."

I was deprived of the precious gift of speech for two and a half hours. I wondered what she considered serious. [12]

She made arrangements for me to go home in an ambulance and to be met by Don. Don helped me to get inside my apartment and asked if I wanted something to eat. I saw my power wheelchair. It was seriously broken. I started to cry and yell hysterically. A bewildered Don kept asking, "What's wrong, Bill? Do you hurt somewhere? Is there anything I can do?"

I didn't hurt physically. I was angry and afraid that my communication could be taken away that easily. I had worked hard to build a life, and I saw how readily it could be taken away from me.

I wanted to call Mom and tell her what had happened. I did with Don's help. I started my tale with, "I thought you should hear this directly from me…"

"What happened?" Mom asked.

After she heard what happened Mom asked, "Do you want me to come to Lincoln tomorrow? If the electric chair is broken, you'll need someone to stay with you anyway."

Don said, "I think that is a good idea. Bill is pretty shaken up."

The next day one of my personal service assistants drew stairs and a ramp so that I would know which was which as a little joke. Mom appreciated the humor more than I did.

I decided that I should get a medical ID bracelet and necklace to prevent a repeat episode. However, neither of us knew who I should put to call.

By happenstance the next day Pastor Howard came to visit me. I told him about my trip to the emergency room. He was genuinely concerned about me. When I said that a woman recognized me and knew that I went to First Baptist, Howard said, "That is wonderful. I'm happy that people are associating you with First B."

Then, I asked him the Big Question: If I could put his name and telephone number on a medical ID bracelet. Howard didn't hesitate a second. He said, "Yes, of course. It would be my pleasure! Please tell me how you communicate without your pointer on, so I'll know if you should need me."

When I tried to give him an out, he got irritated and said, "Bill, I want to do this for you. I'm a big boy. I can say, 'No,' if I don't want to do something. Believe me I have said 'No,' on many occasions. But, I want to do this. Let me do this for you."

Endnotes

[1.] William Rush. "Adding Insult to Injury." *RN,* (September, 1991): 21-25. No longer in print.

[2.] Ibid.

[3.] Ibid.

[4.] Ibid.

[5.] Ibid.

[6.] Ibid.

[7.] Ibid.

[8.] Ibid.

[9.] Ibid.

[10.] Ibid.

[11.] Ibid.

[12.] Ibid.

CHAPTER 14

(Chris' Voice)

What's the First Amendment?

"Bill I am worried about your safety living beside that KKK guy." I confessed. "Is there no way that you can move and get away from him?" I continued and then ranted. "I can't believe that some guy with guns and very scary friends is living beside you. This whole situation is unbelievable to me. In Canada we have fewer guns in the cities and no KKK and shootings are rare here. This sounds like a bad movie, Bill."

I was getting anxious learning that some guy with guns and who propagated hate, had moved in beside Bill. And I couldn't wrap my mind around the fact that the KKK still existed in the late 1990s. Extremist fringe people lived primarily in American movies, not in real life, right? Were they not a remnant of the past, from the southern states of the USA? How is it that someone like this lived in Lincoln, Nebraska, let alone beside Bill?

Even as we lived on the same continent, the differences between our nation's histories were stark. And these differences were significantly impacting our lives. I would never be living beside some KKK guy with guns. But, sadly people in Canada with significant disabilities lived primarily in large institutions and not in neighborhoods.

"This would never happen to you if you lived in Canada. You would be living in an institution with 250 other people." I lamented out loud, about what I had been thinking.

'Yeah and I'd self-destruct." Bill countered. And he added, "I'll take my first amendment and freedom to create my own life over the so-called "safety "of an institution any day."

"What's the first amendment?" I asked honestly.

"Free speech Chris." Bill responded, to teach me about this important aspect of American life. "My KKK neighbor has the right to say anything as long as he's not harming me. He can say hateful things to me because he is protected under the law. He's living in the same apartment unit because he, like me, needs accessible housing. Annoying one's neighbor is not against the law."

"But his guns and KKK friends are really dangerous." I argued. "Bill, you really need to move."

"Moving me is like moving the space shuttle when it's on the ground." Bill explained. "It's a lot of work to move me and to set up all my electronics. Plus any new place needs to be made accessible for me. There are not very many accessible places yet for me to live in Lincoln because society has not adapted fast enough to accommodate for people like me, who need accessible housing, to live in the community. And I don't want to bother my family and Mark."

What I would later come to understand was that Bill was socialized in America to value individual freedom above all else.

He needed control over his life. If he had to live beside a sexist, racist, ableist bigot in order to have it, so be it.

I was not sure that I would make the same choice. But then again, I was not raised in America, faced with the limited choices in housing that Bill now had, nor had I been dependent on my family members in such practical ways for so long, that I believed that I was a bother to them, and was working hard to not ask them to help me.

But I was still worried.

Bill wrote to give me updates on his progress in dealing with the Grand Dragon of the KKK neighbor. I cringed as I read his letters. Bill's humor was still intact but this situation was causing him tremendous amounts of stress.

Dear Chris,

I'm working hard to get rid of my neighbor's vulgar transmitted messages and I'm getting more and more frustrated.

I've tried to problem-solve how to get rid of my KKK neighbor's ham radio messages that continue to transmit into my apartment. One friend called the Federal Communications Commission. The FCC told him that I should get a filter and that there was nothing that they could do because his speech was protected by the First Amendment.

I went to the local phone company and asked them if they could put a filter on my phone. They said that they could and did. But there was a problem with testing the filter. To test the filter, the repairman needed the cooperation of my neighbor and my neighbor wouldn't cooperate. He slammed the door on the repairman.

"I'm sorry but if your neighbor won't transmit his ham radio, there's no guarantee that this will work," the repairman said. It didn't work.

I called my friend and technology expert Mark. He said that my electronic system had many wires and that any one of them could be picking up my neighbor's transmissions. Unless my neighbor cooperated in tracking down the problem, Mark couldn't help me, short of lining my apartment with aluminum sheeting.

I talked to the people at First Baptist about my neighbor. One woman suggested that I should let my light shine for my neighbor. I rejected her suggestion because I had succeeded in getting him to hate me. His bitter soul was not taking in any light. He has guns next door and friends in the KKK. And besides, I can't run away or protect myself against any physical attack.

I need to figure out what is picking up my neighbor's transmissions. So I had my assistants unplug one part of my electronic system at a time, a very tedious task. By very systematically going through all of my electronics I figured out that my Touch Talked voice synthesizer was picking up the transmissions. But how do I stop the transmissions and still talk to you on the phone or write stories into my Touch Talker?

Once the strap that held my foot down on my wheelchair's foot pedal came undone and my leg involuntarily started kicking the wall that I shared with my KKK neighbor.

My Touch Talker was turned on because I was working and my computer started speaking, "Is that Bill Rush that retard, banging his head against the wall? If he sends anybody over to talk about my radio, I'll blow his head off. He can keep banging his head against the wall. I wonder how he graduated from college. They probably gave him his diploma because they felt sorry for him."

Someone said, "Know your enemy." I decided to see if the local paper had done any stories on him. It had. The story painted a picture of a person who had the same logical system as the Mad Hatter. He acquiesced that minorities had the right to equal opportunities to education and to jobs but he deplored "race mixing" by reasoning it leads to "the mongrelization of the races," according to him and to the Mad Hatter. He also insists that the Jews are taking over the country.

It was an interesting theory, considering that Jews make up three percent of the country's population. One of his brochures said that the Holocaust was a hoax, that fewer than six million people had died and that those who did probably died of typhus.

The more I read about him the more I realized that he and the Mad Hatter have a lot in common. HA!

I studied the civil rights movement when I was at UNL to learn how to bring about peaceful change. As a person with a disability, I am fighting for my civil rights, much as King did. I admire King's philosophy that said that a community should be based on "agape" love, a good redemptive love for all humans. King said that agape is the only force that can bring a peaceful community into being because it fosters cooperation instead of competition.

My neighbor, on the other hand studied the survivalist movement, which is preparing for a nuclear holocaust, which would eliminate the races that survivalists think are inferior.

I resent being in the same classification as he is, Chris. Since we both used wheelchairs, society had relegated us to live in the same low-class accessible housing, use the same sorts of personal assistant services and support each other. But he and I have nothing in common. I admire Martin Luther King. He admires Adolph Hitler. And he doesn't realize that people with disabilities were the first to go to the gas chambers in Hitler's Germany.

I wish you were here with me, even though I wouldn't want you to have to deal with my KKK neighbor.

Bill. [1]

Endnotes

[1] Chris Robinson. Personal Communication (1989)

CHAPTER 15

(Bill's Voice)

An Incident with a Semi-Truck

I was coming home from mailing another letter to Chris at the post office. My apartment was 15 blocks from Lincoln's main post office, in my case a nice rotation of the tires or a nice stretch of the legs for those with able bodies. I like to go to the post office and mail my letters to make sure that my letters get out the fastest way possible.

Going to the post office was easier and safer for me than using a corner mailbox. When I tried to use a mailbox, I had to wait by it until somebody came along to help me to get my letter into the drop box. I risked having someone mug me before they put my letter in the box. In contrast, the post office continually had someone on duty that I could ask for help. The postal employee would take the letter from my wheelchair tray pocket or backpack and put it in the mail slot for me. And I wasn't afraid that the Postal employees would take my wallet.

The quickest way to and from the post office was through a warehouse district. Its streets were lined with parked semitrailers. The streets were empty; Sunday evening in Lincoln Nebraska and everyone was at home. Sidewalks and curb cuts were not available so I had to drive in the street. I thought I was safe from the semi-trucks because they were all parked.

On this night I was wrong. My headstick had slipped over my eyes so that I couldn't see. I didn't know that I was heading straight for a semitrailer. By the time I saw the trailer I was under it with my head pinned on my right shoulder. My neck's left side was rubbing against the underside of the trailer's hitch. However I could see the street sign and a street lamp. Somehow, knowing where I was reassured me.

A line from a vintage poem that my grandpa used to recite: "I stood under the old lamppost and thought about that old gang of mine," popped into my head.

While I was sitting under the semi, I thought about that old gang of mine, the kids who were in my segregated elementary school in Omaha. Most of them were living with their families, in nice safe institutions or in their graves -- instead of under trailers.

I made noises until someone saw my peril and got the police. They were getting to know me very well. I bet that they called me the klutz of Lincoln. If they weren't, they soon would be after this fiasco.

The person came back with a police sergeant. "Are you all right, Bill?" the cop asked, "I'm going to pull you out from under there."

In less than five minutes the cop had me back on my wheels and ready to go. "Are you ok, Bill?" the officer asked again.

I lied and said yes. My neck felt like a Tootsie Roll that someone had tried to twist off but couldn't, but I had to get home. I drove slowly home.

When I got to my place, my neck was still stiff.

The bathroom door was open, so I went in there to see if I had any grease on my shirt. I had a grease spot on my neck. I wondered how to get rid of it. I wondered if I shouldn't go to the grocery store to get something to get the spot off my neck. I didn't know what I should get, so I called my adviser. She would know. I dialed my telephone.

"Hello, this is Bill Rush." I said.

"Hello, Bill, how are you?" my adviser said.

"OK."

"What is up with you tonight?"

"I have a question. What cleans grease?"

"What kind of grease? Where did it come from?"

"Automotive. It came off a semitrailer."

"Where is it now?"

"On my neck."

"Pardon me. I didn't hear you. Would you please say that again?"

"On my neck."

"That is what I thought you said. What happened?"

I told her.

"Does your neck hurt?" my adviser asked.

"A Little bit," I said.

"Have you seen a doctor?"

"It's a Sunday night. No transportation. You know that," I said.

"Would you go see a doctor if you had transportation?"

"Yes, but there isn't any transportation," I said.

"I'll call you back," my adviser said.

About fifteen minutes later the on-duty nurse from the home health agency called and said, "You are going to the emergency room at Lincoln General." It was not a question. It was more like an order. "The Handi-Van is coming for you. It will take you to the hospital, so hold on."

I didn't reply. I was in shock. It was a Sunday night. The (Un) handi-van did not run Sunday nights, no matter what. Maybe they would put something like, "Here lies the klutz who made the (Un) handi-van run on a Sunday night," on my headstone.

Still, I resented that the on-call nurse from the agency had told me to go to the hospital, instead of asking me if I wanted to go to the hospital. I would have to talk to her about that sometime.

Fifteen minutes later the (Un)handi-van came to take me to the hospital. The driver was unusually courteous to me. I guess all a person has to do to get people to talk nice to you is to ring your neck.

When I got to the hospital and when the paperwork was completed, a doctor ordered x-rays of my neck. They showed that I hadn't broken it. I had just bruised it. At first the doctor wanted to put a neck brace on me. I pointed out that I used my headstick for everything. If he made me wear a neck collar, I wouldn't be able to do anything but sit and watch TV.

"I see your point," the doctor said, "However I can't do much other than that to help you with the pain."

"What about having my assistants give me neck and back massages after I'm in bed," I asked.

"That sounds like a good idea," the doctor said.

"What about using hot packs, too?" I asked.

"That is a good idea, too. Do you want me to tell somebody or do you want to tell them?"

"I need you to write a prescription for these things. That way the home health agency will be authorized to do them."

"Okay, I'll do that," the doctor said.

I went out to the lobby and was greeted by two of my assistants who had become my friends as well. One greeted me with, "We heard that you went under a semitrailer and were expecting to find you in little bits and pieces. We see that you are okay. How is the semi?"

The doctor came out with the prescription. He laid it on my tray, and I gave it to my friends to give to their supervisor.

Before he left the doctor looked at me and said, "You are lucky, very lucky. You know that, don't you?"

CHAPTER 16

(Chris' Voice)

How to Deal with a KKK Neighbor?

Bill wrote to give me an update about what was happening with the KKK neighbor. Feeling helpless in response to the guy's resistance to helping him solve his technology problem, and anger because of the spewing bigotry, Bill's behavior was deteriorating and he was now feeling ashamed of himself. From Canada, I could read that the situation was getting worse.

Sitting a thousand miles away, I could feel that I was getting physically and emotionally hotter as I read Bill's letter, feeling more and more anger toward a growing list of people south of the border who were not keeping him safe; the KKK neighbor, the city of Lincoln, the League, and the friends and family around Bill and this ridiculous First Amendment thing!

Dear Chris,

> *After two months of listening to my neighbors' tirades, I lost it and now I'm ashamed of my behavior. I'm not a saint and I'm having trouble behaving like a Christian with him.*
>
> *I gave him a taste of his own medicine. I put in a tape of Martine Luther Kind's March on Washington Speech, turned up the volume to maximum and set*

the tape deck to play over and over and then I left to play chess for three hours. Cowardly but clever.

When I came back he was at the mailbox.

"Hello, how are you?" he said.

"I wish you would stop calling me retarded." I said. I decided I didn't like being a coward, clever or not.

"Well if you're going to act that way, you have to expect that." He said.

I turned so that my approximately 200-pound wheelchair was blocking his light-weight wheelchair. It reminded me of a tank blocking a Volkswagen.

"You're interfering with my computer. Stop it."

"Get a filter like the FCC said," he said.

"I did but you have to help me test it. I can't call my friend whenever you get ready to transmit. The FCC wouldn't like to hear you using obscenities on the air." I said.

"I can't understand you and that machine. Have someone come over and talk to me," he said. He started to leave. I blocked him again.

He turned and went the other way. I took a short cut to his apartment door. I blocked the entrance and said, "I want to talk to you now."

"Get out of my way," he said.

"I can't understand you."

"Listen to me, damn you," I said.

"Let me by."

"Not until you listen to me," I said. I knew that I could tip his light-weight wheelchair over, but I resisted the temptation. Then, his nurse came give him insulin. I backed away from his door because I didn't want to interfere with his cares. He hurried into his apartment.

"Come on in before he comes in," he said to the nurse.

"Don't you want your friend to come in," the nurse asked.

"No! Don't let him in... I can't even check my mail..." he said.

I noticed fear in his voice. I went to my apartment.

I had a lot of conflicting emotions. For five minutes I felt satisfaction because I had bullied the bully. Then I began to think, "My neighbor was obviously bitter about his disability and was trying to find every way possible to believe that he was better than everyone around him." I thought I hated him, but then I realized that hate was the wrong response to a person like my neighbor. Maybe I pitied him. After all, someone said that pity was one step away from ridicule.

I felt bewildered at how I reacted to someone I would normally consider a brother. He was my brother in disability, and yet he could not see the logic in anything I believe in and was actually contemptuous of all that I hold dear. Then I realized that just because someone is in a wheelchair doesn't mean that he has instant solidarity with all people who are in wheelchairs.

I feel ashamed. I have let my neighbor win. I have lowered myself to his level. I didn't handle this predicament like a Christian. A more mature Christian would have used love to combat my neighbor by trying to win his understanding and friendship, not humiliating and defeating him. Instead of attacking him, I should have attacked the evil that was inside my neighbor.

Obviously I have a lot of room to grow as a Christian. I am grateful that I am forgiven in Christ, because clearly I am not perfect.

Love,
Bill [1]

Ah Ha! I thought, how interesting! Bill had the opportunity to experience what it is like to be the bully by blocking the neighbor from going into his apartment.

Then I gleefully thought, "Hooray! Good for you Bill! You, the most physically vulnerable person around, intimidated the Klansman!" This was too good! Sweet revenge!

To me, Bill had been quite restrained. He didn't knock him over in his wheelchair when he had the chance. I would have knocked the guy's chair over and rolled my wheelchair and me, weighing a total of approximately 300 pounds, on top of him, if I had been him.

Bill had behaved very immaturely, chasing the guy around the building and blocking him from going inside to try to make him talk to him, in an attempt to try to fix the problem. It was almost comical! But it was also very sad.

Always the thinker, Bill believed that this guy could just "decide" to help him with his computer and together they would solve the problem, like adults. Bill was forgetting that he was trying to use logic with one of Hitler's friends!

My behavior would have been far less Christian than Bill's. I could think of nothing sicker than picking on vulnerable people such as an adult with a significant disability like Bill. Bill had enough on his plate to deal with everyday to just survive!

I enjoyed entertaining my fantasies about all the things that I would gladly do to this despicable man and his scary friends. And I felt no shame for my sick thoughts.

But, unlike me, Bill didn't want to behave badly towards anyone. He truly desired to reflect Christ in his life and this was most admirable to me. I was far from thinking about reflecting Christ, as I read Bill's letter. I wanted safety for Bill. I wanted him as far away from this KKK guy as possible. Someone able-bodied could take on the task of sharing Christ's love with this lunatic.

Bill was feeling ashamed that he was not behaving like his friends at First Baptist were telling him to do. With anger I thought, "What hypocrisy! How dare these Christians with intact neurological systems living in safer neighborhoods, tell Bill, who is physically vulnerable to the point that he can't defend himself against a flea, (and who has to live next door to the Klansman because of their shared disabilities) how to act when he was being verbally abused and being threatened with physical harm?! How often had they rolled in his wheels? What was wrong with his Christian friends? This was not the time to debate how one is supposed to live a Christian life. It was time to take action to keep a vulnerable man safe! Get Bill out of there! He needed to move now!"

I understood Bill's whole dignity in risk argument from the disability rights movement. People living in institutions might be cared for, but without any risks (or responsibilities) in their lives, they did not have dignity. But this situation that Bill was living in, was far from dignity in risk. This was nothing short of dangerous! Anyone (able-bodied or having with a disability) living beside this guy was not safe.

The guy had told Bill on a few occasions that he wanted to see someone blow his head off. He was threatening physical violence towards Bill and had the people to carry it out for him, and the guns for them to do it.

From my vantage point all the way north to Canada, I could see that Bill was a sitting duck, ready to get his head literally blown off by one of the neighbor's "friends".

I was feeling an all-consuming righteous and protective anger as I finished reading Bill's letter. Why was Bill not working harder to find another place to live, when his life was at risk? What was wrong with all the people around Bill in Lincoln? Had Bill and his friends and the authorities all lost their collective minds, putting protection of the right to free speech above Bill's safety? And why was Bill's safety not of higher value to the Christians that Bill was hanging with, than pressuring him to be Jesus to the KKK neighbor? He wouldn't have a cheek to turn, if he stayed in his place much longer. I was feeling like I wanted to go to Lincoln and organize a crew to move Bill myself!!

Endnotes

[1.] Chris Robinson. Personal Communications (1990)

CHAPTER 17

(Bill's Voice)

Disaster in Toronto

I was making another visit to Chris in Canada. She was now living in Toronto and I was looking forward to spending time with her there. While visiting, Chris and I would speak as a couple with a Relationship and Sexuality Group of teens who experience physical disabilities at ErinOak, an Ontario Children's Treatment Centre on the outskirts of Toronto. Chris had a network of people in the "helping professions" who wanted us to share our wisdom with younger people about dating when one of the partners experiences a disability.

I was certainly no expert in the relationship department. My history with women before Chris was atrocious. Chris and I were just trying to figure this thing out one day at a time. We didn't have any answers. But we could share what we had learned so far to my younger brothers and sisters with disabilities. Being a part of the disability rights movement, it was my responsibility to encourage those who would come after me, so I agreed to do this gig with Chris.

We talked about what we would say to the teens and how to best make ourselves available to them. We wanted to show who we were as a couple when Chris visited me in Lincoln, and for that reason Chris insisted that I would need my power wheelchair. We would hold hands throughout the presentation as a visual symbol of our relationship to the teens. If we weren't experts, we could at least look like we knew what we were doing.

Chris and I talked about the advantages and disadvantages of having my tag along assistant Don, come with me to Canada. Having an assistant come with me had the advantage of built in help. But the assistant didn't get any time off. Plus Chris and I had to figure out what to do with the assistant when we didn't want to have them around. We decided to try to get attendant care help in Toronto. After all it is a very large city.

I have never seen anyone work as hard as Chris did in preparation for my visit. She coordinated my personal service assistants (in a country that was still in its infancy of personal service assistant programs). She had to do what I used to have to do, which was beg and bribe people to be personal service assistants for me. I had to do it for survival; she did it for love.

Chris borrowed a lift-equipped wheelchair van from the parents of boy with cerebral palsy. I took my seating system and Chris would scrounge a power base for it in Canada. She had to co-ordinate this with a wheelchair dealer in Toronto.

Murphy's Law says, "If anything can go wrong, it will." This axiom seemed to be working overtime on this trip.

First, I can't get a direct flight from Lincoln to Toronto because they don't exist. I had a layover in Chicago. But my plane from Lincoln to Chicago was late, causing me to miss my connection. I had to wait in O'Hare to catch the later flight to Toronto.

Sitting in my manual wheelchair in the Special Needs Area, waiting for the next flight to Toronto, I wondered if I had bit the bullet this time. I could be left here indefinitely if someone didn't respond to my attempts to get them to talk to me and make sure they put me on that next flight. To say I was nervous was an understatement. I was feeling really vulnerable. I could hear Chris saying that she thought I was crazy trying to do this trip by myself. Maybe she was right.

I was worrying about Chris arriving at the airport and finding that I wasn't on the flight. She would panic and I couldn't help her.

By hollering and flinging my arms around, I managed to get an attendant's attention and asked them to call Chris' place and leave a message telling her that I was on the next flight.

But Chris had already left to go get the van and travel to the airport and didn't get the message.

After what seemed like hours, an attendant came and helped me to get on the flight to Toronto. When I was finally in my seat on the plane, I realized that I had travelled now more than eight hours without a potty break. It was going to be one long hour flight. Prayerfully it wouldn't be bumpy.

Chris arrived at the Toronto airport and realized pretty quickly that I was not there. She went to the airline and asked for them to check the logs to find me. She tried to be calm but she was getting upset, imagining that I was left abandoned and sitting alone in some back hallway in O'Hare.

After waiting for what seemed like an eternity, the airline figured out that I had caught the next flight. They could confirm to Chris that I was in the air and on my way. Hooray! I was on the way.

Chris quickly calculated that amount of time that must have passed since I left Lincoln and figured out that I had not used the restroom for more than eight hours now. She knew that either I would have dried up or my back teeth would be floating. She thought the latter.

Oh Canada! I thought as my Boeing 737 flight touched down in Toronto. I was never so excited to be out of O'Hare, and to Canada, to see Chris and get to a restroom.

"Please remain in your seats. We have a medical emergency," a flight attendant said over the speaker.

Oh great! Someone else is having a bad day! I thought to myself.

Was I dreaming? Chris and some young guy I assumed was an assistant Chris found were walking down the aisle toward me. Chris was smiling and looked relieved. The young guy with her grinned, looking like he was enjoying making everyone on board wait in their seats while the two of them boarded my plane as soon as it touched down.

Oh I'm the medical emergency! I thought to myself with relief, and delight and a big smile on my face as I watched Chris walking toward me.

"Thought you might need the restroom right away" Chris whispered to me as she and the assistant guy put me into the aisle chair and started to haul me down the aisle and out of the plane.

How did she get through security? Well, there was no stopping her! I thought with pride.

"Bill, this is Phil. Phil this is Bill. Phil is going to be one of your assistants while you're here." Chris said.

Phil and I went quickly to take care of my most urgent need.

Murphy had followed me to Toronto and had taken root here. Chris gave me the bad news.

"I got back to my apartment last night, and the front of the building is all torn up. They're doing some kind of construction. I don't know if we can get your manual wheelchair into the building," she said.

"This wheelchair has been almost everywhere. It can take any abuse you put it through." I offered trying to lighten her stress.

"Goodie, I get to take out my frustrations by destroying your manual chair," Phil said jokingly.

When we got to Chris' apartment, I saw what she meant. Her apartment building stood in a ring of bulldozers and other tractors. The bulldozers had dug a mini-mote around the entire building. Thin wooden planks served as makeshift drawbridges.

"Bill, you'd better mind your manners, or Chris will make you walk the plank. Are there any alligators in there?" Phil asked while gingerly pushing my manual wheelchair over the waterless mote. "That would be an interesting security device, don't you think?"

"I don't know how I'm going to get you out of here by myself when Phil isn't here," Chris worried out loud. "I guess I could always get someone to help me."

When the time came, Chris called on a good friend to come and help to get me out of the apartment building. Chris and her friend scrounged for the widest plank they could find, which was about an inch wider than my wheelchair, and put it across the mote. They lifted my wheelchair with me in it onto the plank. Then, Chris gingerly pushed me across it.

"This is ridiculous!' Chris fumed. "Why would they pick this week of all weeks to build a mote around my apartment!"

The apartment building problems grew day by day and I watched Chris slowly disintegrate from frustration into despair. One morning we woke up to find all the refrigerators in the hallways. This left little room for my wheelchair and me to get through the building.

Then one evening when we were returning from talking to the teens at ErinOak, the electricity went out in our city block when Phil came to help me get to bed. Chris' apartment was on the third floor. We didn't know how long the power failure would last. So Chris and Phil took me out of my manual wheelchair and used a modified firefigher's lift to get me to the third floor apartment. They lay me on Chris' living room floor. Then, they had to go down to get my wheelchair. While they were doing that, the power came back on.

"Well that gave us a workout," Phil joked when he and Chris returned with my manual chair. Chris was not laughing and I was worried about her. The stress was mounting.

On another night another personal service assistant didn't show up. We waited for an hours. Chris tried to call the person and got no answer. Finally Chris said, "Why don't I help you get to bed?"

"You are tired and don't have the energy to help me," I said.

"If I don't do it, you will have to stay up all night. That isn't good for your body."

I tried to disagree with her between yawns. She won the argument.

But neither of us was happy. We both knew that too often the able-bodied partner of a person with a disability is faced with this choice. If the partner is faced with this too often the average couple splits up because of resentment.

Chris had bought us tickets to the Phantom of the Opera. However, by the evening of the operetta, Murphy's Law had mutated to: "Everything goes wrong all at once in a big way."

When she took me to the van in my manual wheelchair, Chris put her purse on my wheelchair. She asked me to keep an eye on it while she got someone to help us get across the Mote.

When we got to the theater, the purse, which had our tickets and her credit card, was gone.

Chris begged the usher to let me stay and watch the show while she tried to find her purse. She was crying, and I was dying inside. A small part of me watched the program. The rest of me went with Chris to look for her purse. A little before the intermission Chris came back. She hadn't found her purse, but she had decided to cancel her credit card and to relax and watch the operetta.

After the play we went back to Chris' apartment. We found a note taped to her door. An honest neighbor had found her purse in the apartment hallway. Diogenes would have been delighted.

I wasn't delighted. I was ashamed because I had lost the purse. I was frustrated because I knew if I had my equipment and if the front of Chris' apartment building hadn't been torn up, I wouldn't have lost Chris' purse. I cried in frustration because I had worked hard to be self-sufficient and I was seeing how easy it could slip away.

I said that I felt like I had made an institution for myself outside an institution. It had become obvious that I couldn't travel anywhere because the support system for people with significant disabilities was not portable.

Chris reassured me, "We got my purse back. The system that you have built in Lincoln is phenomenal. You should be very proud of it," she said.

Murphy's mutated law was still in effect. After a personal service assistant finished my morning routine, Chris went down to get something out of the van. Fifteen minutes later she came back in tears and said, "I hate this city. The van has been towed. I have to go get it from a compound across the city. The subway is not accessible, so I have to leave you here. I don't want to do that," she said between sobs.

I told her that I would be okay.

"I need $200 to pay the fine. I asked that idiot superintendent if it would be all right to park there, and he said yes. This morning it was in the way of the construction, so he let them tow it. It's not fair," she said. "I have my credit card... No, I don't. I canceled it last night. This is a nightmare."

I had taken some crisis intervention training. It was time to start using it. Chris was in crisis. It stressed breaking the mess down into manageable parts. That way the person can deal with little problems rather than a big crisis.

"We have $200 from the time with the teens. You can use that to pay the fine," I said.

"I guess I could that. Thank you," Chris said, "This city drives me crazy. It's so big. Will you be okay? I'll get there and back as fast as I can."

I nodded. She put the phone where I could get it and she left.

Sitting there waiting, I realized that I couldn't live with Chris in Canada. I needed the supports that I had built in Lincoln. I wanted to have more than this cross-border wonderful thing with Chris but I knew that it would be disastrous to try to have a relationship here.

I also knew that Chris loved Canada fiercely. She would have to make a choice between me or Canada. In the past when a woman felt that something had to go in her life, it was me. So, when Chris got back, I asked her if she would rather that I went back to Lincoln.

"No. Do you want to leave?" she said.

"Of course not. I just thought it would be easier on you if I went home," I said.

She had a new resolve about her. "I want to get out of this city," she said. "It's too crowded, too fast, too big. Too much of everything. I have a friend in Hamilton who may be able to let us stay at her place. I'll call her now. Maybe Phil would meet us there."

We went to her friend's place that afternoon. I didn't ask if we could get an "I love Toronto" T-shirt. The farther away from Toronto we got, the calmer Chris got.

Having minored in sociology, I was well aware of the effects of over-crowding has on people. This had been the first time I had seen the effects so graphically illustrated.

"I feel like God hit me on the head with a frying pan this week, Bill. We can't do this relationship thing here in Canada. I probably needed this kind of disaster to convince me and I'm convinced. I can't have both you and Canada. I'm going to have to make a choice."

Chris said to me while driving in the van out of the big city. She was silent for a while.

I stayed silent and let her think.

"I'll have to think about moving to Lincoln. That's really big Bill. I love Canada. This is my home." she said and then was silent again.

Oh. Chris <u>was</u> thinking what I was thinking, I thought to myself.

I left her in her thoughts. I knew enough not to push her but I prayed incessantly storming the gates of heaven, "Please God help Chris to move. She is a gift and a miracle and I need her."

With all of me, I wanted to beg her to come back with me to Lincoln, even with my insane KKK neighbor. I loved her and needed her in my life.

But I knew she had to figure this out for herself or she would resent me forever for pushing her.

CHAPTER 18

(Chris' Voice)
A Spouse Role Model for Chris?

"Bill, I'm thinking about taking that new job." I said to get his reaction.

"Good for you." Bill continued. "Sounds like it will give you some more valuable experience. You're not ready to move here. It's not time yet, Chris."

Wow! I thought. What common sense. He was right. I wasn't ready to move, but I had to admit to myself that I wanted to. More importantly, I was happy and relieved when I realized that at least one of us had a mature mind thinking about if and how we might drive this relationship forward.

OK. So if I wasn't ready to move to Lincoln, maybe I could get some sense of what it was like to be in a marriage with someone physically like Bill, I had been thinking to myself. Was anyone else doing this? I didn't know, so I asked.

"Bill, do you know of anyone who has a significant disability like yours who is married and deals with lots of personal care assistants?" I asked him. And then, I added what I was really looking for, "Maybe it would be helpful for me to talk to another woman who is living in this situation."

"Sure." Bill responded, always the resourceful one. "I know someone you could speak with. Call this couple on the east coast of the US and talk to this guy's wife. I think they have been married for a few years. She could talk with you and answer your questions." He gave me their number.

"OK. I'll do that. Thanks Bill." I said and hung up.

Taking the plunge I called the couple Bill knew in the US. I talked with the guy's wife for about a half an hour. She was very happy to talk with me. But I was horrified.

This man's wife did *all* of his personal care. She said that she enjoyed it and didn't want it any other way. She didn't like having people coming into her home anyway. So this had worked out the best for them. I thanked her for her time and hung up.

In tears, I called Bill. "The guy's wife does ALL of his personal care." I said, through sobs. "So much for finding me a role model spouse!"

"Oh no! I'm so sorry Chris. I didn't know that about their relationship." I could hear Bill's voice synthesizer speaking, while also hearing his body moving about in an agitated state in his wheelchair. "I wouldn't have told you to call them if I had known that."

"Chris, I'm sorry. There isn't anyone like me who wants what we want and who is married, I guess. I am a pioneer and so are you, whether you want to be or not."

Carefully Bill ventured a little further, "We can chart our own course. I have supports in Lincoln and I can find you what you need here, Chris."

I listened carefully, soaking in his assurance that I could feel a thousand miles away, over the phone. His body had settled down, no more body jumping around and rattling his chair. Just the sound of his voice synthesizer, slowly and carefully, each headstick tap speaking another word of confidence, as Bill plotted out our next steps together.

"Next time you come to visit I will set up some time with Marlene from the League and you can ask her any questions that you might have. Pastor Howard will come too and answer anything you need to know about my church family. They will both help us in any way that we need." Bill finished.

"OK Bill. That sounds like a good plan. I was horrified when I spoke with that woman. I don't want her life. I think that I want to be with you, but I don't want to be your personal care assistant." I said, clearly articulating what I had learned about myself. Perhaps the call had been a good exercise, after all.

'You are not my personal care assistant. You are my girlfriend. I will protect you from having to do my care." Bill stated.

Wow, I thought. He labeled it and he was right. I was his girlfriend.

And, he so clearly stated that he would keep me from becoming his attendant. I immediately felt protected from a role that I never wanted with him.

He was taking the lead in our relationship. I was grateful for his strength and his willingness to assume the lead.

And, I was also leaning on his ability to clearly think of calculated and small steps forward for us. Baby steps were all that I could handle in Nebraska.

Figuring out how I could leave my world and move into his was overwhelming enough for me.

CHAPTER 19

(Bill's voice)

The Open Air Taxi

I was not making any headway displaying my Christian love toward my KKK neighbor, who I found out was a Grand Dragon for them. His sexist, racist, ableist tirades were unending and the threat of physical violence to me was becoming very real. Chris was right. I couldn't afford to NOT move.

So in July 1990 I found a fun new apartment a good distance away from my neighbor the KKK Guy. My new building was a former furniture warehouse that had been converted into apartment buildings. It offered apartments to both able-bodied people and also to people with disabilities.

Since I believe that people with disabilities should be integrated with able-bodied people, this place seemed to be the perfect fit. In fact, when I had gone to visit the new place, no one called the police to say that I had run away from the state institution, like had happened in my old neighborhood.

My family and my friend Mark came to haul all my stuff and electronics over to my new place. It was a mammoth job. I just tried to stay out of their way.

I left no forwarding address with the KKK Grand Dragon. I felt relief to get away from him and to live in a peaceful building, with a lot more security.

Chris was coming again. I was excited to show her my new place in the fun Haymarket district of Lincoln where I now lived. This time she was flying into Lincoln. I wanted to meet her at the airport myself. So I called the (Un)Handi-van a week before Chris was to come to schedule a ride.

"Sorry," the (Un)Handi-Van dispatcher said, "We can't take you. Your ride to the airport isn't a priority ride. It's in the evening and we don't offer service after 5 pm unless it's a necessity."

Not a necessary ride? My girlfriend was coming from Canada and needed a ride to my apartment. It sounded like a priority to me.

"What is a priority ride?" I asked.

"Medical, work and school trips," the dispatcher said.

I hung up, trying to keep calm. I didn't like hearing someone say that I could only make trips to medical, work or school appointments. That was no life. I wanted to meet my girlfriend coming from Canada at the airport.

Ignoring the fact that my monthly phone bill to Canada was now approximating the national debt, I called Chris and told her what the dispatcher had said.

"I could take a taxi," she said, "Why don't I do that? It would be easier for everyone."

I considered and then answered, "Your way probably would be the simplest solution."

"Then, why don't we do it that way? I don't mind, really."

"But, I want to be hospitable to you. Having you take a cab from the airport doesn't seem like I'm welcoming you to my home."

"Whatever you're able to work out is fine with me," Chris said.

Before I met Chris, I had to make all of the telephone calls to people with whom I wanted to have a relationship. Arguably, a part of this was a matter of logistics. I had to be ready to talk when people called. However, it had sent a very clear message to me. I had to make the overtures or risk losing contact with some people.

Chris, on the other hand, was calling me as much as I called her. She was single-handedly subsidizing Bell Canada, the national phone company in Canada. And we were now adding United Airlines to the corporations we subsidized in our relationship. We really had to figure out something before we both ended up in bankruptcy court.

I wanted to meet her at the airport. So I convinced Leon, the owner of a medical supply company and a friend, to give me a ride in the back of his pickup. He was reluctant at first.

Then he said, "Isn't this woman Chris—the one you keep talking about?"

I nodded.

"Then we have to think of a way to get you to the airport. We can't have her using a taxi, can we? That wouldn't be cricket," Leon said, teasing me.

Chris had said that Nebraskans have a propensity for meeting people at airports. This was really odd for her, being from a very large city where people use transportation services all the time to get to and from the airport. I tried to tell her that is because people rarely visit the state of Nebraska. When someone does visit, Nebraskans flock to the airport to mark the event.

"Well, I suppose that you have asked the Handi-Van?" Leon queried.

"Yes, I have. It's a night flight, and the (Un)Handi-Van won't give me the ride because it's not a necessity or a priority." I lamented.

"Figures," Leon retorted.

"I know you can take my power wheelchair to your shop using your pickup truck, so I just thought you could take me in it to the airport," I said, like it was no big deal.

"That's right. We do transport it back and forth in the pickup. However, you aren't usually in it? Aren't you afraid of falling out?" Lean asked, with some trepidation in his voice.

"No, I'm strapped into this chair in four places. How could I fall out? I'm not Harry Houdini. I'm not sure that I could fight my way out of a paper bag," I laughed.

"I don't know," Leon said and chuckled. "How could you? I guess you have a point there. You aren't Houdini, are you? And we can secure your wheelchair down so it doesn't go anywhere. Yeah, we can do this."

I said, "Thank you." Then added, "How's about a trial run the night before, so we know if it will work?"

"That's a good idea," Leon said. "I'll pick you up at seven-thirty on Wednesday night, okay?"

On Wednesday night Leon took me out to the airport. It felt exhilarating to have the wind blowing through my hair and seeing the beginning of a sunset on the Nebraska prairie. I felt a part of something much grander than I would ever know. I started to sing that grand old biker's song, Steppenwolf's "Born to Be Wild."

When we got to the airport Leon and his friend who had come along helped me to get down out of the bed of his pickup. He asked, "What was wrong? We heard you groaning, but you looked okay, so we kept going."

"Nothing was wrong. I was singing," I said.

"Oh. Don't give up your day job," Leon said. We both laughed.

The airport was empty. As I showed Leon where we would go, I thought about Chris. She had said that she hated airports because she was always using them to leave the people she loved. I didn't fully understand this until I roamed the empty airport. Someone always has to say good-bye in this building.

However, this building had brought much healing to me because Chris was using its facilities to be with me.

The next night, before Leon and I left to head over to the airport, Chris called from Chicago, where she had a layover. Her flight from Toronto had missed its connection in Chicago. She was stranded for the night. She said that she would catch the first flight to Lincoln in the morning.

I called Leon and told him what had happened. Leon and I headed out the next morning to meet Chris at the airport.

I was waiting for Chris with a big smile on my face as she came up the jet way into the airport.

She came over and gave me and hug and a kiss and I beamed.

"Hi Chris, I'm Leon. I'll be your transportation today." Leon then said to Chris with a smile. "Bill's riding in the back and you and I are riding up front in my pickup." Chris threw her luggage in the back of the pickup and jumped into the front.

With absolute delight that Chris was back again with me in Lincoln, I rode in the back of Leon's pickup along the streets of Lincoln singing Elvis' Burning Love on our way to my new apartment. "Your kisses lift me higher-like the sweet song of a choir-you light my morning sky-with burning love." I didn't care if I couldn't sing. I was one happy dude.

I was endlessly amazed by Chris. She didn't want to be called a miracle but she was. She was my miracle of love, and had just touched down in Lincoln one more time. And my city slicker girlfriend rode around in a pickup with me in the back like she did this all the time.

With the wind blowing through my hair I thought to myself with pride, *This might be an unusual ride, but Rush you pulled it off. You did meet Chris at the airport and give her a ride back to your place!*

CHAPTER 20

Meeting Bill's Support System

"Hello Chris. It's so good to meet you." Pastor Howard said with a booming voice and a large smile as he extended his hand for a handshake and then gave me a big hug. Bill beamed as he watched Howard and me chatting together. I took an immediate liking to Pastor Howard. He exuded joyfulness and sincerity.

A woman quietly approached us.

"Hello Chris. I'm Marlene from the League of Human Dignity. I'm happy to meet you." said the woman with a soft voice and a smile toward Bill who was grinning as she introduced herself to me. She introduced herself to Pastor Howard and then said, "Hello Bill," in the tone of a friend to a friend.

The fact that both of these people knew and loved Bill as a friend was not lost on me.

We met in an enclosed outdoor patio in Lincoln's Haymarket District where Bill now lived. Umbrellas provided some shade from the blazing Nebraska sun and the heat of this summer day.

Bill had been busy strategizing how to give me both the information and support I needed to think about exploring this relationship with him in Lincoln. It had been twenty-one months since we first met and I was beginning to look seriously into the possibility of moving into Bill's world. He wanted to show me how much support he had in the community of Lincoln, through the League and also through his church, First Baptist. So he asked Pastor Howard and Marlene to meet with us.

"Bill is an integral part of our church family. We love Bill." Pastor Howard began.

"He comes to worship service on Sundays and says Amen through his communication device when he likes what I am saying from the pulpit. It's nice to have someone give me an Amen every once in a while." Howard said and then laughed.

"Bill and I have been working on getting an elevator at the church so that Bill and others who need it can go downstairs to the fellowship hall for weekly Bible study and church functions. We want everyone to be a part of worship, fellowship, service and teaching and much of it happens on the lower level of the building. We are making good headway and hope to have the elevator installed soon."

"Sounds like Bill is a real part of the community at First Baptist," I said out loud. "How do people respond to Bill at church?" I asked because I was curious.

"Most people say hi to him. Few actually stop to talk to him for long. People are a little nervous but they want to include Bill and do their best." Howard responded honestly.

"One of the deacons gives Bill communion and four of them got him into the tank to be baptized last year. And we didn't drown him." Howard laughed heartily.

"It was such a joyous occasion." Howard added.

"I am here for Bill and I am here for you Chris. Whatever you need, I am here to help," he concluded with genuine sincerity.

"Thank you Howard. I really appreciate your support," I said with delight. I was amazed. How wonderful I thought, this pastor is able to think outside of societal norms of what constitutes a typical able-bodied couple and support our relationship. It was refreshing to say the least.

Marlene had been asked by Bill to come and answer my question about if it was possible for Bill to marry and not have his wife do his personal care. He had also asked her to provide information on the disability rights movement, relevant disability-related legislation and his work in the disability rights community.

"Chris, Bill has said that you had questions about what happens if Bill were to marry." Marlene started.

"Yes. I do have lots of questions." I replied. "I spoke with a woman on the east coast of the US who is married to a man who uses a computer to speak and has physical needs similar to Bill's. She said that she did all the care for her husband. Is that the only option for Bill if he marries? I wouldn't want to become Bill's personal care attendant."

"You wouldn't necessarily have to become Bill's attendant should you marry him." Marlene said. "However I have to tell you that Bill's services are covered by Medicaid, a state funded program with income guidelines that require the household income be very low. This means that if you were to continue to work after Bill got married your combined income would most likely disqualify you from the program."

"Are you saying that we would have to live in poverty?" I asked in horror. "But Bill and I both have university degrees. We need to be contributing to society not living off of it." I said with disbelief.

"Unfortunately no one else has done this in Nebraska." Marlene continued in her calm voice. "Couples live together and don't tell the state so that they can keep their earned income or they get married and live according to the income guidelines. One couple in Nebraska got divorced last year so that the woman could have access to state-funded Medicaid, and not lose their resources and income. Bill keeps the small amount of income that he makes from his work editing a newsletter for Nebraska Advocacy Services. He also earns money from publishing stories, but state and federal laws are not yet set up to allow Bill to have income above poverty guidelines and still have access to needed Medicaid- funded programs."

This is sounding really bad, I thought. Bill had to live according to poverty income guidelines. Someone was forced to get divorced in order to continue to get the needed care and not lose their income and resources? Was she going to say that marriage was totally out of the realm of possibility for Bill?

I tried to listen to what Marlene was saying but it was hard to concentrate. Plus she used words that were so foreign to me. She talked about the "movement", second-class citizenship, civil rights, state and federal legislation and regulations. What did all of these terms mean? People in this "movement" have their own language I thought. I was feeling very much the Canadian outsider.

"But I can also speak to Bill's advocacy work and ability to move things forward for all people with disabilities. I can tell you about the work that Bill has been doing in the movement." Marlene continued in the same calm and paced manner.

There was that movement word again. In my Occupational therapy world "movement" was used to talk about bowels, but surely it was a short form for the disability rights movement. She was speaking so positively about Bill's ability to control his own life. Can Bill change this? Is this is what she is suggesting? I thought to myself.

"Bill has always been motivated to live independently and to not have second-class citizenship and he has worked through several barriers already in his life." Marlene affirmed in her soft calm matter-of-fact voice. "I have confidence that he can work through this barrier as well. Bill's roots taught him how to not settle for second best, he learned how to advocate from his parents, when they pushed for him to be able to go to grade school and then supported his work to go to UNL."

Well Chris you at least know a little more now about Bill's upbringing, I thought to myself. And you did already know about his need to live the most normal life possible.

"Bill has always wanted to be in control of his life. He has always been involved in decisions that affected him. It started with the technology for his welder's cap that he uses to create his headsticks. He learned from his parents how to find skilled people to make them. Then when he was at UNL he was a pioneer willing to try things that would increase his independence, including the Ability Phone that he now uses at his apartment."

OK. I was back with the conversation now, but the "poverty and divorce" words were still ringing in my ears.

"Bill used his typewriter and now uses his computer to make and maintain connections at the local and state level to push for full inclusion for people with disabilities into society. He has done the hard work of building coalitions one person at a time to support passage of national and state legislation such as the Civil Rights Restoration Act of 1987. More recently Bill worked hard to push for the landmark Americans with Disabilities Act of 1990 that just passed through congress in July of this year. This legislation is going to literally change the landscape of America." Marlene concluded on a positive note.

Was Marlene really saying that Bill could work to change these regulations or bills or whatever they were called? Are you kidding? I thought. Do Americans really think that they can work to change laws and regulations? Wow. This was astounding to me because I sure didn't think that way.

My mind was whirling, trying to understand this advocacy mentality. I had heard of fringe environmental activists in Canada who took on big business by blocking loggers from cutting trees.

But Marlene was not talking about fighting with corporations she was talking about lobbying government. And she was telling me that Bill had done lots of this for years with others to bring about the support he needed to live in the community. I didn't know that people with disabilities had been doing this across the USA.

"What is this Americans with Disabilities Act that just passed?" I asked.

"It's a Civil rights law, a 20th century Emancipation Proclamation that was passed only a month ago, July 26, 1990 to establish clear and comprehensive prohibition of discrimination against people with disabilities. The purpose of the law is to address major areas of discrimination faced day-to-day by people with disabilities in employment, public transportation, state and local government, and communication systems. The goal is for people with disabilities to be in the most integrated setting possible while maintaining personal choice. The original intent was for a flat-earth bill to pass creating a flat America within 2 years of passage, meaning all of America would be physically accessible to Bill."

"That would be amazing," I said, thinking about how many stairs there were in stores and malls, restaurants, movie theatres and work places. Now that. I did understand.

"Unfortunately Chris it had to be watered down some in order to get it to pass through congress. The ADA that passed tries to balance the needs of the individual for accommodation with the need to not imposing undue hardship on corporations."

"Oh so it's not so simple after all."

"Bill was part of the hidden army who pushed through this very important legislation that will come to help him and other Americans with disabilities who will come after him. The bill passed because of the grassroots movement of many people like Bill. Plus many congressmen have or know someone with a disability; Bob Dole, Edward Kennedy, Tom Harkin, Orin Hatch and of course President George HW Bush, whose three year old daughter had leukemia and who has a son with a learning disability. Bush's support of disability rights helped him win his election campaign and in return we got the ADA. Bill personally sought out and gained Senator Kerry's vote for passage of ADA. It was a difficult task because of the business community's lobby that it would cost them more money. Bill successfully argued that businesses were not able to access one tenth of the market share, with their inaccessible shops. Put up a ramp and people with disabilities would soon pay for the ramp by their purchases and then the businesses would profit. Everyone in the underground disability rights movement played a part in this bill's passage and Bill did his part in spades."

This was an awful lot for me to digest. And much of the information I just didn't understand.

I would come to understand that Marlene was telling me that there were regulatory barriers to Bill getting married and keeping his own personal care attendants and medical insurance. On the other hand she was clearly saying that if anyone could make it happen, it was Bill.

Marlene and Howard left and Bill and I sat in the courtyard. I wondered if I looked as overwhelmed as I felt.

"Chris, I want to take you to the new Indian restaurant for supper. Is that OK?" Bill asked, looking at me and smiling. He knew that all this information was too much for me to digest and he thought it best to move on to enjoy time with him in his new fun neighborhood and let all the complexities have time to settle.

Learning from previous trips that it was most enjoyable for both of us if Bill ate ahead of time so that we could spend time alone and talk while I ate, Bill had arranged his personal attendant schedule to eat a little earlier and free him up for dinner with me.

When it was time to go to the Indian restaurant, we used an accessible side door. I approached the door and a waiter was quick to help with the door so that Bill could roll inside. We were seated quickly and easily when the waiter simply removed one of the chairs. Bill enjoyed watching me savor spicy Indian food while we chatted. And no one stared.

Leon was not on duty for my return trip to the airport. Bill had not wanted to push a favor too far. Instead I took a much less fun car taxi ride out to the airport.

Even though I knew that we would continue to mount up debt to our phone companies, living in two countries was becoming really difficult. Bill didn't need his communication device to speak this time. His eyes were saying I don't want you to go back to Canada. With tears in my eyes and caressing his shoulder I looked at him and said, "I'll call you when I get to the airport." and left.

When I called back to his place I heard Bill say, "Chris, I know this is a lot harder than you probably thought it was going to be." He carefully approaching the subject that we had purposely ignored for a couple of day.

"Yes Bill it is really overwhelming. I don't understand how you can just change government regulations to get married." I said.

"I know." Bill said. "But I will make it happen Chris. If you decide to come here, it will happen. You will not become my personal care assistant, live in poverty or hide your life from the state. I will honor you. I will get it done. But it will probably take another 8 years. I understand if that is too long. Chris can you wait that long?"

"I can wait Bill. I can" I responded without hesitation. "Love you, Bill. I have to go. My flight is boarding."

Somewhat numb by what had just happened, I floated down the jet way, boarded my flight and managed to get myself into a seat and buckle up for the flight.

I had just made the biggest commitment of my life, to a man who was committed to change whatever state or federal regulations it took to marry me. This brilliant, witty and passionate man would do everything in his power to honour me and take care of me. He would lay down his life for me if I needed it. I would not and could not say no to that no matter how difficult the next eight years might be.

Oh yeah, I thought to myself, he will get it done. Of that, I was certain. There was no stopping Bill and that was what one thing I loved about him.

…But how was I going to legally move to Nebraska? I wasn't a US citizen. I couldn't just move here. I could travel here for up to 6 months as a Canadian but I couldn't get a job or stay here. More barriers I thought…

CHAPTER 21

(Bill's Voice)

Senator Exon and the Free Trade Permit

"Senator Exon, I need to find out when Occupational Therapy is going to be added to the list of jobs included in the 1989 Canada-US Free Trade Act. My girlfriend is moving from Canada and she is an OT and needs a job. Can you research this for me?" I asked.

"Absolutely Bill. I will ask my contacts in DC who deal with international trade treaties and see what we can find out for you." Senator Exon replied.

I had rolled over to Senator Exon's downtown Lincoln office to see if he could get any inside scoop. Today's visit to the Senator was particularly enjoyable for me. Instead of my usual petitioning for equal access and opportunity for people with disabilities to be enacted in various legislative bills and acts, I was petitioning for help for Chris to move from Canada.

Using my Journalism school research skills, I was finding very limited options for Chris to legally move to the US. She would have to enter the US on her own merit because I did not have the resources required to sponsor her. Under normal circumstances she would need a work visa that could take years to obtain from an employer who would have to prove the need to hire a non-US citizen.

However, God was showing me a potential parting of the red sea, a way for Chris to get into the US. Canada and the US were coming out of a recession in the late 80's and were anxious to grow their respective economies through the US-Canada Free Trade Agreement just passed in 1989. I was holding out hope that this treaty would also grow our relationship in Lincoln.

A nice chat with a reference librarian at a Lincoln City Library got me a copy of the trade treaty. Reading through the ponderous details of the legislation I found the list of occupations that the two countries were "trading". Physical Therapy was listed but not its sister profession Occupational Therapy. My hope was that Senator Exon could find a more recent version of the trade act that had added OT to the list of professionals, and thus slide Chris into the US economy with limited fanfare. Through this treaty, Chris could get a one year work visa and we could continue to explore our relationship in the same city, instead of between two countries. It would certainly help our pocketbooks to no longer support two telephone companies and United Airlines. On the other hand, I thought with a smile, these corporations might go bankrupt without us.

I went home and called Chris to give her an update on my research.

"Sounds like it might work, assuming that OT gets added to the list," Chris responded when I told her what I had been researching.

"I will need to come as a traveler to the US and find an employer willing to sponsor me for a Free Trade Permit. Then I will have to get to a Canada-US border point to re-enter with a work visa. I will start wrapping up my work here and come sometime in December."

"My brothers will come to Canada with their cattle truck and pick up your things if you want," I offered, knowing that my brothers would really do this if I asked them to. I was concerned that Chris was not going to be able to bring her belongings with her. I wanted her to be as comfortable as she could possibly be when she came.

"I can only come with a couple of suitcases Bill, because I am coming as a traveler. The border agents wouldn't let me bring in a truck load of items for a vacation. They might get suspicious." Chris laughed. "Bill I don't need much. But I will need to find a place to stay and few pieces of furniture." She added in a more serious tone.

"I will find you a place and get you some furniture." I declared, and began to think about where Chris could live. She needed to be in a wheelchair accessible place or I would never be able to visit. And she needed to be close enough to my place so that she wouldn't have to travel far when winter came. She said she was going to sell her car in Canada before she came so she would need to have access to public transit. The more I thought about it, the more I realized that getting Chris an apartment in my building would be the most convenient and safest for her. But I would have to convince the landlord that they should rent to Chris.

I went and paid the landlord a visit.

"Bill, we are not supposed to rent to illegal aliens," the landlord said. "Is Chris going to get legal status to stay in the US?"

"Yes. She is going to come and get a job that will sponsor her to get a Free Trade Permit to work here." I replied with astonishing assurance, considering that the Free Trade Act did not, as of yet, include her profession.

"Have her send us a down payment for an apartment and I will hold one for her starting December, Bill. But she will need to get me proof of her legal status here as soon as she gets it so that we don't get in trouble with the INS," the landlord said in a stern tone.

"Absolutely," I said, trying not to show my excitement that I had managed to convince my landlord to set aside an apartment for my most alien girlfriend.

Finding furniture for Chris would be a piece of cake. My family had lots of old stuff stored at the farm house where my parents now lived in rural Nebraska. My brothers would bring her whatever she needed.

My job was now to keep an eye on the Free Trade Act for Chris' job title, bug my brothers and pray.

God don't let me down now, I prayed fervently and incessantly, just as the scriptures had taught me to do. *Part the red sea so that Chris can legally get at job in the America and stay here with me.*

CHAPTER 22

(Chris' Voice)

Arriving in Nebraska

"Where are you going in the US?" the US customs officer at Toronto's Pearson International Airport asked me.

"Nebraska." I responded remembering that it was best to answer only the question I was being asked. Praying that he wouldn't ask me when I would return to Canada, so that I wouldn't have to lie, I looked him straight in the eye and worked hard to keep myself calm.

"What are you doing in Nebraska?"

"Visiting friends," I responded in an easygoing manner.

"Have a good trip," the customs officer said and the ordeal was quickly over.

I entered the USA bound United Airlines/Air Canada terminal passenger lounge one more time. Bill and I had both frequented this terminal several times in the past 26 months. I was excited that I was going to go be with Bill. But I was also feeling terribly sad about leaving Canada.

From my window seat on the aircraft, I could see many Air Canada planes at their designated gates, all with red maple leaves on their tails. With tears streaming down my face, feeling a rip of separation from my beloved birth nation, I looked out my small window, watching my plane pull back from the gateway. The various airliners with their individual Canadian emblems and then the Toronto skyline disappeared as we took off for Chicago.

Goodbye Canada, I thought as silent tears rolled down my face throughout the first leg of my journey.

My plane landed at O'Hare and taxied into one of the now very familiar to me United Airlines terminals. The tears had subsided. I had said my good-byes and I was moving on to what would come next for us. With growing excitement, I made my way along the underground walkway from one terminal to another to catch my second plane that would take me to Lincoln and to Bill.

Nervous and also delighted, as I thought about being able to stay for some time with Bill, and not have to come back through this airport again in a few days, I boarded the plane for my final leg of the journey.

Without delay at O'Hare, my flight took off. My excitement grew during the hour flight. I felt a sense of total relief, as we touched down in Lincoln.

"Welcome to the Good Life Chris!" Jeff, Bill's friend said, smiling at me, declaring Nebraska's Logan, to me, the newcomer. Then looking to Bill who was smiling broadly, he added, "Bill asked if I would like to be a part of his greeting party. And I didn't want to miss this."

I had stayed with Jeff and his wife Cathy during a couple of my visits. These friends were neighbors of Bill's when he lived in his first apartment. They had been gracious hosts, giving me space to come and go as I pleased and letting me have free reign of their kitchen to find anything that I needed and didn't get over at Bill's place.

"Welcome home," Bill said to me, looking both relieved and elated.

"I'm here Bill. I'm here." I said whispering in his ear as I wrapped my arms around his neck.

"Well let's get you both loaded up and over to Bill's place." Jeff said picking up my luggage and starting for the door. I pushed Bill, who had used his manual chair to get to the airport in Jeff's minivan. We got Bill into the passenger seat, carefully putting his Touch Talker on the floor of the van and then putting Bill's tray and the manual wheelchair behind the back seat.

Back at Bill's place, I was savoring the fact that this was not yet again, another time limited visit. Having all the time I could ever want to be with Bill was wonderful. Sitting curled up in the corner of Bill's couch while he sat in front of me, we chatted about his plan to get me some furniture for my apartment. Then Bill rolled away from me toward his large custom designed desk.

"I have something for you Chris." Bill said. Using his headstick, he pulled a document off his desk to his wheelchair tray. Bill rolled over and sat again in front of me. He then pushed the government-looking document off his tray and into my lap.

"What is this?" I asked trying to figure out what it was.

"It's the latest draft of the US implementations of the Canada-Free Trade Agreement, dated December 10, 1990. Chris. Look at the highlighted part on the second page."

I turned the page to look for the highlighted section. There, well marked in yellow, were the words *Occupational Therapy*, added to the list of professions that could be "traded" between Canada and the USA.

"Senator Exon's office found it for me in Washington, DC. They said that the border offices don't even have it yet. So when we go to get you a work permit, we will need to take this copy to show them." Bill said with a very satisfied look on his face.

"Wow. This is amazing. I just arrived and my profession got added this month? The timing is unbelievable Bill! Someone is looking after us!" I said with absolute amazement and pride that Bill had found this.

"And Jeff has offered to drive us to the Canadian border at Manitoba and back again when you are ready – it's 600 hundred miles one way. All you need is a job Chris and you can stay here, at least for a year." Bill said and smiled.

"Now all I have to do is find an employer willing to hire an alien." I said laughing. "It's funny to think of myself as an alien. Am I green with funny antennae?" I joked with Bill.

"You are my alien miracle Chris. USA didn't make what I needed so God had to outsource to Canada to find me an alien." Bill said, laughing with sheer delight and involuntarily jumping up and down in his wheelchair.

Reprint of the Federal Register, Vol. 56. No. 4, January 7, 1991.

482   Federal Register / Vol. 56. No. 4 / Monday, January 7, 1991 / Rules and Regulations

nor does this rule have Federalism implications warranting the preparation of a Federal Assessment in accordance with E.O. 12612.

List of Subjects in 8 CFR Part 214

Administrative practice and procedure, Aliens, authority delegation, Employment, Organization and functions, Passports and visas.

Accordingly, part 214 of chapter I of title 8 of the Code of Federal Regulations is amended as follows:

PART 214—NONIMMIGRANT CLASSES

1. The authority citation for part 214 continues to read as follows:

Authority: 8 U.S.C. 1101, 1103, 1184, 1186a, 1187, and 8 CFR part 2.

2. Section 214.2 is amended by revising paragraph (b) (4) (i) (D) (1) to read as follows:

§ 214.2 Special requirements for admission, extension, and maintenance of status.

*   *   *   *   *

(b) * * *
(4) * * *
(i) * * *
(D) *Sales.* (1) Sales representatives and agents taking orders or negotiating contracts for goods or services for an enterprise located in Canada/the United States but not delivering goods or providing services.

*   *   *   *   *

3. In § 214.6, paragraph (d)(2).(ii) is revised to read as follows:

§ 214.6 Canadian citizens seeking temporary entry to engage in business activities at a professional level.

*   *   *   *   *

(d) * * *
(2) * * *
(ii) *Schedule 2 to Annex 1502.1 of the FTA.* Pursuant to the FTA, an applicant seeking admission under this section shall demonstrate business activity at a professional level in one of the professions or occupations set forth in Schedule 2 to Annex 1502.1. The professions or occupations in Schedule 2 and the minimum requirements for each are as follows:

Schedule 2 (Annotated)

—Accountant—baccalaureate degree
—Architect—baccalaureate degree or state/provincial license [1]
—Computer Systems Analyst—baccalaureate degree
—Disaster relief claims adjuster—baccalaureate degree or three years' experience in the field of claims adjustment
—Economist—baccalaureate degree
—Engineer—baccalaureate degree or state/provincial license [1]

—Forester—baccalaureate degree or state/provincial license [1]
—Graphic designer—baccalaureate degree, or post-secondary diploma and three years' experience
—Hotel Manager—baccalaureate degree and three years' experience in hotel management
—Land surveyor—baccalaureate degree or state provincial/Federal license [1]
—Landscape architect—baccalaureate degree.
—Lawyer—member of bar in province or state, of L.L.B., J.D., L.L.L., or B.C.L.
—Librarian—M.L.S. or B.L.S. (for which another baccalaureate degree was a prerequisite)
—Management consultant—baccalaureate degree or five years' experience in consulting or related field
—Mathematician—baccalaureate degree
—Medical/Allied Professionals
  —Clinical lab technologist—baccalaureate degree
  —Dentist—D.D.S., D.M.D., or state/provicial license [1]
  —Dietitian—baccalaureate degree or state/provincial licenses [1]
  —Medical technologist—baccalaureate degree
  —Nutritionist—baccalaureate degree
  —Occupational therapist—baccalaureate degree or state/provincial license [1]
  —Pharmacist—baccalaureate degree or state/provincial license [1]
  —Physician (teaching and/or research only)—M.D. or state/provincial license [1]
  —Physio/Physical therapist—baccalaureate degree or state/provincial license [1]
  —Psychologist—State/provincial license [1]
  —Recreational therapist—baccalaureate degree
  —Registered nurse—state/provincial license [1]
—Veterinarian—D.V.M., D.M.V., or state/provincial license [1]
—Range manager (range conservationist)—baccalaureate degree
—Research assistant (working in a post-secondary educational institution)—baccalaureate degree
—Scientific technician/technologist
  —Must work in direct support of professionals in the following disciplines: Chemistry, geology, geophysics, meteorology, physics, astronomy, agricultural sciences, biology, or forestry.
  —Must possess theoretical knowledge of the discipline.
  —Must solve practical problems in the discipline.
  —Must apply principles of the discipline to basic or applied research.
—Scientist
  —Agriculturist (agronomist)—baccalaureate degree
  —Animal breeder—baccalaureate degree
  —Animal scientist—baccalaureate degree

[1] The terms "state/provincial license" and "state/provincial/Federal license" mean any document issued by a state, provincial, or Federal Government as the case may be, or under its authority, which permits a person to engage in a regulated activity or profession.

—Apiculturist—baccalaureate degree
—Astronomer—baccalaureate degree
—Biochemist—baccalaureate degree
—Biologist—baccalaureate degree
—Chemist—baccalaureate degree
—Dairy scientist—baccalaureate degree
—Entomologist—baccalaureate degree
—Epidemiologist—baccalaureate degree
—Geneticist—baccalaureate degree
—Geologist—baccalaureate degree
—Geophysicist—baccalaureate degree
—Horticulturist—baccalaureate degree
—Meteorologist—baccalaureate degree
—Pharmacologist—baccalaureate degree
—Physicist—baccalaureate degree
—Plant breeder—baccalaureate degree
—Poultry scientist—baccalaureate degree
—Soil scientist—baccalaureate degree
—Zoologist—baccalaureate degree
—Social worker—baccalaureate degree
—Sylviculturist (forestry specialist)—baccalaureate degree
—Teacher
  —College—baccalaureate degree
  —Seminary—baccalaureate degree
  —University—baccalaureate degree
—Technical publications writer—baccalaureate degree, or post-secondary diploma and three years' experience
—Urban planner—baccalaureate degree
—Vocational counselor—baccalaureate degree

*   *   *   *   *

Dated: December 10, 1990.

Gene McNary,
Commissioner, Immigration and Naturalization Service.
[FR Doc. 91-152 Filed 1-4-91; 8:45 am]
BILLING CODE 4410-10-M

8 CFR Part 264

[INS Number: 1295-90]

Applicant Processing for the Legalization Program

AGENCY: Immigration and Naturalization Service, Justice.

ACTION: Final rule.

SUMMARY: This rule amends 8 CFR 264.1 by requiring those aliens adjusted from temporary resident status to permanent resident status pursuant to section 210(a)(2) of the Act, to submit the Form I-90 to the Director of the Service Center having jurisdiction over their place of residence. This change is necessary to properly process the large volume of one-time applications as a result of section 210(a)(2) of the Act.

EFFECTIVE DATES: This final rule is effective January 7, 1991.

FOR FURTHER INFORMATION CONTACT: Janet Charney, Deputy Assistant Commissioner, Legalization, (202) 514-0106.

SUPPLEMENTARY INFORMATION: On May 16, 1990 a final rule was published in the

CHAPTER 23

(Chris' Voice)

Settling In at First Baptist Lincoln

"How's the job hunting going Chris?" Pastor Howard asked with concern and interest.

"Not every employer wants to hire an alien for a year. I need one who is willing to work with me to get a Free Trade permit." I said, feeling insecure about my job prospects.

"Chris, you'll get a job." Pastor Howard said complete confidence and a broad smile.

Pastor Howard and I were chatting while I was waiting in the church's nursery for the small children to arrive. We were looking out the window at people arriving in the parking lot.

Some friendly church friends of Bill's had slid me into the vacant childcare position as a way of helping me to earn a little cash. Looking back, I assume that these friends didn't think of me as an alien because I am white and am Canadian. After all, don't many Americans joke that Canada is the 51st state? However, because I did not have residency status, I knew that earnings from any source including babysitting in the church's nursery were illegal. Justifying it to myself by saying that babysitting money was not taxed, I seized the opportunity to make a few bucks without telling the church that they were not supposed to pay me.

For the first time I was experiencing what it was like to be the new immigrant, trying to get status in the US while also trying to support myself to live. I mooched off of Bill, eating at his place and spending down my savings on my apartment.

It was tough to make ends meet, even if I had so much going for me; I was privileged, white and educated, yet I too needed a little hand up until I could get my well-paying job and become a tax-payer. This experience gave me new eyes of compassion for the millions of non-resident immigrants of color, living in the US because they want to be with their loved one(s), but who are far less fortunate than I in terms of race, education and job opportunities.

Pastor Howard interrupted my thoughts.

"Aw Here comes Bill, one of God's choicest creatures!" Pastor Howard affectionately announced, when he spotted Bill rolling through the parking lot of the church in his power wheelchair while we looked out the window.

Yes! I thought to myself, what a great way to describe him. Bill is most definitely one of God's choicest creatures! He was indeed of high quality and also clearly chosen by God for the task of opening doors for others with disabilities, that would come after him. Bill was growing in his faith and devotion to Jesus. As one of God's choicest creature, I trusted that he would also be used, to lead others to Him.

Bill's finer qualities of courage, wit and determination, were the result of the refiner's fire of perseverance. He had learned to never give up, finding humor in his often, dire circumstance, while fighting societal prejudices, one day at a time, so that he might get through university and then build a system, an infrastructure of supports to keep himself out of a nursing home and in the community. Now I was entering Bill's community and also learning from his experience. I would come to see Bill as the greatest teacher of my life, sharing constantly, with and without words, from the adversity that he had overcome.

I began to think about my first few visits to First Baptist Lincoln. I started attending church with Bill in December of 1990. The response of people at First B to me being with Bill ran the gambit. I put people's responses into three groups, the supporters, the assumers, usually consisting of those who assumed that I was Bill's attendant, and the nosy ones. Bill would be more generous than I and say these people were just curious.

Words of welcome by a couple of individuals and families suggested that they, like me, were able to find Bill in the midst of all of his essential technologies and under his significant disability. These supporters valued Bill as a person, and thought that he was worthy of having a relationship with me.

Several people at First B addressed me with, "Oh you must be Bill's nurse." When I corrected these assumers by saying that I was Bill's girlfriend, some were apologetic, realizing that they made an incorrect assumption. Others, who couldn't get past their own assumptions just stared with a look of incredulousness. Bill taught me to not waste my energy on these people. It wasn't my job to change anyone's preconceived notions about ability and relationships.

Finally, there were the nosy ones. Some people asked socially appropriate questions, such as where I was living and what I did for a living etc. One nosy incident however stood out from the others, for its sheer audacity.

An older woman whom I had never spoken with before, came up to me and very candidly asked, "Can Bill have sex?" in the same tone one would use to ask, "Where is the restroom?"

I was horrified by the woman's question. I was feeling violated and wanting to run away. Even though the question was about Bill, it was being directed towards me. This older woman dared probe into Bill's and possibly my private life, something that I had assumed was off limits in society at large, and especially in the church.

"Absolutely," I responded working hard to keep as serious a face I could muster. The tone of my voice was probably defensive, if not outright hostile. I turned to leave the woman as quickly as I could. With my heart racing and feeling horrified by what had transpired, I went to find Bill, my comfort and security.

"Bill you are not going to believe what that older woman said to me." I said to Bill, feeling a mixture of horror and disgust. "Why are people so nosy? It's none of their business." I said angrily.

"We need to go talk with Pastor Howard." Bill said and off we went to find him. He was used to this kind of discrimination. I wasn't. And it showed.

Howard's response was as expected. "That is really off the wall. It's a violation of Bill's privacy let alone personhood and a violation of your own privacy Chris." he exclaimed.

I felt better hearing Pastor Howard validate Bill's personhood and our privacy. He was a balm to my injured soul. Bill was sadly resigned to this, yet another questioning of his sexuality and personhood. I was the one who was in shock and needed Pastor Howard's affirmation. I had a sickish feeling in the pit of my stomach.

In spite of the rush of emotions that Bill must have been feeling, he went straight to a problem-solving mode to try to protect me from further questions. He said, "I would like to introduce Chris to the congregation through a note in the newsletter. Would that be OK Pastor Howard?"

"Sure Bill, write what you wish and we'll see about sending it out in the weekly newsletter. That way, the truth of who Chris is will be out there for all to read. And hopefully the questions will cease."

Bill did write a small piece, explaining that I was his girlfriend and not his attendant, and that we were exploring a relationship, now that Chris was in Lincoln. Bill requested that people respect our privacy and not ask probing questions about us.

Bill's introduction helped greatly. The nosy ones settled down and stopped asking me questions. The assumers began to assume that I would be at church with Bill. The supporters continued to be there for us, just as they had always been.

CHAPTER 24

(Bill's Voice)
Inaccessibility Makes Romance Tough

"Do you want to check out that new ramp tonight at Cinema 1 and 2?" I asked Chris, hoping that she would be open to the idea. "After all for the past two years while you were living in Canada, you had to listen to me gripe about this theatre not being accessible."

I felt like a little kid showing off a new trick to a playmate. I was rejoicing that I had won a three-year fight to get the city's only inaccessible theatre to put in an accessible entrance.

"Sure," Chris said.

For three years I had been demanding entrance into Cinema 1 and 2. When the owners tried to placate and ignore me, I had started a boycott and a picket line outside the theatre to make the public aware that the place wasn't accessible. The owners hoped that I would go away like a bad case of pimples.

I didn't go away. I filed a discrimination suit with the Commission on Human Rights and the owners got an attack of social conscience. They agreed to put in a ramp at the exit door of one of their auditoriums and to rotate the movies once a week. This way every movie would be shown in the accessible arena eventually. I knew that it was a compromise. As the lawyer at the Commission on Human Rights had reminded me, it was better than what I had when I started.

On one Sunday in late January of 1991 I checked on the progress of the ramp.

"Yes, the ramp is installed," the theatre manager said. "Which movie do you want to see?"

"I'll come back later," I said.

I wanted to share my victory with Chris for reasons other than I had used her to gripe to. I wanted to share this with her because she was an important person in my life.

When Chris and I bought our movie tickets at the theatre on a bitterly cold night, the clerk said, "Go to the door that is in the alley. Someone will be with you shortly."

It sounded easy enough. So we went in the alley.

At that moment, I wished I could talk so I could do an imitation of Humphrey Bogart starring in Casablanca, asking Chris what a nice girl like her was doing in a place like this. The alley was dark and I bumped along in my power wheelchair toward the side entrance.

Then Chris asked, "Which door? There are two doors here."

We walked back and forth like Russian sentries on patrol in northern Siberia, looking for the usher with the new ramp to appear.

After about five minutes of doing this, Chris said impatiently, "This is crazy. Where is the man with the ramp? We should have been in the warm theatre five minutes ago instead of out here in a freezing cold alley."

"Welcome to my world," I lamented silently. I had gotten used to using inaccessible accessible entrances, but she hadn't. Did loving me mean she had to give up using the front door?

Before Chris entered my life women had lost interest after the first or second date. No wonder! When I was in college, eleven years before I was here with Chris, I had asked another woman if she would want to go out with me again. She had honestly articulated the problem: "I don't think so Bill. By the time we got you and your manual wheelchair in and out of my car, got you in and out of your chair and found the accessible entrance to the place, I forgot who you were."

Inaccessibility, meaning a lack of accessible transportation to the party and then a hassle to find an accessible door into the place we were going, had derailed that relationship from the first date. To make matters worse, I wasn't able to talk with her while we were getting to the party, and a lack of communication with me felt to this woman like she had "lost me."

While I had grown in self-efficacy as a person with a disability, thanks to the support of my advisors at the League of Human Dignity, inaccessibility continued to plague me. I had to fight to make companies comply with the requirements of ADA to allow me to have quality time with Chris, in public places. This fiasco was getting worse by the moment.

Looking at the total picture some people might say that accessible theaters were the least of my problems. But, sitting in the cold alley waiting for a ramp and watching Chris fume, I didn't think she considered inaccessibility as a small problem. When people are on a date, they try to put their best foot (or wheel) forward. I was trying to do that on this date but wasn't having much success.

About five minutes later an usher came out of the theater with the ramp in hand announcing that the ramp needed bolts and that he didn't know where they were.

"Damn," I said in frustration. "This ramp was a compromise. We wanted United Artist Company to put a wheelchair lift inside the building, from the lobby to the theatres. But they had said that a lift would cost too much money."

"Couldn't they see that if they put in a lift, more people could get into the theater meaning more business? Can't you sue them since this ramp isn't working?" Chris asked, now totally exasperated.

I shook my head no. "The ADA only covers newly constructed buildings and mandates that the owners make "reasonable accommodations." To the owners of Cinema 1 and 2, a ramp into the back door fulfills their legal obligation. So I can't sue them. Besides, I signed a pretrial agreement that said I wouldn't sue the owners in exchange for the installation of a ramp."

All of this discussion was academic. The ramp wasn't working. Chris and I were being left out in the bitter cold. We could have rented a movie. But we wanted to go out like real people do.

When the usher went to look for the missing bolts, I could see steam coming out of Chris' nostrils. She wasn't used to being a back door person, nor had she been trained to tolerate others' incompetence. I had been.

"You look so cold, Bill." Chris said. There was genuine concern in her voice.

"So do you. Why don't you go on in? I will be in shortly." I offered.

"And leave you out here? Don't be silly. We came here together. What other couple uses different doors when they go somewhere?" She had a good point.

"The Commission didn't tell me that the ramp would be like this. They had said it would be permanently attached to the building, "I said. "Of course, they were only going by what United Artist had promised them."

Finally the usher found the bolts. He installed the ramp and helped me onto it. On the first try the wheelchair didn't make it up the terribly steep ramp. So I tried to back off and get a running start, but it didn't make any difference because the alley was too bumpy.

On the third try, the usher got a second pair of hands to help push me up the steep ramp. Chris guided me so that I would stay on the ramp. Getting the first space shuttle back to Florida couldn't have taken more effort.

When we finally got seated in the movie theatre, I apologized to Chris for the crazy ramp. She said, "At least we got in here. That is more than we had before you started bugging them to do something."

During the movie, I thought about what Chris had said. I knew that she was trying to salvage something from this botched victory celebration and to make me feel better.

I couldn't help thinking that this fiasco was my fault. Perhaps if I had pushed harder, perhaps if I had insisted on seeing the ramp before I signed the pre-trial agreement, perhaps if I had checked on the ramp before I asked Chris to the movie or perhaps if I had met with the owners personally, things would have been different. After all, I was supposed to be some kind of a hotshot advocate for people with disabilities.

This was when I realized that I was doing just what a rape victim does after an attack. That is, I was blaming myself for something that wasn't really my fault.

During the movie I tried to figure out why I was feeling so angry. I had gone in worse entrances.

Then I realized that I was so annoyed because Chris experienced what it's like to be treated like a second-class citizen. She had to endure the excuse that partial accessibility was the best the builders could do. I loved her and wanted to save her from that.

I was used to this. When I was young, my dad, uncles and brothers carried me up and down stairs. In college, attendants and friends hauled me, and my manual wheelchair, up and down stairs. However, now that I was an adult, it was no longer practical or dignified.

In the eleven years of living on my own, everything had changed but really nothing had changed. I now had a serious girlfriend. I lived in downtown Lincoln so that I could roll on my dates with Chris. This eliminated the need for her to transfer me into and out of her car. And, I always checked to make sure that I know where the accessible entrance is before we go anywhere.

However, despite all my precautions, I still had to contend with inaccessibility. If these inconveniences were unavoidable, I wouldn't have minded, but they were avoidable. People who really care have made inaccessible buildings very accessible.

In the 1960's blacks faced the same indignities. They had to use separate (and inferior) drinking fountains and had to ride in the back of buses. They had heroes who said that it wasn't right to make people use the back door.

Similarly, people with disabilities had to fight hard for equal access to public buildings and transportation. The Americans with Disabilities Act was the result of decades of work by many people. As a result of this legislation, some buildings now have permanent ramps that everyone uses.

But there was still often a more subtle kind of discrimination present, such as when a business puts in a ramp that was hardly worth the hassle to use it.

CHAPTER 25

(Bill's Voice)

Exorcizing My Demons

"Bill I'm worried about you." Chris said with genuine concern.

I looked to her as she continued. "You are doing fine with me, but all the terrible things that people have said to you over the decades, about you not being able to have a relationship with a woman, are still haunting you. Do you think it might help to go see a counselor and work on redefining your masculinity?"

She was right. I did need some help. I couldn't stop the audiotapes that continually played in my mind. Society had told me for my entire lifetime that I was not masculine, that I was not a sexual being and that I couldn't have what I most wanted and needed in my life, a woman-like Chris.

Now that she was living in my world in Lincoln, I was terrified that I would mess up the relationship and then she might leave. No matter how often Chris said that she wasn't leaving, I had a hard time believing it.

So I went to see a counselor and spent a couple of very helpful sessions identifying my demons to begin to exorcize them. Societal messages from my past, redefining my own masculinity, and my concern about the discrimination that Chris was now facing because of my disability became the focus of my discussions with the counselor.

"Before I met Chris, other women had flirted with me. They played games with me. When I got serious, they ran away. So, I decided that I couldn't and wouldn't trust another woman with my heart. This was not because of my disability. It was because I had been burnt and I was afraid and angry. Chris has demonstrated her love for me by moving here. She loves, honors and cherishes my heart and yet I'm still afraid and angry."

"Bill you need to give yourself some time to grow into this relationship with Chris. You trust her implicitly. It shows. The pain of the other experiences will fade with time." the counselor said with an encouraging tone.

"I want to protect Chris from the discrimination that she is now experiencing when she is with me. I'm angry that she has to experience it too. I have watched how people respond to Chris. Society's response to Chris is reminding me of what I have been told for years." I told the counselor.

"And what is that?" the counselor continued.

"That I am damaged goods, and no one wants inferior merchandise. And now I see people telling Chris this about me too. She gets frustrated by it and I get terrified that she will get tired of it and leave."

"She finds it disconcerting when we're out on a date, having an intimate conversation, and people come up and look at how I'm talking. They stick themselves between my Touch Talker™ and us and ask, "How does he do that? Is that his real voice? Can he hear me?"

"I'm used to this rudeness, but it hurts me to have Chris experience the same dehumanization. Sometimes, I wonder how I can have the audacity to expect people to comprehend that Chris loves me when they don't even understand that I'm a person."

"So you are seeing your fears being played out," the counselor astutely summarized.

"There is greater scrutiny of our relationship than there would be had I been able-bodied. People ask Chris why she moved down here from Canada. She tells them she came to be with me, a person who is a free-lance journalist, who doesn't have a steady job and who has a disability. They just look at her like she has lost her mind. They don't say, 'That is wonderful," or, "That is terrible." They just stare at her with silent curiosity like she is an oddity. She sees so many faces of ridicule, curiosity, fear and pity when she says that she has a boyfriend with a disability."

"People who can only see my disability have told her that she shouldn't get involved with me because she might hurt me. Those who can't see me for all of who I am, think of me as being vulnerable. When Chris met me, I was vulnerable; not because of my disability, but because I was alone."

"Most people think that Chris is either a saint or some kind of deviant for wanting to pursue a loving relationship with me. She is neither. She is human. She gets frustrated with societal bigotry against people with disabilities, and towards those like her, who choose to have relationships with them. She also gets tired of my low self-esteem."

"Bill I don't think you have low self-esteem." the counselor countered. "After all you have what it takes to work through this relationship with Chris. You are figuring it out one step at a time. Rather, it would seem that you have been hurt in your past and you are trying to protect yourself. That's only smart."

The counselor then added, "But, from what you are telling me, I hear that Chris loves you and is not playing games with you like the other women did."

"Yes Chris does not play games. She is honest and honorable. And I don't want to lose her." I replied truthfully.

"How do you deal with the discrimination when you are alone?" the counselor continued.

"I try to understand that to be human is to be curious, and I teach people to understand that I am a person by talking to them. But I can't expect Chris to do this about our relationship."

"You have a great sense of humor. Do you use humor to deal with obnoxious and ignorant people, Bill?" the counselor questioned.

"Yes. I could show Chris how to use humor to deal with some people's strange behavior. I need to feel empowered to help Chris."

"You of all people Bill know that you can't change how people react to you and Chris, but, you can change your response. You can teach Chris to do the same thing. You are a team. Teach Chris how to respond to people's curiosity when it's appropriate and how to handle bigotry when it happens."

I moved on to my concern about my lack of a definition of my own masculinity. "Unlike me, Chris had her womanhood affirmed in her teen years. She was supposed to date and then marry an able-bodied man. I can't be the tough guy that Hollywood spoon feeds us. And I don't have any role models." I said.

"What does Chris need from you? Perhaps that is how you can define your masculinity?" the counselor suggested.

"She wants a man who will give her emotional support, listen to her and love her." I responded without hesitation.

"How does that resonate with you as a context for defining your masculinity Bill? More broadly speaking, sexuality is about emotional connection and not just Hollywood erotica. You have explored this idea in your writing in the context of disability, haven't you? What have you written that you can revisit?"

"I wrote from the perspective of the person with a significant disability being limited to two options in dealing with their feelings of love -- the road of fantasizing or the road of expecting and accepting only platonic love. I was wrong, thank God! And now I have to figure out what to do now that I have attained what I most wanted."

I continued, "Chris is *the road less travelled.* She is someone with enough courage, honesty and love to go against societal prejudices to see that I, a person with a significant disability am capable of loving and being loved. And now I have to figure out how to love her back."

"Sounds like you have been doing it for a long time already, but that you haven't fully grasped what it is that you are doing. You will figure it out as this relationship continues to develop. Then you will have redefined your masculinity into something that fits for you."

The counselor moved on to the topic of role models, "Here's another thought, to help counter Hollywood's stereotypical erotic images of masculinity; do you know of any male TV or movie characters who experienced a disability and could be a role model to you?"

"I loved Ironside." I responded quickly. "He was intelligent, powerful and taken seriously. I'm going to go home and see if I can find him on channels that show old TV programs."

"Sounds like you have found some tools to begin to move forward Bill," the counselor concluded, as we wrapped up my final session.

CHAPTER 26

(Bill's Voice)

Ironside as "Roll" Model

I went home and told Chris about my final session with the counselor. I was feeling better because I knew what I could do to begin to redefine my own masculinity. I also knew how I could support Chris to deal with the discrimination she was facing when she was with me in public.

Back in the driver seat of my life, the past relationships with women, and what my society had told me in explicit and subtle ways, no longer had power over me. I shared with Chris that I needed to find some role models of men who experienced disabilities and were confident of their masculinity.

"Are there any fictional characters on TV that might be helpful?" Chris asked, giving me the same advise as my counselor.

"Ironside. When I was a teenager he was my "roll" model."

I told Chris what I had remembered from watching him as a teenager:

"...I saw a strong man who was a key part of his community. The character, like me, also used a wheelchair, but that seemed secondary. I saw a man who was respected (and sometimes feared) for his abilities instead of being pitied for his disabilities. I also saw a man who accepted his disability. This, in return, allowed others to accept his disability. [1]

Finding that Ironside re-runs played on the Nostalgia Channel, I got reacquainted with him. Raymond Burr, playing Ironside, a Special Department Consultant to the San Francisco Police Department had been paralyzed from the waist down when a sniper shot him. He used his brains and initiative to solve cases.

Thinking back to when I was a teenager, I remembered that I had modeled my interactions on Ironside's premise that people would follow my lead and accept my disability, if I showed them that I accepted it. It took a lot of effort on my part but most of the time it worked.

"Now -- some twenty years later -- when I watched the series again, I still marveled at Ironside's control over his life. He surrounded himself with people who supported him without smothering him. His attendants helped him without interfering. He had his dignity, and he and his attendants fought to keep it. He had used his intellect to earn a living and contributed towards the greater good for society. [2]

"Ironside had always given me a yardstick by which to measure my own success." [3] I thought to myself.

And without realizing it, I realized that I had also been using it also as a measure of my masculinity, even if, in the series, Ironside didn't have a significant relationship with a woman.

Similar to Ironside's character, I had and continued to fight hard to keep control over my life. I worked to keep my relationship with my attendants such that they supported me without smothering me. I took charge of my care in my dealings with the home health agency that was providing my attendants.

My writing and advocacy work were my contributions to society. I was doing writing and editing jobs to earn as much money as I could without infringing on the Medicaid income guidelines. I was advocating for changes to state and federal laws and regulations that would allow for me to become a part of mainstream society and eventually become a tax payer.

But now that Chris was added to the equation, I was fighting to keep her in the role of a girlfriend and not be used as a substitute attendant when someone couldn't come. I knew that this could become a very slippery slope that might leave Chris feeling resentful towards me. So when an attendant was not available, I would tell the home health agency that Chris was not an option and demand that another attendant be found.

I was also working to keep my relationship with Chris private from the attendants. Attendants were curious people. When they would ask questions about Chris I would explicitly tell then that our relationship was off limits.

Perhaps the counselor was correct. I already had a definition of my masculinity thanks to watching Ironside as a teenager. I just didn't know it.

With Chris in my life, it was simply a matter of adding to my definition of masculinity. I would expand it to include protecting Chris's boundaries with my attendants as well as making sure that her needs were met.

A couple of sessions with a counselor and revisiting my teenage "roll" model Ironside helped me to feel much better.

Endnotes

[1.] Bill Rush. "A Perfect "Roll" Model." *Nebraska Rehabilitation and Community Newsletter* December 1994. Reprinted with permission.

[2.] Ibid.

[3.] Ibid.

CHAPTER 27

(Chris' Voice)
A Job and A Border Run

"I have a job interview in Omaha, Bill." I said. "I think I should go and check it out." I concluded even though I was concerned about the fact that Omaha was a 50-mile commute from Lincoln. I knew that many people lived in one city and worked in the other. However it still seemed a bit daunting to me.

Bill looked concerned but said, "I'll find someone's car that you can borrow."

I had been searching for a job for a couple of months since arriving in Nebraska. I was broke and needed money to pay for my apartment. And I needed to get started into some sort of a work routine.

I loved being this close to Bill, being able to spend endless amounts of time with him without having to worry about the cost of phone calls. But I was desperately homesick. I missed my family and my home. Perhaps getting a job would help to connect me into the larger culture here so that I wouldn't still feel like such an outsider. Hopefully then I would not feel so homesick.

Borrowing a car that Bill found for me I drove to Omaha to the job interview. My potential employer wanted to know why I moved to Nebraska. I was honest. I said I had moved here for love. The potential employer smiled in response.

Perhaps it was my love story that made my new employer offer me the job offer. I'll never know. But I was told that they would do whatever I needed them to do in order for me to get my Free Trade Permit. With a letter offering me employment in my hand I drove back to Lincoln. Now all we had to do was get to the Canadian side of a US border to get my Free Trade Permit from a border customs officer.

On a cold March morning before dawn, Jeff and I loaded Bill and me into his minivan and started the six-hundred-mile trek to the Manitoba, Canada border. The further we travelled, the colder it got and more snow was piled on the sides of the roads.

The first day we drove as far as Pembina North Dakota, just south of the border between the USA and Canada and found a cheap motel room. Being the gracious men that they were, Bill and Jeff slept on the floor and let me have the bed. Jeff and I managed to help Bill with the minimal care that he would allow us to do for him, in order for him to make the trip.

With a stack of legal and professional documents including Senator Exon's updated Free Trade Permit professional occupations list, we crossed into Canada. Jeff got out of the van take a picture of Bill hanging his head out of the van in Canada with the Canadian flag in the background to prove that we had been there. Literally twenty-five feet into Canada we did a U-turn and headed back to the US border crossing.

I entered the small border crossing building with my stack of papers to talk with the customs officer.

"I don't see Occupational Therapy listed on the professional occupations list," the officer said to me, after reviewing the letter offering me employment and referring to his official Free Trade treaty document. Without saying a word, I pulled the updated version of the Canada-US Free Trade Treaty from my stack of papers and gave it to him. The officer stared at the highlighted words, "Occupational Therapy."

"I think we are set then." he said with a smile. "Just let me fill in these forms and you will be on your way."

Within ten minutes I was out the door and back in the van. Bill let out a holler of relief and delight when I showed him my Free Trade Permit.

"Thanks to your work with Senator Exon's office," I said to Bill as I gave him a hug. "They didn't have the updated treaty. It was a good thing we brought our own."

"Let's go home!" Jeff declared, as we started our trek back down through the cold snowy Dakotas to warmer Nebraska.

Goodbye Canada, I thought sadly, as we drove away from the border office.

And also, with excitement I thought, *Hello, America, my new home!*

CHAPTER 28

(Chris' Voice)

Ramps to Relationship

During the summer of 1991 I watched as one by one the buildings in my neighborhood of downtown Lincoln became accessible to people with physical disabilities. Even if the ramp was a metal plate to allow Bill to roll over one small step, it was a symbol of the success of the disability rights movement to push for rights of integration that would hopefully lead to attitudes of inclusion.

The fun local coffee shop built a concrete ramp to the patio and side entrance. Bill could now enjoy hanging out on the patio with me while I drank cold tea and chatted with him. Simple pleasures, like chatting at the coffee shop, taken for granted by the able-bodied world, became new routines that we enjoyed together.

These might seem like small victories for able-bodied people who frequent public places all the time with ease. But for those of us with significant people in our lives who had been, until recently, physically excluded from many community buildings, every ramp represented a new welcome mat, welcoming us together, into the mainstream of American life. I celebrated the construction of each and every ramp that we could see, in the 20 square blocks where we lived, with Bill.

One hot Saturday afternoon in May of 1991 I had gone ahead to get in the line-up at the busy main post office across the street from our apartment building to mail a package to my family in Canada.

Bill was going to come over to meet me at the post office before we went around the corner to check on the progress of the construction of the new ramp on the side of an old building in the Haymarket district.

Having spotted the beginning of the construction a couple of weeks before this day, Bill and I often trekked over to check on its progress. We were both anxious to use the ramp and celebrate its presence by getting some gourmet ice cream together inside the building.

"Why don't you have someone drive you over here? Wouldn't that be safer?" I heard a woman asking Bill as he was coming toward me in the post office.

"How would you suggest that I get money to pay for a van and a driver?" I heard him ask the woman in response.

"Aren't there programs to pay for things like that for people like you?" I heard the woman say and I cringed, imagining what funny things Bill was possibly thinking about "people like her."

"No there aren't programs to buy people vans and drivers. I need to use the post office and so I roll over." Bill responded.

"Well. I could find that out for you. I'm a private investigator." the woman said, and I almost laughed out loud, finding it ridiculously ironic that she was suggesting that Bill might need her to find out about programs at the state. After all, Bill was the quintessential expert on all things disability related at the state. She gave Bill her business card and left.

Bill came rolling over to me and said wryly, "She thinks that she is going to find me a van and a personal driver."

"I heard." I said and laughed, enjoying the joke with him. Bill was teaching me incident by incident how to laugh at the ridiculous things that people said to him, to me and to both of us.

After mailing my things at the post office, we went to check out the ramp to gourmet ice cream shop. The railing was not on but a large and wide ramp was completed. Excited to see that the building was now accessible to him, Bill took off up the ramp at warp speed. He waited for me at the door that I found to be locked. I went around through the front door to get some help to unlock the door. Bill came rolling into the building, visibly excited to have access to it.

We found our way to the ice cream shop and ordered French vanilla for Bill and Belgian chocolate for me. Savoring the cold and sweet treats, we also celebrated the hard won ADA that had allowed Bill access to this building to share in a regular part of American life, with me.

Bill appeared to be deep in thought about how wonderful it was to be welcome into the ice cream shop and to be able to enjoy this with me. What I didn't know was that he was planning ice cream runs for us, something that the ramp would now allow him to do.

A couple of weeks later, when I was hanging at Bill's place, he asked me if I wanted ice cream. He called the ice cream shop and asked for a pint of "International Special", consisting of French Vanilla for him and Belgian Chocolate for me. He asked them to please open the door so that he could get into the building.

Bill rolled out of his apartment and over to the ice cream shop.

As I waited for Bill's return, I was thinking about the timing of so many amazing things that were happening to support our relationship going forward. Implementation of the ADA, resulting in the creation of these ramps to inclusion was a seemingly God-timed and really important part of what was unfolding for us.

How the Canada US Free Trade Act had just "happened" to add my job title to the list of professions being "traded" between the two nations, the month I had "moved" to Nebraska, continued to stun me, whenever I thought about it. That timely piece of legislation had left me awed by a God who would care enough for me to be in boring legislative details.

Pastor Howard's confident presence and assurance that God would help us to find our way, and the supportive attitudes of many at FBCL, unknowingly providing sanctuary for us, from a gawking world that was not yet ready for us, gave us emotional space where we could be and be seen.

And of course, the physical presence and endless support from people, such as Marlene, the League of Human Dignity could not be understated.

About twenty minutes later, with a big smile on his face Bill returned with the "International Special" in his wheelchair backpack.

My Bill was finding his way, learning who he was and who he wanted to be, in his relationship with me.

And I was learning to laugh off the very strange and ignorant things that people who didn't know us would sometimes say about Bill, or me or about both of us.

CHAPTER 29

(Bill's Voice)

Pressing Charges Against the Dragon

Suddenly awakened in the middle of a hot night to the sound of my phone ringing, I lay alone in the dark, unable to move or communicate, hearing my answering machine pick up and start to record the message.

"There are people beating up niggers outside your apartment building. And you're next, I hope, you drooling bastard," said the all-too-familiar voice, Larry Trapp of the KKK, blasting out into the stillness of my quiet apartment. [1]

With absolute terror seizing my mind and body, I realized that I had not evaded my former KKK neighbor by moving away from him. I was awake for the rest of the night.

When Chris came to see me the next morning before going to work, I told her about the phone call. I was still pretty shaken about the thought that my neighbor wanted to cause me harm. He could easily follow through on his threat, given the thugs that he had as so-called friends.

"I moved to get away from him and he is still harassing me." I said, petrified and exhausted by this seemingly never-ending nightmare.

"This is a death threat, Bill." Chris said, after listening to the message. She was looking as terrified as I felt.

"He has to be stopped. Press charges against him. You have evidence on your answering machine tape." She argued, before heading out the door to get to work.

Chris was right. I had fled from my KKK neighbor and he had followed me to my new apartment. I had nowhere to hide. It was time to take action.

I rolled over to the City-County Building with my material evidence in my wheelchair backpack to speak with the police and the city attorney. [Terror now mobilizing to anger welling up inside of me], I requested that charges be pressed against Larry Trapp and that no deals should be made with him. [2]

The city attorney, hearing the tape and listening to my concern about my safety, filed the charges that were available to them. Given the evidence of the recorded message, a misdemeanor of disturbing the peace was all that they had on Larry. It was a weak case. But, at least they had at least sufficient cause for the law to go after him.

A notice was sent for Larry Trapp to appear in court.

As it turned out, this was just what the Lincoln Police Department needed. More than one person wanted to stop Trapp-or at least slow him down. [3]

In addition to leaving messages on my answering machine, the former KKK neighbor had been escalating his attacks against others in the community. He had made death threats towards people who spoke out for all that he hated; multiculturalism, tolerance, and equal rights. Donna Polk, a prominent leading woman of color, had been receiving death threats against her too.

An activist in the Coalition of Black Women and now Director of Counseling Services at the Indian Center, Donna frequently spoken out on television against racism. Sadly, because she was a woman of color, she was used to people disagreeing with her opinions and being disrespectful towards her. The KKK neighbor, furious by her outspokenness on television sent her a hate poem and included flyers that had pictures of three people labeled "race-traitor scum" hanging from nooses. Donna was scared enough to carry a gun with her at all times.

The same week that Larry Trapp had left me a harassing message, he had also left a message on the White Knights hotline to alert the KKK to "pay Donna a visit", giving out her address and phone number. Knowing the history of the KKK, and the fact that there were cross burnings in Lincoln as recent as 1980, Donna like me, in a state of terror, went to the police and also to the FBI. [4]

She was told, just as I had been, that the neighbor could legally tell White Separatists on the hotline to "pay her a visit." She was also told that the neighbor was being picked up that day for harassing me because my voice machine tape provided enough evidence to arrest him for disturbing the peace. [5]

On the day scheduled for the arraignment of my former neighbor, a bomb threat was received at the City County Building and it had to be evacuated. The timing seemed to be lost on everyone but me; I wasn't surprised.

Having failed to show up for his arraignment, a warrant was issued for the KKK Grand Dragon's arrest.

The police loaded the Grand Dragon of the KKK and his wheelchair into their car and took him to the inaccessible city county jail where he spent the night. Wishing that they would keep him there indefinitely, I was able to sleep well for that one night. Released the next day on a $50 personal recognizance bond, the Klansman was assigned an attorney for his trial that would begin August 28, 1991.

I would be at the trial to speak my peace and to see the end of this man's hateful behavior towards me.

Endnotes

[1.]   Kathryn Watterson. *Not by the Sword,* (New York: Simon and Schuster, 1995), 132-135.

[2.]   Ibid.

[3.]   Ibid.

[4.]   Ibid.

[5.]   Ibid.

CHAPTER 30

(Chris' Voice)

Going to the Chief

"In America, we look after our own family member's medical and financial needs," the austere state senator said to Bill and me, in an authoritarian and condescending manner.

Bill had taken me with him to meet with one of the Nebraska State Senators he knew from his work advocating on behalf of the rights of all Nebraskans with disabilities with the Nebraska Advocacy Services Board of Directors. I was learning that using your government network to advance your disability rights agenda was a significant part of the movement's advocacy work. We went to talk with the senator about the Nebraska Administrative Code 469 2-006.01.

It says, "Consider income and resources of spouses living in the same household as available to each other, whether one or both are eligible for Medicaid." (Medicaid was the state program that provided funding for Bill's attendant care. If we were married, my income would make Bill ineligible for the program.)

I quickly realized what the senator was suggesting; I would be expected to pay approximately $8000 a month for Bill's medically necessary attendant care services, should Bill and I get married. That would mean that I would need to earn $96,000 a year to pay for Bill's care, plus additional income to pay for our living expenses.

As an Occupational Therapist, who was new to Nebraska, I was making significantly less than the median Nebraska household income of $40,000. On my income I was paying for my living expenses with a little extra cushion. I quickly calculated that I was going to need to earn at least $136,000 to be able to cover Bill's attendant care cost in addition to our living expenses. Considering that $40,000 was the highest salary that any Occupational Therapist was making in the state of Nebraska at the time, what the senator was suggesting was not feasible.

Paying for healthcare was a foreign concept to me. As a Canadian, I was socialized to believe that healthcare was a right for all people, to be funded primarily through taxation with minimum out-of-cost to the consumer. This concept, however now shifting to more being paid by the consumer in Canada, because of limitations of public funding, still had strong roots in a belief in universal health care.

Is this what happens in America? I thought to myself. *Are people expected to pay for medical care regardless of the cost? Was he saying that I would work around the clock and go into bankruptcy to pay for Bill's attendant services or do it all myself? No wonder spouses (primarily wives) were doing the attendant care in America,* I concluded. The prevailing governing bias was toward the family either paying for attendant care for their loved one or doing it all themselves.

"I understand that the state's point of view is that the family unit must be responsible for the partner's debt." Bill responded, assertively and clearly, without becoming angry. "However, the state forgets that many families have health insurance, which helps with overwhelming expenses. My personal care expenses are approximately $8000.00 a month. This is clearly an overwhelming expense for any family."

I was impressed with Bill's willingness to courageously stand up to the government that held the purse strings to what was needed for his life, and ask for more. I would probably fluctuate between the extremes of passiveness and aggressiveness at the ends of the passive aggressive paradigm; flying by the middle and for advocates, coveted stance of assertiveness in the middle.

"Bill, our state regulations are guided by federal statutes. This is out of my control to change," the senator responded, clearly deflecting his responsibility back onto the feds after Bill had made his compelling argument.

"Leslie Shannon from Health and Human Services in DC was in contact with me about this Nebraska statute. She claims that the feds can do nothing about Nebraska statutes," Bill countered, as quickly and as clearly as he could get his Touch Talker to articulate.

"Well, you are going to have to get back in touch with Leslie Shannon, Bill. Rules regarding income requirements for Medicaid come from the feds," the senator countered.

"I will get in touch with the feds again. Thank you for your time," Bill responded, ever respectful of the elected official's position and then we left the senator's office. I wanted to say some less kind words but followed Bill's polite lead and kept my mouth shut.

When out of earshot of the Senator I dumped on Bill, "Does he expect us to live in a tent and for me to work 24 hours a day to pay for your attendant care?"

'Both the feds and the state are playing politics Chris. It's a hot potato issue and we are caught in the middle. I'll go back to the feds and pin them against each other and keep us out of it." Bill responded confidently. His facial expression said, "Trust me. I'll get this mess sorted out."

'OK. Have fun writing another letter. I'll do the labeling and folding thing later. Got to go. Love you," I said in haste, leaving him to do whatever he would do next in his day. I needed to find my car and get going to drive to my job in Omaha.

When I returned to Bill's place after work that evening, I could hear his dot-matrix printer tractor feed spewing out paper to the floor as the printer head made its characteristic high-pitched whine/buzz sound moving across the paper. Bill's latest letter, petitioning for changes to federal and state regulations regarding family income limits to allow him to marry, keep my income and still keep his attendant care services from a home health agency was coming out of his printer, hot off the press.

Many individually addressed letters to Congressional Representatives and Senators were folded on the floor in front of the printer where they landed after being printed. After affixing labels on more than one hundred envelopes, I started to carefully separate the sheets of paper that had come out of the printer and fold them. Starting from the last of the letters printed and working toward the first, folding and enclosing each in their appropriately addressed envelope, I finally held the first letter that Bill had printed. It was addressed to George Bush, President of the United States of America.

Wow! Bill has the courage and skill to write to the President of the United States again! I thought. The first time I had folded and stuffed a letter from Bill to the President, I was in awe. I was no less amazed this time because Bill was continuing to petition the President to get the regulations changed so that we could marry. He was going all the way to the top. And he would not stop until it is done.

How many guys would do this, I thought to myself. I stared at the page for a minute, marveling at Bill's determination before I read what he had written in his clear and concise prose.

George Bush
President of the United States of America
The White House
Pennsylvania Avenue
Washington, DC 20500

Dear Mr. President:

Thank you for responding to my letter of August 5, 1991, but your response didn't solve my problem. It is my fault because I didn't clarify my situation.

As I have told you, I'm a thirty-six year old man who is in love. However, I also have cerebral palsy which means my body isn't coordinated so I use my head for everything. With the back of it, I control my power wheelchair. I also have a headstick to operate my portable voice synthesizer (which brings up the fact that I can't talk.) I have to have attendant services for eight hours a day. With this service I can live by myself in an apartment and be a freelance journalist.

Your office had Leslie Shannon from the Department of Health and Human Services contact me. She tried to help me but under system, there was nothing that she could do.

The problem is the regulation, 469 Nebraska Administrative Code 2-006.01. It says, "Consider income and resources of spouses living in the same household as available to each other, whether one or both are eligible."

I know that this is a state regulation and that the federal government cannot change it. However, people in the state government are saying that there are federal guidelines which required this state regulation to exist. If this is true, please change it.

I'm aware that this state regulation has an exception. The exception is if people are on a Medicaid Aged and Disabled Waiver Program, their spouses' income is not considered. However, the Waiver program only pays about $1500 a month for attendant services.

In July 1991, my attendant services cost $8839.60. This would leave $7339.60 a month uncovered if I got married. My girlfriend, if she became my wife, would have to pay this. She cannot do this. Furthermore, it wouldn't be healthy for our relationship if she did.

On the other hand, I could fire the agency that I now have and use private pay attendants. I have done this before and it is very stressful. When I started to live independently, I tried using private providers. Often I would get up in the morning, hear that my bedtime attendant couldn't come that night and spend the day searching for someone to put me to bed. Or, I would have an attendant just not show up. This living situation causes tremendous stress, and it is not an option.

I understand the state's point of view that the family unit must be responsible for the partner's debts. However, the state forgets that most families have health insurance, which helps with the overwhelming expenses. And, $8839.60 a month is an overwhelming unavoidable expense.

People have suggested that we just live together or have a bonding ceremony. We want to get married. Why shouldn't we have that option? Why should an archaic law decide this most personal life choice?

If I didn't get married, that state will still have to pay for my attendant care. Why can't they continue to do that even if I'm married? Nothing will change except I'll be happier and healthier.

Thank you for your time and help.

Sincerely,
William L Rush
335 North 8th Street
Apartment #403
Lincoln, NE 68508

I finished reading Bill's letter to the President and then carefully folded it and placed it in the appropriately envelope addressed to go to the White House. Sealing the envelope, I placed it in the box with the rest of the petition letters, and then put the box in Bill's backpack so that he could take them to the post office the following morning. As I did this, I thought about the right to petition the government, and how it was definitely an upside of the First Amendment of the US Constitution.

This first amendment thing gave Bill the right to free speech and the right to petition the Government for a redress of grievances. An American right, derived from my British ancestors, it could be traced as far back as the English Declaration of Rights, written in 1689, which states that subjects of the King are entitled to petition the King without fear of prosecution.

Bill was not only advocating for what we needed in our life together. His actions were teaching me something essential to any civil rights movement, like the disability rights movement. Any civil rights movements mobilized the power of its people, guided by the premise that "We, the people" are "We, the government," to bring about change.

September 6, 1991

George Bush
President of the United States of America
The White House
Pennsylvania Avenue
Washington, DC 20500

Dear Mr. President:

Thank you for responding to my letter of August 5, but your response didn't solve my problem. It is my fault because I didn't clarify my situation.

As I have told you, I'm a thirty-six-year-old man who is in love. However, I also have cerebral palsy which means my body isn't coordinated so I use my head for everything. With the back of it, I control my power wheelchair. I also have a headstick to operate my portable voice synthesizer (which brings up the fact that I can't talk). I have to have attendant services for eight hours a day. With this service I can live by myself in an apartment and be a freelance journalist.

Your office had Leslie Shannon from the Department of Health and Human Services contact me. She tried to help me, but under the present system, there was nothing that she could do.

The problem is the regulation, 469 Nebraska Administrative Code 2-006.01. It says, "Consider income and resources of spouses living in the same household as available to each other, whether one or both are eligible."

I know that this is a state regulation and that the federal government cannot change it. However, people in state government are saying that their are federal guidelines which require this state regulation to exist. If this is true, please change it.

I'm aware that this state regulation has an exception. The exception is if people are on a Medicaid Aged and Disabled Waiver Program, their spouses' incomes are not considered. However, The Waiver Program only pays about $1500 a month for attendant services.

In July, 1991, my attendant services cost $8,839.60. This would leave $7,339.60 a month uncovered if I got married. My girlfriend, if she became my wife, would have to pay this. She cannot do this. Furthermore, it wouldn't be healthy for our relationship if she did.

On the other hand, I could fire the agency that I now have and use private pay attendants. I have done this before and it is very stressful. When I started to live independently, I tried using private providers. Often I would get up in the

September 6, 1991   George Bush   page 2

morning, hear that my bedtime attendant couldn't come that night and spend the day searching for someone to put me to bed. Or, I would have an attendant just not show up. This living situation causes tremendous stress, and it is not an option.

I understand the state's point of view that the family unit must be responsible for the partners' debts. However, the state forgets that most families have health insurance, which helps with overwhelming expenses. And, $8,839.60 a month is overwhelming unavoidable expense.

People have suggested that we just live together or have a bonding ceremony. We want to get married. Why shouldn't we have that option? Why should an archaic law decide this most personal life choice?

If I didn't get married, the state will still have to pay for my attendant care. Why can't they continue to do that even if I'm married? Nothing will change except I'll be happier and healthier.

Thank you for your time and help.

Sincerely,

William L. Rush
335 North 8th Street
Apartment #403
Lincoln, NE 68508-1348
(402) 477-3996

CHAPTER 31

(Bill's Voice)
An Elevator Brings Healing

I wasn't used to accessibility without exerting a lot of pressure. When I was in college, administrators met my requests for better accessibility with reminders that I was only one person and that it wasn't cost effective to change a building to accommodate a single person.

Shortly after I became a church member at First Baptist Lincoln, people came forth during our worship services to say how much the church needed an elevator. One man recalled how he had to carry his brother with a disability up to Sunday school. Another person who had had a foot operation said an elevator would have helped her while she was recovering from her operation.

Such a healing time for me! I was hearing that I was wanted no matter what it took. People who had little knowledge of the disability rights movement were saying that it was morally right that all people with mobility problems be given full access to a public place.

During the six years it took, from the first congregational meeting to the elevator installation, my church didn't lose sight of the meaning of accessibility.

One Sunday Pastor Howard said, "We're starting to offer interpretation for the members who are deaf during our corporate worship. At first it will be hard not to be distracted by it, but it will help us to sharpen our focus on the Lord."

I wondered what Pastor Howard would say if I suggested having Braille bulletins. He probably would say that it would help us to sharpen our feel for the Lord.

A cardboard elevator appeared where the real one would be built. I played games with the children by asking them why the cardboard elevator wouldn't work when I touched its cardboard buttons. They patiently told me that the buttons were only make-believe.

About midway through the project the church found out that the planned elevator was too small for an adult size wheelchair. So the committee had to go back to the congregation to get approval for more money. To my amazement the congregation voted unanimously to spend the extra money.

It looked like it would be just a matter of time before we had the elevator.

But in July, 1990, the State Fire Marshall refused to give the church a permit to install the elevator until the church agreed to put in a sprinkler system.

"I don't suppose he would let me have a garden hose, sit out on the lawn and wet the building down every once in a while?" I offered.

Pastor Howard chuckled.

Then, more seriously I added, "I don't understand why he would do this. It's so frustrating. Doesn't he understand how much this elevator means?"

"We can't fault him," Pastor Howard said, "He is doing his job. If the elevator is God's will, He will show us the way. Remember, Bill, all things are possible with the Lord. Maybe this will be just the thing to make this congregation pull together."

After a lengthy debate, the church decided to put in a sprinkler system. I pointed out during the congregational discussion that Baptists love to get wet.

The church did pull together, including the youth group that decided to raise money for the elevator instead of raising money for something that they had wanted for their group.

On June 1, 1991, my church dedicated its new elevator. I participated in the festivities by writing a speech, which was read by Pastor Howard:

> *Tonight I am happy because Lincoln has one more accessible church. But my happiness goes beyond being a pleased advocate for people with disabilities. I would like to think that it was my consistent, relentless grumbling about this building being inaccessible that has made this night become a reality, but I know that it was your compassionate commitment to serve this community.*
>
> *When I decided to join First Baptist, I needed a sense of belonging and this congregation provided that the best you could with the barriers imposed by this building, which was all I could ask. You have taken your friendship a step further by removing the barriers that kept me from becoming a full member.*
>
> *There have been some well-meaning Christians who have tried to tell me that God could heal me if I only believed He could. I think that they were offering their love conditionally. And, by not making themselves accessible many churches are saying the same thing. However, by putting in an elevator you have assured people who have or will acquire disabilities that the thing that makes them people is not in their unconventional muscle movement, nor in their wounded nervous systems, nor in their difficulties in moving, but in the God-given self, which no disability can confine.*
>
> *It is true that we aren't the first church to put in an elevator. A neighboring church put in an elevator. However, their elevator is at the back door. Ours is in the center of the building. To me this signifies that this congregation really values all of its member's participation.*
>
> *Often, as with our friends at that neighboring church, people with mobility limitations are*

expected to enter through the back way and to be happy about it because it was the best the build- ers could do. But this congregation said that way of thinking was not right and made this place totally accessible from the front door. I think this building will serve as an example of what can be done if peo- ple really want to make their building accessible. One of the missions of any church is to model to a community. We have done this with style and grace.

It is true that pride is a sin, but I think that God will forgive us if we pop a few buttons over what we have done to His house. [1]

A week after the elevator dedication, my church honored the woman whom I met at my first fellowship meeting, for her work in the Sunday school in the basement of the building. Her fight with cancer was nearly over. She was using a wheelchair now and needed continuous oxygen to breathe. Everyone was saying it was only because of elevator that she was able to get to the celebration event.

We all knew that she was dying. But somehow I could sense that she had an inner peace about it.

I greeted her and asked her how she was doing.

She looked at me and said, "You have taken this church so far in its thinking. You have taken us light years from where we were before we knew you. Thank you, Bill."

She was wrong. I hadn't taken them to greater understanding of what accessibility was. If I had that power, the entire country would have been totally accessible years ago.

But I may have been God's reminder of their mission to serve everyone who needed their ministry.

Endnotes

[1.]   Bill Rush. "First Baptist Lincoln Gets A Very Special Thank You!" *The Messenger- American Baptist Churches of Nebraska*, Summer 1991: 7 Reprinted with permission.

CHAPTER 32

(Chris' Voice)

The Dragon's Trial

"You know Chris you don't mess with the Klan. They have people who can knock you off anytime and anywhere," a black woman told me at my workplace in Omaha when I shared with my colleagues what was happening with Bill and the KKK neighbor and that the trial was wrapping up this day of September 1991.

The look of terror on her face spoke volumes about the atrocities that her race, if not her own family, had faced at the hands of the KKK. I was too afraid to ask her to explain what she meant, so I didn't.

Besides I really didn't want to know. I wanted to remain naïve and ignorant. Growing up in what was predominantly white Southern Ontario, I had never experienced the KKK. My only contact with this hate group was in my school's history textbooks, where the KKK was a relic of the past from a far off place. And that was where I wanted to keep them.

So instead of heeding the warning of the potential danger to Bill (and myself) from Bill taking the KKK's Grand Dragon to court, I chose to ignore the fear that was rising inside of me, in response to this Black woman's statement of concern for us.

"Bill doesn't have a choice. This guy has to be stopped. The city of Lincoln finally has something to stick to him and they are going after it, because they are tired of him harassing Bill." I said, naively, hiding my apprehension and also praying that Bill would not become a target of the KKK for showing up at the court to challenge the Grand Dragon. I did not know, at this time, about all the others whom the KKK guy had been threatening.

I rationalized that this man was really a puppet leader, even if he had all the paraphernalia of the KKK, including the guns, Klan rings and swastika tattoos on his fingers. He physically couldn't do anything to Bill because he was blind and literally didn't have legs. He was dependent on people to follow his orders and carry out his plots of hatred. I prayed and rationalized that his followers had long since deserted him because he had been arrested.

Part of me wished I had taken the day off to go with Bill to the final day of the trial. Another part of me was too terrified to show up. Bill never asked for me to go with him and I had not gone to any of the trial dates. But I could have insisted that I go along...at least this time.

I was in a state of denial. New to America, and very young emotionally, I didn't want to admit that evil exists and that some will allow their dark sides to rule. And I couldn't, for the life of me, wrap my mind around the fact that the KKK would let this guy with a pretty significant disability, be their Grand Dragon. Like Bill, I was trying to find logic in what was totally bizarre.

You're chicken, I thought to myself, feeling nervous and quite sick to my stomach. It's a good thing that Bill has more courage than you have.

My gut understood the gravity of the situation, even if my head didn't.

I remembered what Bill had reported back to me about the trial so far.

"The judge and attorney called me Mr. Rush or sir- titles that mean respect... I kept expecting my dad to amble in because he was Mr. Rush in our family. [No one ever called me Mr. or sir, Chris.]"

"And they actually wanted me to speak. I had a turn. I was amazed because most people tell me to shut up, ignore me or dismiss me. Too frequently, most people do all three, leaving me with the expectation that no one should be interested in what I have to say. Now people wanted to hear what I had to say. [1]

"It felt really good being asked to speak about the neighbor's harassment of me. The court seemed to care that this man has been harassing me."

"But Chris, "I was nervous. I didn't wait for the attorney to finish asking some of his questions."[2] I was worried that I couldn't speak fast enough. I tried to head nod yes and no to help make things go faster but that was not admissible, so I had to say it anyway and that really slowed things down."

"I had to point out the neighbors speaking patterns [to prove it was his voice on the message tape]. It was hard to reproduce his vocalics with an acceptable degree of accuracy. I thought of bringing this to the manufacturers of my device, but what would I say? Would I say that I couldn't call Afro-Americans "niggehs?" Somehow I didn't think the manufacturers would lose any sleep over that defect in their baby" [Bill added and then laughed.] [2]

"I am so proud of you Bill," was all I was able to say. He had spoken up for himself against this horrid person and had done a fine job in a very stressful situation. The pressure for him to respond quickly must have been enormous.

Bill must have had to work very hard mentally to speak up during court. Because of his nervousness in this stressful situation, his jerky uncontrolled body would have been even more difficult to control. He would have had to harness all of his mental abilities to keep his body calm and controlled enough to allow him to use his headstick to talk with his Touch Talker, at the fastest, only eight words a minute, in a situation where people were used to witnesses speaking at least 120 words a minute. He would have been trying to edit his thoughts to make them more concise while simultaneously trying to control his body and use his headstick to type. It must have been nothing short of exhausting.

I desperately needed to hear the verdict and how Bill was doing on this, the final day of the trial. After work I raced back home to

Lincoln and was relieved to find Bill at his apartment, exhausted but ecstatic.

"Chris, Judge Doyle found the neighbor guilty of disturbing the peace!" Bill exclaimed and then let out a holler and jumped up and down in his wheelchair in his excitement.

"She told him, "You are to stay away from Bill Rush. You cannot call him or harass him in any way. Bill has the right to not be harassed.""

"Hooray!" I exclaimed. "It's about time that someone started putting limits on this man's first amendment rights! Now we can live our life without being afraid of some guy and his scary friends harassing you."

"A November sentencing date has been set. Doyle said that he could spend up to six months in jail and pay a $500 fine."

"I hope he gets the maximum." I said, secretly hoping he would rot in jail but knowing full well that was not likely.

"Chris I am so happy and relieved that he is finally going to leave me alone. I had to go to trial to get him to stop harassing me. And I did it," Bill said, with obvious exhaustion, slowly moving his headstick across the keys of his TouchTalker™ to select the icon sequence he needed to tell me this. He then lifted his head to look at me.

I looked at Bill's dark tired eyes and his worn body, literally hanging in his wheelchair, using the side supports to hold him upright, and thought about how exhausted his body must be feeling from this courtroom ordeal.

Bill never complained about any pain or discomfort he might be feeling, but he did once say that sitting in a wheelchair all day long felt the same as it feels to sit in a car all day long. I took this to mean that he was stiff and sore after a day of sitting in his wheelchair. This had been one long stressful day of sitting in his wheelchair while trying to talk as fast as he could and his body showed it.

But Bill pressed on. There was more that he wanted to share with me and he continued talking, pushing one icon button at a time, slowly communicating why this experience had been so valuable to him.

"Somehow testifying has given me back my self-respect. For someone who has had his personhood questioned many, [the judge's verdict] was a victory in itself." Bill said to me with a satisfied smile.

He then lowered his head again to use his headstick to type out his final thought on his Touch Talker. I waited quietly, knowing that Bill needed time to think out loud and to be heard. What he said was not only profound, it was also disturbing. I listened as each word and then the complete idea was uttered.

"Somehow testifying has given me back my self-respect. For someone who has had his personhood questioned many times, [the judge's verdict] was a victory in itself." [3] Bill said. He then slowly lifted his head to look at me.

With tears in my eyes, I looked into Bill's eyes and said, "I'm glad that your experience in court affirmed who you are. But I'm horrified to hear that you had to go to court to get it. That is really sad Bill..."

Bill looked to me and with very sorrowful eyes nodded his head "yes", affirming that his revelation was indeed sad. Knowing that he was exhausted but still very much wanting me to be with him, I simply relaxed while I watched Bill push the buttons on his power wheelchair to allow the chair to position his body in a semi-reclined position. He then took off his headstick and lay back to rest in the chair and looked over to me. We were both deep in thought about what Bill had just said.

Endnotes

1. Reprinted from [William Rush. "My Turn to Speak." *Communication Outlook*, Vol 13 Number 3: 19. (1992).] No Longer in Print.

2. Ibid.

3. Kathryn Watterson. *Not by the Sword,* (New York: Simon and Schuster, 1995), 136.

CHAPTER 33

(Chris' Voice)
Exams and Canoe Trips

I had two things on my mind as my first summer in Nebraska approached. I had to write and pass the National Board for Certification in Occupational Therapy exam in order to continue to work in the US and I wanted to find a way to be able to spend some fun time in the outdoors with Bill.

Having grown up spending at least a part of every summer on the lakes of Northern Ontario, I had come to appreciate spending time in the outdoors. In the years immediately prior to moving to Nebraska, I had done canoe-trips with friends in the lakes and bays of Killarney and Temagami Ontario, returning to civilization invigorated from the strenuous exercise and fresh air. I wanted to find some way to share this experience with Bill.

Call me crazy for wanting to take Bill along on a wilderness adventure but I did. I wanted to share what I enjoyed with Bill, just as he had been sharing with me all the things that he enjoyed doing in Lincoln.

"When I get done with my exam, I want to do a canoe-trip stateside." I said to Bill.

"With me? I'm not much of a paddler." Bill replied, using his odd-ball sense of humor, and then laughed.

"Yeah with you," I responded laughing at his disability humor. "I want to share what I like to do with you, just as you have been sharing with me what you like to do here in Lincoln."

"For you, I'd make myself a mosquito buffet. They love to eat me Chris." Bill responded continuing to make jokes, while also showing affection for me, through his words.

"We'll take lots of bug spray and keep you covered so it won't be so bad. Besides maybe we could swim and I know you love to swim." I offered, trying to make the trip more palatable.

"OK. I'll go do some crazy wilderness trip with you if you will learn to play chess with me. Deal?" Bill countered.

"Sure. I'll try chess." I responded, with trepidation knowing that I was really awful at strategy games. I would honor Bill's deal after the trip.

While I crammed for my exam, Bill worked to find us a canoe trip. His research led him to Wilderness Inquiry (WI). Headquartered in Minneapolis Minnesota, WI provides outdoor adventure throughout North America and the World. The trips are accessible to everyone, regardless of age, background or ability. Started in 1978, the passion of this organization is to make high-quality outdoor experiences accessible for everyone of differing abilities, including those who do not typically get out and enjoy the wilderness.

The organization sounded perfect for us. They were used to assisting adults. They could provide lots of strong arms to help to move Bill into and out of the canoe and back into his wheelchair. They would also provide a large marine lifejacket for Bill to use, in case we tipped or if Bill wanted to have a swim in the river.

With trepidation that he would be giving up his independence for a couple a days as well as setting himself up to be a buffet for mosquitos, Bill signed us up for a two day canoe trip down the St. Croix River in Wisconsin. A quick flight to Minneapolis and an overnight with Bill's Uncle Alan and Aunt Merry Ann would get us a quick visit with them and a ride to our pick up/ drop off point in Minneapolis.

Meanwhile, I continued to study all the American Occupational Therapy textbooks that I could get my hands on for my exam. I was told that I had only one chance to pass the exam. No do-overs allowed. Because I was licensed to work in Canada, and had missed the required Canadian certification exam by graduating one year before it was instituted, the National Board for Certification in Occupational Therapy in America, decided that I must prove myself by passing the American exam in only one attempt. If I failed the exam, I would lose my provisional Nebraska Occupational Therapy license, provided by my Free Trade Permit, and would be required to move back to Canada.

My test site was set for July 1991 at the University Of Nebraska at Lincoln. I marveled at the convenience of my exam location. Literally a few blocks from where we lived, Bill was able to show me the building where I would take my test ahead of time so that I would know where to go on the exam day.

My faith and trust in God was growing as I saw God was taking care of this next step for us, in concrete ways. My job was to study hard. God would take care of the rest.

Even as I was learning to trust God, on the Saturday of my exam, I woke with a massive migraine headache. Knowing what was at stake, Bill was equally stressed; his worried eyes and serious face spoke louder than words. He rolled over to the building with me to make sure that I didn't get "lost".

"Get 'er done Chris," Bill said, using the local colloquialism meaning apply yourself and succeed. He then sat outside the building, having a prayer vigil, hanging out with God, until I was finished with my exam.

After one hour of test time had passed, all of the recently graduated young people, who were taking the test with me, had finished their exams. I was the only one left in the test room, working systematically through each and every multiple-choice question. I still had a third of the exam to complete.

I chose to ignore the fact that I was the slow poke of the group. My life in Nebraska with Bill was on the line. I needed to be exceedingly diligent.

After reading and re-reading the questions for two hours to make sure that I had done my best, I was finished. Saying a prayer that I would pass, I gave my paper to the test adjudicator and left the assigned testing room.

Sitting where I had left him was Bill with a red rose on his tray for me. He looked both relieved and delighted.

"It's done Bill. Prayerfully, I did OK." I said in total exhaustion, with my splitting stress headache still present.

"You'll pass." Bill said confidently and then added, "Let's go get you something to eat. The canoe trip is next week. It'll be good for you to get away while we wait for the results."

"Yes. Thanks for agreeing to go with me. I hope there is something special on this trip, just for you." I added.

Friends from church helped us to get to the airport with all of Bill's low tech stuff. With some help from the airline attendants, we loaded Bill, his manual wheelchair, tray and bags of personal belongings onto the 737 Boeing aircraft. Before long we were racing down the runway and taking off for Minneapolis, St Paul.

Uncle Alan and Aunt Merry Ann met us at the Minneapolis airport. From the time that Bill and Uncle Alan saw each other until we were dropped off to go on our canoe trip they didn't stop grinning and acting like silly teenage boys. Uncle Alan enjoyed telling jokes to Bill and dragging him up and down the stairs of his house to show him his latest electronic toy. This trip had been worth it already.

We drove to the canoe-trip pick-up site the next day. Trucks loaded with canoes and some passenger vans lined the streets, indicating that we had found the correct meeting place.

"Hello, you must be Bill and Chris," one of the staff said approaching us with a broad smile.

"Bill would you like to check out the lifejackets?" one of the staff asked.

"Sure I don't want to sink if we capsize," Bill responded trying to keep things light.

I was impressed by the WI staff. They were friendly and helpful without being maternal or patronizing. That is a hard line to keep when you are working with adults with disabilities, who need various degrees of support. Furthermore, they assumed that Bill had intelligence and spoke directly to him rather than to me. I really liked that.

Getting Bill into the canoe was simple because we had lots of help. Two young people helped to lift Bill into the middle of the canoe, and helped to make him comfortable by providing soft padding underneath his bottom.

When all the canoes were loaded, we started our trek down the river. The bright sun on the water meant that we all needed sunglasses, including Bill who wore his big stylish wrap-around sunglasses and a cap with a visor. Listening to the swish of each paddle stroke, I enjoyed being on the water again, even if my arms were tiring quickly.

In the warm afternoon the WI staff asked if we would like to go swimming and float down the St. Croix River. *Ah! Now there was something that Bill and I might be able to enjoy doing together,* I thought.

Bill was game to try floating and drifting in the current so we got him, still in the military lifejacket, into the water and helped him to lie on his back. Staying really close to him and holding his hand, I drifted alongside of Bill down the river, feeling the current slowly pushing us forward.

I looked over to see how Bill was doing. His face was serene and his body was quiet. Ah! he was enjoying this part of the trip and so was I. I loved the feeling of my body being quiet while the current pulled it along slowly. Watching Bill get to experience what I also enjoyed was double the pleasure.

Later, when Bill was back in his manual wheelchair with his headstick and his Touch Talker, I asked him how he liked the floating on the river.

"Water is the only place where I can experience freedom of movement. I loved it." Bill replied.

"That's what it looked like to me." I responded.

"Swimming is something that we can do together in Lincoln for exercise," Bill said, thinking out loud. "I'll find out where I can get one of those marine lifejackets."

"I'm so glad that someone has come out of this crazy trip already. You have been a good sport doing this." I said laughing.

When supper came, Bill offered to stir the spaghetti sauce with his headstick. He needed to feel like he was contributing something to the success of this trip.

"Sure Bill. I'll help you to come over here and stir this sauce," the staff person responded and got Bill close enough to the pot so that he could use his headstick as a stir stick. Delightful, I thought and took a picture of Bill helping in his own crazy way.

Unfortunately, when night fell the mosquitos did try to make Bill the buffet table. *How did they know that he couldn't defend himself?* I thought to myself.

Lathering him in bug spray and covering as much of his body as I could with clothing including his hands with socks and his head with a balaclava we had brought along for him, I attempted to keep the mosquitos away but many still succeeded to feed on him. I felt awful. Bill was right. They did love to eat him.

Relieved to be going back to civilization the following day, Bill said, "I'm going to teach you how to play chess when we get home."

"OK." I said and then we started to board our flight back to Lincoln.

CHAPTER 34

(Bill's Voice)

Getting into the Swim

"I'll hold Bill steady here while you hand me that Mae West," George, the sixty-something year old man said with a laugh and then looked at me and Chris. Understanding the reference, we both laughed. George was using the term that the Allied Forces used for a life preserver during WW2 in tribute to the sex symbol of the day, Mae West.

He was talking about a lifejacket sort of like the one that I had used when we did our Canoe trip to Wisconsin with Wilderness Inquiry. After the trip, I found an identical military-style life jacket for sale. My mom always concerned that I get more exercise, gladly paid for it. Here it sat, brand new and ready for me to use at one of the local YWCA's open Co-ed swim times.

Returning to Lincoln from our Wisconsin canoe trip to learn that Chris had passed her National Certification in Occupational Therapy exam with flying colors, much weight had been lifted off our our shoulders. With delight and confidence about her ability to stay in Lincoln, we were building more routines into our life together.

George, a regular swimmer and former military guy, stepped up to help when Chris, I, and Susan, the head lifeguard were trying to figure out how to get me into the pool. Getting into the swim was taking some ingenuity but we had silently agreed that it would be more than worth the time and energy to help me to get some exercise.

We first tried the accessible lift chair because it appeared to be the obvious way for me to get into the swim. Chris maneuvered my manual wheelchair to the lift chair and helped me to stand and make the transfer to the seat. Without bracing of my feet and hips, I can easily slide out of any chair. I tried to sit still in the chair as it shook violently, swiveling and then starting to make its way slowly down to the water.

George, who was in the pool looking up at me, saw my terrified expression. "This is a chair from Hell, Bill. I've jumped out of airplanes and I wouldn't want to sit in that thing. Let's try lifting you in from sitting on the edge of the pool." I looked to George and tried to communicate with my eyes that I thought his idea was a better one. Chris and the lifeguard stopped the lift chair and helped me to transfer back into my manual wheelchair.

I liked this guy George. He not only had a great sense of humor, he also had compassion. Even though he had just met me, he talked to me and not at me. He assumed that I had intelligence and was able to read my non-verbal communication surprisingly well. Lots of people, including people in the so-called 'helping professions' couldn't do that.

Furthermore, I was relieved that George had a plan B for getting me into the pool and that the lifeguard didn't baulk that we were not going to use the "handicapped" access. I didn't want to badmouth the lift chair. After all it provided some needed accessibility to the pool. But it wasn't the right fit for my shaky uncoordinated body. I was terrified that I would slip down into the water and drown before anyone was able to make sure that I was lying on my back so that I could breathe.

Chris maneuvered me back around to the end of the pool. She asked me if I thought it would be best to get the lifeguard to help her to lift me down to the sit at the edge of the pool. That sounded like the safest idea to me. George would then put on my lifejacket while Chris kept me sitting on the edge of the pool.

I felt safe when George lifted me off the edge of the pool and down into the water, so safe that I leaned my body into his and placed my head on his shoulder. He carefully and slowly helped me onto my back and stayed with me until Chris got in the water to swim with me.

I started kicking my legs. George started swimming beside me and we took off down the pool without Chris for a little guy chat time.

Looking over at some woman in another lane who had many tattoos all over her body, George asked me, "What do you think of ALL those tattoos Bill?" and then laughed. I turned my head to see the tattoos and was stunned to see a woman with tattoos everywhere. I looked back to George, nodding and laughing to indicate that I too thought that they were quite amazing.

"What's so funny?" Chris asked as she caught up to us half way down the pool by this point.

"Oh nothing, "George responded with a grin. "Let me know when you are ready to leave and I'll help you to get Bill back out of the pool," George said and took off swimming in the far lap lane.

"OK. I'll swim alongside of you and make sure you go straight," Chris offered, doing a sidestroke to keep her eyes on me while I kicked my way down the pool. Enjoying the freedom to be able to use my strong leg movements in the water, I kicked and swam with Chris, only taking breaks when she turned me around at the ends of the pool.

Once George grabbed one of my legs and pulled me backwards as he swam past me. I hollered and then the lifeguard asked Chris if I was OK. Chris told her that George was teasing me. I felt safe and welcome with Chris swimming beside me, the lifeguard watching me and George, my new swimming friend in the next lane. We swam for 40 minutes until my assistant came at the end of the session.

"Wow Bill. This is cool that you can swim. Lots of other people I help would love to be able to do this." the young assistant exclaimed as he helped Chris to get me back into my chair. I had arranged with my home health agency for my night assistant to first come to the pool before meeting me at home for my bedtime routine. I had argued that exercise was a part of health and that I would not cost the state more money or take more than the time allotted for this visit.

The home health agency agreed to my plan, without me needing to pull out my full armor of advocacy weaponry.

Chris went to the women's change room to get changed, and I and my assistant headed for the guys' room. My assistant quickly got me dressed but Chris still beat us. We all left the YWCA and Chris and I walked back to our apartment building.

The assistant met me back at my place to help with my night-time routine. We completed it quickly so that I wouldn't take more time than usual.

With teamwork, we had pulled this off. I was delighted and a little surprised to find the YWCA staff and George, my new swimming friend, so welcoming and helpful. I was proud of my home health agency for working with me on this. Feeling tired and relaxed after a good swim, I slept well that night.

CHAPTER 35

(Chris' Voice)

Advocating Both Levels of Government

With the Dragon's trial and my exam behind us, Bill, the disability rights advocate, was back at his unpaid day job. In addition to supporting Nebraska Advocacy Services, Inc., The Center for Disability Rights, Law and Advocacy, on their Board of Directors and continuing to work as a part of the larger disability rights community as advocacy needs arose, he diligently learned existing federal and state regulations regarding marriage and Medicaid and wrote letters to officials at both the state and federal levels of government to try to get our problem solved.

I asked Bill to explain the advocacy work that he was doing for us. He responded, "Since Medicaid is both a federally and state funded program I have to work with both governments. Because we are the only couple in Nebraska who needs a program or regulation that doesn't currently exist, we don't stand a chance of getting new legislation to support us. We have to find another program that would protect your income and that already exists to put alongside of my current Medicaid-funded program. The problem is going to be finding the two puzzle pieces that will fit together well."

Bill was playing some kind of strategy game with the state and federal governments, trying to get them to talk to him and to each other, to work out a possible solution within the context of available programs. He used his persuasive writing style to consistently articulate why he needed changes to the system to both levels of government at the same time and refused to give an inch on what it was that he and I needed.

I didn't offer to help Bill because he, by training and background, had been groomed to be our best advocate.

Also I, unlike Bill, have a disability in the area of strategic thinking. My valiant attempt to learn how to play chess, tried only because I had said that I would do it in exchange for Bill coming on a canoe trip with me, displayed my significant disability in strategic thinking.

I succeeded in frustrating even Bill, who patiently tried to teach me before allowing me to give up. I struggled with keeping multiple pieces of information about each chess piece in my head at one time while trying to plan my next chess move. Bill had written me a guide for each piece but even with this aide, I was still the world's worst chess player. And I didn't enjoy playing the game.

Being more of a gestalt thinker, and not understanding the government as Bill did, it took me some time to understand the system, let alone what we needed. Over time, I was able to put some of the pieces of the puzzle together about the overall concepts of what Bill was doing in his advocacy for us.

I understood that Bill's primary concern was to make sure that I not be saddled with the $8,000 plus cost per month for his personal service assistants per month. And he was going to work until he was more than certain that this would not happen. He did this by continuously reminding government officials that this was too great of a burden to ask of any spouse. I was not going to stop working and become destitute with Bill in order for us to qualify to have Bill's care paid for by the Medicaid system for low income families. Because I was not a US citizen, this was not an option anyway.

My visit to the state senator with Bill had taught me that there was a prevailing assumption in government that spouses should pay for one another's needs, regardless of the financial burden. This attitude was one of Bill's biggest concerns, because he knew that, even if we found a state program to support us, we would be going against the prevailing attitudes and as such, could have our funding pulled at any point.

A letter that I saw on Bill's desk from a federal Member of Congress confirmed that this belief was not only an attitude, but was also an embedded premise within state and federal laws.

Dear Mr. Rush:

Thank you for writing to me regarding the potential loss of your Medicaid-funded attendant caregiver if you get married. As you probably already know, Medicaid is funded by a combination of Federal law and state statutes.

Contact has been made with the Nebraska Department of Social Services for clarification of the issue you raised. It is important to understand that under Nebraska law, spouses are held to be responsible for each other, just as parents are responsible for providing the necessities of life for their children. I have asked that your situation be reviewed to determine whether it is one of which an exception can be made.

Occasionally proposals have been made at the Federal level to pay relatives to be caregivers in various taxpayer-funded programs. However, none of these proposals have become law because of the long-held traditional — and legal- recognition that family members are responsible for the needs of each other.

I would like to take this opportunity to note that I appreciate your visits to my District Congressional Office during which you share your opinion on various issues of concern to you.

Best wishes,
Doug Bereuter,
Member of Congress

(Bill Rush. Personal Communications).

In this note to Bill, Representative Bereuter clearly articulated the premise behind the law, that spouses were ultimately responsible for each other. Given the high cost of his care I, like Bill, was very concerned about the long-term implications of this legal precedence relative to our situation.

But, I was also delighted to see that Representative Bereuter was reaching out to work with Nebraska Health and Human Services to try to figure out how to get around this problem. Maybe it was possible, that different levels of government could work together.

Bill was no longer playing monkey in the middle. He had succeeded to get the governments to talk to each other to try to solve our problem. And that was no small feat!

CHAPTER 36

(Chris' Voice)
Trust the Government Solution?

Later in 1991, Bill heard back from the feds at the Department of Health and Human Services in Washington, DC. Amazed and impressed that Bill managed to get the feds and state to talk to each other, and that they appeared to be working together to try to come up with a solution to our unique situation, I read the following letter:

> *Department of Health and Human Services*
> *Health Care Financing Administration*
> *6325 Security Boulevard*
> *Baltimore, MD 21207*
>
> *Dear Mr. Rush,*
>
>   *I am responding to your letter to President Bush concerning a Federal Regulation which requires that we consider income and resources of spouses living in the same household as available to each other for purposes of determining Medicaid eligibility.*
>   *You are correct that there is (such) a Federal regulation...that rule is set forth at 42 CFR 453.723*

> *We discussed your situation with MS. Mary Jo Iwan, Nebraska Medicaid Department of Social Services. Ms. Iwan indicated that one possible option available to help you with your attendant care services is a home and community-based waiver. You indicated that in July 1991, your attendant services cost $8,838.61. She confirmed, as you have noted, that there is a $1,500 monthly cap under the waiver on attendant care. However, the state is exploring the possibility of whether an exception to this cap can be made possible in your case.*
>
> *I hope that this information, and our efforts and those of the State, are of some assistance to you.*
>
> *Sincerely yours,*
> *Christine Nye*
> *Director for Medicaid Bureau*
>
> *(Bill Rush Personal Communications)*

On first glance it appeared that the state and feds had come up with a simple plan. Bill could apply to a "waiver" program through Medicaid to have my income waived and still received his attendant care but it would require an exception to the waiver for him to continue to have his costly attendant care that was provided by a home health agency.

"What do you think of this offer?" I asked Bill.

"I'm not willing to gamble our lives on an application for a waiver, Chris. There are problems with this; we are not guaranteed a slot in the program, and also my costly care greatly exceeds the limit of the program. I would need an exception and there are no procedures for getting or keeping one and without procedures, a bureaucrat could just pull it when there is pressure to cut back on spending. Plus I have concerns about you being the first younger person with a good income to use the Spousal Impoverishment Program piece of the program. It's too risky." Bill concluded.

"What is Spousal Impoverishment?" I asked.

"The Spousal Impoverishment Program is used by community spouses of older people who are going into nursing facilities. The community spouse, that would be you even though I would also be in community with you, is allowed to keep their money after an initial assessment."

"So the state would look at my bank accounts, etc. before you could be on the program?" I asked.

"Yes. There would be an initial entry limit. The state said that they would not care about what you make after that. Given that older people usually decrease their savings and sometimes need money, they are more concerned that you would have enough to live on. It could work but it still scares me. Being the first to use this program as a younger person, they could renege, once they realize that you make money and could start asking you to pay for my care. It might work but I'm not convinced yet." Bill explained.

Bill continued to be concerned that the state might find some way to get their fingers into my checking account. With the help of Senator Wesely he pushed for further discussion about the issue of spouse for spouse responsibility, within the context of Medicaid programs.

Meanwhile, with help from Marlene at the League of Human Dignity, Bill found that, because the cost of his care at home though a home health agency was higher than the average cost of institutional care, he would not be waiver eligible. Bill was hesitant because he could be asked to return to the cheaper option of hiring and firing his own attendants in order to use the waiver.

When he first started to live on his own, Bill had used private providers. Often when he got up in the morning, he would hear that his bedtime attendant couldn't come and would spend the day searching for someone to put him to bed. Or he would have an attendant just not show up. This living situation caused tremendous stress, and it was not an option for Bill or for us. Bill was determined that he was not going to put our marriage at risk, by requiring us to live under this never-ending extreme level of stress.

Bill met with his Medicaid Income Maintenance Worker in December of 1991 to start the process of moving over to the waiver. However, terrified of his worst nightmare coming true, Bill did not complete his application.

On the other hand, Bill did secure assurance that any future application for a waiver would be processed without delay and that he would not have to wait for waiver services, should he decide to apply at a later time.

Some people in the disability rights community said that Bill should have just taken the waiver program being offered. Probably because it wasn't their own lives at stake, they were able to trust that Bill would be given a waiver slot, that he could continue to receive his attendant care from a home health agency and that the Spousal Impoverishment Program would work fine with my lower middle class income. After all, hadn't the governments worked together to create a solution? And, furthermore, wasn't Bill setting an example by becoming an exception could eventually lead to more rule changes? some in the DR movement argued.

From Bill's point of view, however, what seemed to be such a simple solution according to the government officials was turning out to have too many risks to take what was being offered.

Bill wanted to create at least one back-up or alternative option for us and push for larger system change. He was not comfortable with what he thought was a duct-taped solution to our problem, a single exception to a waiver regulation --- that could very easily be ripped off or withdrawn when financially hard times hit the state.

CHAPTER 37

(Bill's Voice)

An Active Member

"I'd like to volunteer to be a part of the Maundy Thursday Last Supper dramatization," I told Richard, the brilliant liberal arts professor who had requested male volunteers to recreate the famous painting by Leonardo da Vinci with narration as part of the Easter worship services at First Baptist Lincoln in 1992.

"Sure." Richard responded casually, even though his body language suggested at least surprise if not hesitation.

"Would there be a problem with me participating?" I continued to get the issue out in the open.

"No, why would there be a problem?" Richard responded, even though I suspected that he was wondering how this was going to work.

"They didn't have wheelchairs in those days," I said, stating the obvious that I was going to ruin the Last Supper picture, similar to what would happen if someone put a goatee on the Mona Lisa. I didn't want to ruin the visual effect but I did want to participate.

"Don't worry about it Bill. You are the first to volunteer and we need to find twelve more guys. That is going to be our biggest problem. Besides, this will save me the trouble of figuring out how to reproduce Leonardo's da Vinci's famous painting."

"That is what they call artistic license. Besides our rounded sanctuary makes it impossible to do it exactly as it is written. I don't think that Leonardo da Vinci would mind…" [1] Richard rationalized.

203

"Great. The Last Supper painting is now wheelchair accessible and complies with the Americans with Disabilities Act," I joked and then added, "I would like to be Judas."

"Sure Bill. I'll have your lines for you next Sunday." Richard said with a smile and I knew we were off and running.

I wanted to be Judas because, honestly, I felt the most affinity to him; I had turned my back on God.

If anyone had told me five years before I played Judas that I would be in a church presentation, I'd have laughed in their face. I was anti-church and anti-God because of how I'd been treated at my neighborhood church when I was a child and then how some Christians treated me at the University of Nebraska Lincoln.

My experience in church in the 1960's and 1970's was symptomatic of American society at that time. No one with a significant disability was seen in public, let alone at church.

I became my church's Tiny Tim and I hated it. Members came and put their sloppy kisses on my forehead. I was told to keep quiet and wasn't allowed to interact with other members.

I was seen as an object of pity and not whom I was, a subject, a person, made in the image of God. I desired to be a participant and not just a recipient, in my relationship with God, and with others at church.

So I became angry at my fellow Christians and at God. And I stopped going to church.

At the University of Nebraska Lincoln in the late 1070's and early 1980's, Christians tried to tell me that I was not able-bodied, because I didn't have enough faith. They fueled my belief that I was not welcome in the church or by God because both they and He saw me as defective and not whole. These "Christians" confirmed my belief that the church considered me primarily as an object of pity and shame. At the other extreme, some Christians thought that I was especially blessed by God and had an unusually close relationship to God because of my disability.

I am neither divinely blessed nor damned because of my disability.[2] I am merely a person, needing God's grace and mercy as much as the next person and desiring a relationship with God the same as any "TAB", disability slang for temporarily able-bodied people.

Also, while at the University of Nebraska Lincoln, I joined the League of Human Dignity and entered the disability rights movement. This group gave me a place where I was accepted for who I am, disability, warts and all. They encouraged me to continue to not be bound by the meaning someone else imposes or tries to impose on me about my disability. They reminded me that disability is a natural part of life and they encouraged me to embrace what I knew was my God-given ability to accept my disability. But they couldn't lead me back to God.

Now here I was five years later preparing to play Judas in a reenactment of the Last Supper, thanks to the 'Hound of Heaven' [3], and my mother's urging. I was coming back to God through the ministry of inclusion at First Baptist.

Being an active member at First Baptist was helping me to reconnect with God and as a result, I was beginning the work of forgiving the Christians who had harmed me in the past. I was making headway when I saw them for who they were, people who simply didn't understand who I am in God's eyes.

I was excited to tell Chris that I was going to play Judas.

"That should be fun," Chris responded with delight, when I told her that Richard was fine with me participating in the Last Supper Reenactment. "I can help you to program your speech into your device if you like," she offered.

Richard gave me my speech the following Sunday at church. The following Monday afternoon at one o'clock I started to program it into my TouchTalker™. Storing it in my TouchTalker™ turned out to be as much work as memorizing it.

"I started the speech which was 3,726 characters at one o'clock in the afternoon and, when Chris came at six o'clock, I was still working on it. The results didn't please me."

Chris saw that I was frustrated and said, "Why don't I help to program since I have ten fingers?"

Besides having ten fingers, Chris has a good ear. She could hear what programming sounded the best. If we put in the speech with only the usual punctuation, the TouchTalker™ would say it too fast. If we put in a comma after each word, it sounded so monotonous that Chris started to rock when she heard it. Fortunately, Chris was a pianist and had a feel for the rhythm of my speech. [4]

After Chris typed and edited a small portion of the speech, I saved it. However, when I tried to retrieve and combine parts of the speech together, the pauses between the sections were uncomfortably long. So we saved the speech in sections until it was all ready to go and then combined it into one storage place on the TouchTalker™ .

Then I thought about the voice. I didn't want to use Perfect Paul, my regular voice, because I wanted some way to disassociating myself from Judas. I didn't want to hear Judas when I was talking. [Even as I felt an affinity with Judas], I chose Doctor Dennis because it sounded harsh and sinister.

After we got the speech precisely the way that we wanted it, I backed it up on my hard drive, on a disc, and on a friend's online bulletin board. The greater the effort, the more backups. [5]

At the first rehearsal the rest of the guys were still learning their lines. They were stumbling all over the place, nervous, missing and forgetting some of their speeches. Then came my turn and with my TouchTalker™ , I was able to recite my speech perfectly the first time.

"OK! You should all be more like Bill! I mean, first time, letter perfect! What an example!" Richard chided and all the guys laughed.

There were five rehearsals and I went to all of them. I joked with the others that they might do better if everyone had a TouchTalker™ to say their lines. In return, they warned me that my Touch Talker might get laryngitis. Boys will be boys.

Behind my teasing and badinage, I felt proud that I could contribute to the Maundy Thursday worship service at my church. Also, I felt pride knowing that I didn't need any modifications to the speech. [6]

On Maundy Thursday, I came to church and found that one of my twelve co-stars had finished making a ramp so that I could get up on the altar at the front of the church.

Martha, a matriarch in the church and a creative furniture upholsterer, dressed all of us in robes and sashes.

The sanctuary of the First Baptist church in Lincoln was hushed.

I ascended the ramp with the help of one my fellow apostles and found my place behind the Last Supper table, two places to the left of Jesus. George, one of the men who had lifted my chair into the baptismal tank for me to be baptized, and who was the sound person for this service, had placed a microphone near my place at the table so that I would be heard.

Solemnly the worship service began and we took the poses that Richard had assigned to us, to replicate the postures of each apostle in the Last Supper painting. I took my position, looking over to Jesus with my head held high, in a look of accusation and anger.

The service began with scripture and a hymn, "And Can It Be That I Should Gain?" to set a mood of reflection about the Last Supper. The drama was introduced by Arch, the Colonel who helped me to take communion.

We then began our living dramatization of the Last Supper, portraying possible reactions that each apostle would give, when Jesus said that one of them would betray him. One by one, each apostle told how it was that we had met and then followed Jesus. We then recounted our own relationship with Jesus and finally asked, "Is it I? Is it I?" questioning whether we might be the one who would betray Him.

Portraying Judas, sitting in my very large power wheelchair with a frame above my head and a headstick on my head, I spoke my soliloquy at the appropriate time and worked very hard to keep my body still and in pose throughout the dramatization.

Identifying with Judas, the one who betrayed Jesus and defended his own actions, I had had my reasons for turning my back on God. As Judas, I said, "But I have my reasons. My soul isn't as black as some think it is, nor is your soul as white!"

"After the service, my mom, who had come to see my performance said, "You did a really good job. Your TouchTalker™ was so clear and loud that I really could hear and understand it." [7]

People would tell us later how realistic our portrayal of Leonardo da Vinci's masterpiece had been. Even though having me present at the Table was like a goatee on the Mona Lisa, we still managed to pull it off.

And, becoming an active member was helping me to draw closer to God and to work on letting go of the past.

Portrayal of Jesus' Last Supper with His Twelve Disciples, taken in the Sanctuary of First Baptist Church, Lincoln, Nebraska, By Richard Terrell, Maundy Thursday Evening April 16, 1992. Photo Courtesy of Richard Terrell

Endnotes

1. Bill Rush. "the perfect memory." *Prentke Romich Inc. Current Expressions Newsletter* (Summer 1992) Reprinted by permission from publisher.

2. Nancy Eiesland. *The Disabled God: Toward a Liberatory Theology of Disability.* (Nashville: Abingdon, 1995), 70.

3. Francis Thompson, "The Hound of Heaven" in *The Works of Francis Thompson.* (Ann Arbor: University Press, 1913).

4. Rush, "perfect memory."

5. Ibid.

6. Ibid.

7. Ibid.

CHAPTER 38

Liberating Myself With the Liberator™

Only once in our relationship did I give Chris reason to be jealous – when I laid eyes on the Liberator™. I actually drooled over it, and my drooling was unrelated to my cerebral palsy.

A consultant from PRC showed me the Liberator™ on a summer night in 1991. I was impressed with its many functions. It could even sing the University of Nebraska's fight song. However, I had my TouchTalker™. It had served me well for four years, so I didn't want to change horses or devices in midstream. The consultant respected my choice. [1]

However "Memorizing" my "speech" for the Maundy Thursday performance had convinced me it was time to start the switch from my TouchTalker™ over to the Liberator™.

Storing [my lines] in the TouchTalker™ might seem like an advantage, but it was as hard as committing it to memory. I tried to program it in myself. The biggest problem was that the TouchTalker™, unlike the Liberator™, wasn't designed to store whole paragraphs.

Plus, my TouchTalker's™ editing software hadn't been upgraded so that I could do any sophisticated editing.

I even called Prentke-Romich's service department in hopes of getting a hint on how I could download the speech into my TouchTalker™ . The tech said that I couldn't download anything into the TouchTalker™ besides its entire Minspeak™ vocabulary.

"However, if you had the Liberator™," the tech said, "you could do what you are talking about. The Liberator™ can download any text file from your computer and store it as a notebook."

In about 3500 BC, the Sumerians invented the wheel. The wheel consisted of two or three wooden segments held together by transverse struts that rotate on a wooden pole. It transformed transportation, warfare and industry. However, about 400 BC to about 300 BC, a Chinese work described wheels with 30 spokes, dished wheels for greater strength, and the shaft chariot. I thought I knew how the Sumerians could have felt after they heard about the Chinese wheel. [2]

"Had I had the Liberator™, I would have used the Liberator's™ notebook to enter, edit and store the speech." [3] I would have been able to do it without Chris' ten able-bodied fingers. However, I still probably would have needed her sense of rhythm and intonation to program the device. But it still would have been easier.

"Maybe it's time to get a Liberator™," I said to Chris, as she had worked to type each word into my TouchTalker™ for me while checking for rhythm and intonation.

"Well, you are getting into doing more and more stuff with your voice," Chris had said thoughtfully, "It wouldn't hurt to look into getting a Liberator™."

I started with the rehabilitation technology specialist at the Nebraska Assistive Technology Project. I thought he would be supportive. He wasn't.

"Do you know how many people want a communication device who don't have one? Yet you're asking for a better one," he said.

I felt like a Sumerian being chastised for wanting to try a Chinese wheel. Shame on me.

I looked at the rehabilitation technology specialist. I wanted to introduce him to Thomas Henry Huxley. [3]

This British biologist, best known for his active support of the theory of evolution, Huxley had said, "The rung of a ladder was never meant to rest upon, but only to hold a man's foot long enough to enable him to put the other somewhat higher." [4]

It became clear that I would have to make the case of why I needed the Liberator™ myself. As a journalist, I knew that a good solid story had to answer six questions: What? Who? When? Where? Why? And, How?

The who, what, when and where of this story were obvious. I decided to concentrate on two questions: Why did I need to change communication devices? How would the Liberator™ improve my ability to communicate and my life?

With the TouchTalker™ I had started to give speeches for my local independent living center. To give a speech I would have to dump a majority of my device's vocabulary to fit the speech into the machine. Then, after the speech I would have to load the vocabulary back. In between I would have to pray that I wouldn't need the part that I had dumped. With the Liberator™ I could have about 75% of the Bible or 100,000 words at a time stored into the device and still have the software saved that I need to be able to talk.

Besides the better communication options the Liberator™, I had learned through several conversations with the people at PRC, could be used to take notes. This interested me because for a decade and a half I had been looking for a way to take notes when I was away from my base computer. I had tried using a tape recorder. The problem with that was that I couldn't transcribe fast enough and the tapes sometimes failed. This left me without notes – a nightmare to most journalists. However, the Liberator™ had notebooks, that I could use to store large blocks of text.

This meant I could go to where a story was and type my notes into my Liberator™. Since the Liberator™ could upload to my base computer, I could upload my notes into my base computer's word processor via a radio link. Then, I could write the story. Not only would the Liberator™ help me with my face-to-face communication but it would also help me with my journalistic efforts. It would be my communication device and my laptop computer.

The Liberator™ also had the advantage of using Minspeak™ – the same system as my TouchTalker™ used, so I wouldn't have to learn a different system.

I was beginning to feel like Pavlov's dogs. The more I learned the more I drooled.

I started to make my case to the State of Nebraska, whom I needed to pay for the device for me. I asked the people with whom I worked to send letters saying that getting a Liberator™ would enhance my communication. They did.

I needed a speech pathologist to sign off on my work. I found a speech pathologist. She insisted on doing her own investigation because it would be her name and her reputation on the line, both figuratively and literally.

Her research proved me right – the Liberator™ was the best communication device for me. I resisted telling her, "I told you so," and was amazed by my maturity.

The State of Nebraska also thought it was the best communication device for me. It bought the Liberator™ for me in August, 1992 – 13 months after I had been introduced to it.

Even before my Liberator™ came I started to call it, "My Libby." Chris pointed out that I had never named another piece of my equipment. I laughed, but then thought. She was right. I have called my old dilapidated manual wheelchair "a hunk of junk," but I have never called a piece of my equipment a name of endearment because I had always believed that inanimate objects shouldn't have endearing names.

The Liberator™ could do so many things for me. It was almost as if PRC had taken my deepest communication needs and wants of my soul and made a device to satisfy 80% of them.

I remembered an old television series called Knight Rider, which was about a car that had been infused with a person's soul. The car had a name of Knight Industries 2000, and its owners called it "Kitt." It seemed only fitting that I named the Liberator™ because it seemed like it had been infused with my spirit because anything that I could dream of doing was possible with the Liberator™...

One of the first things I did was load Shakespeare's balcony scene from Romeo and Juliet into my Liberator™. I edited out all of Juliet's lines. Then I went to Chris' apartment, sat outside her second story window and recited Romeo's lines from the balcony scene.

When it became obvious that the mosquitoes would have eaten me all up before Chris heard me, I went inside the apartment building and sat outside her apartment door and recited Romeo's lines.

I occasionally serve as worship leader at my church. I look up the week's scripture that will be used, copy it to a text file and download that file into the Liberator™. I also helped with the church's puppet ministry, by doing the voices of the puppets.

I wouldn't put any limits on how far the Liberator™ and I could go. In fact, a friend who is active in the Disability Rights Movement said that she and her group had gotten the National Republican Party to promise that it would have a person with a disability address its national convention in the year 2000. I think my Liberator™ and I would have been up to that, even if it would mean we had to change our party affiliation! [5]

Endnotes

[1.] William Rush. "Liberating Myself." In Speaking Up and Spelling It Out, edited by Melanie Fried-Oken and Hank Bersani, Jr, 148-152. Baltimore: Brookes, 2000. Reprinted with permission from publisher.

[2.] Ibid.

[3.] Ibid.

[4.] Thomas Huxley Quotes. BrainyQuote.com, BrainyMedia Inc, 2018. https://www.brainyquote.com/quotes/thomas_huxley_101466, accessed November 29, 2018.

[5.] Rush, "Liberating Myself."

CHAPTER 39

(Chris' Voice)

What the Grapevine Says

"Hey Bill what's this letter from Marlene at the League about?" I asked Bill.

"It's an update about funding for my current attendant care and the waiver program that we will need to get married, based on what the disability rights grapevine is saying." Bill responded.

"What is the grapevine saying?" I questioned, curious and amazed that there were so many networks of communication that Bill had to keep up with, in the disability rights movement, in order to advocate for programs that he currently had as well as ones we would need to get married.

"There's some concern about possible state budget cuts coming. The state has a seven million dollar deficit in the Medicaid budget. We are going to have to work hard to hold the line on the existing optional Nebraska-funded personal attendant care program through a cut, possibly in the spring of '93. The waiver program is also pretty limited and in this climate is not going to expand anytime soon."

"Uh oh, this is not sounding good." I said with great concerned about what this might mean for us.

"The grapevine is saying that even though the state offered us the exemption to the "cap" under the waiver, Nebraska apparently still goes by the eligibility description, "can be safely served at home

at a cost not more than Medicaid would pay for nursing home care."
That will not work for me.

The League is talking with the disability rights group ADAPT
(Formerly Americans Disabled for Accessible Public Transportation,
now Americans Disabled for Attendant Programs Today), in
Colorado and the Independent Living Center in Topeka, Kansas to
see what they know about how the "cap" is determined. ADAPT is
saying that it is a biased formula that is lower than the daily rate for
living in a nursing home, probably in order to support the nursing
home industry. The nursing home lobby is very strong at all levels of
government.

"What is Nebraska going to do?" I asked.

"There is a Nebraska Government Task force that is looking
specifically at this "cap" issue."

"So what do we do about all of this?" I asked, not sure what
Bill's role might be.

"Chris, we will work to hold the line on the funding I already
have through a budget cut. Meanwhile I will keep pushing for some
more options, like a Medicaid Buy-in program that would allow for
us to have income, making Medicaid operate more like an insurance
program for us.

It's not wise to put all our eggs in one basket. By taking the
waiver without a back-up plan is still not smart. Besides, taking what
has been offered might not be possible for the government to deliver,
anyway." Bill concluded, with concern.

CHAPTER 40

(Chris' Voice)

Threats of Institutionalization

It was early March 1993, and, one evening, I was sitting cross-legged on Bill's couch reading the Omaha World Herald to learn what had happened that day at the Medicaid Hearing at the State Capitol in Lincoln. Johnny Cash's distinctive baritone voice was soulfully carrying Amazing Grace through Bill's stereo system. I kept my focus on reading the newspaper. It wasn't the time to think how sad I was and to mournfully sing along with Cash; Bill needed me to be there to listen to him.

With eyes filled with sadness and an exhausted body that was collapsing into his wheelchair, Bill sat in front of me, waiting quietly for me to finish reading the newspaper article that he had given to me. This would save him from having to explain all that happened that day at the State Hearing for Medicaid cuts, by typing one icon at a time on his Liberator™. He could save his energy for what he needed to tell me.

I read, ""If you make these cuts, they would be disastrous for me and for countless others," said Bill Rush of Lincoln. "If you cut the Medicaid budget, you will discourage people from living full lives. Rush, 37, who has cerebral palsy, said he has depended on services paid for through Medicaid to live on his own for nine years.

Dozens of disabled Nebraskans pleaded with legislators Wednesday not to take away their dignity and ability to live on their own by eliminating services covered by the state's health-care program for the poor." [1]

Some state senators were threatening to pull funding for several Medicaid programs, because Medicaid costs were rising too fast and were taking up a larger portion of the state's budget each year. They could cut programs that were not federally mandated to save state dollars, including Medicaid-funded attendant care.

I was reading that Bill and 149 other people with disabilities had filled the hearing room and the front of the capitol building to petition against the impending budget cuts to Medicaid. Bill told me that The League of Human Dignity had arranged for accessible buses to bring people with disabilities from across the state into Lincoln for this rally.

When I finished reading I looked up to see Bill's dark eyes trying to talk to me. He sat forward and began to type. Word by word, Bill slowly communicated the depths of his despair, while Cash continued to serenade us with his soulful gospel tunes.

"Chris, the state is threatening to put me in an institution. The legislators would put everyone with a disability who needs assistance into a nursing home to rot, in order to save the state money. If this legislation goes through, there would go my life and any chance of us ever building a life together…because I assume you would not want to marry someone who lives in a nursing home…"

Bill completed his thought and then repeated the entire message. He looked at me and a tear started to roll down his cheek.

My articulate disability rights advocate had spoken so nobly and intelligently to the World Herald newspaper reporter about this legislation's power to "discourage the lives of people with disabilities". At home I was hearing and seeing the broken heart of my weary warrior.

"Oh Bill this is really awful," I responded, suddenly feeling sick to my stomach.

I was beginning to realize the implications of such a budget cut to Bill and now to us. It was bad enough to realize that we would always be at the mercy of the state to pay for Bill's attendant care, for every step of our lives together. But now it was sounding even worse.

Our needed funding for attendant care was being tossed around for political gain or posturing. It felt very crass. Politicians could and would threaten to do away with our needed program, if it would help them to look like they were looking after the state's coffers, or to further their own political agenda.

It was becoming very clear to me that the government really did not care for their citizens with disabilities like Bill, who relied on such a program to be able to live in the community. Otherwise, his life would not be used so casually for the politicians' own gain.

"This is yet again, another slap against my personhood. The state sees me as a pawn for political games, someone without power, whose life can be used as a political football. It's sick and it sickens me. Biblically it would be called an abomination, because it is," Bill said with disgust.

He continued, "I don't trust the government because they do this kind of thing all the time to people with disabilities. This is why I can't trust the exemption to the "cap" that has been offered to us."

Now I really understood why Bill had been so cautious about the so called, "exemption" offer from the state. This offer was a state-level knee-jerk response to pressure from the feds. But, it could be pulled just as fast, as it had come forth, regardless of how well meaning any one person at the state might be, who was offering this to us.

"We can wait to get married until we feel that the risk is not too great Bill. We have to get past this fiasco first." I responded, trying to not let this crisis be any bigger than it was. It had taken the wind out of Bill's sails.

Bill continued to pour out his heart and I listened, "I've been working to increase options for people with disabilities to work, be tax payers and have families. This kind of government sentiment feels like a real slap in the face and sets the disability rights movement back 20 years. It takes all I have to fight to have a real life. I'm so tired."

I thought about how much power the government had over the lives of people with disabilities. Everything Bill had worked for his entire life and all that he still wanted to achieve, could be taken away with the passage of one legislative bill. I felt scared and vulnerable for Bill and for my life with him.

I looked over at Bill and could see that the sadness in his face was slowly changing to a steady resolve. He had laid out his heart and now his strength was rising once again.

He now said with conviction, "We have to be a visible presence at the legislature because the government thinks that all people on Medicaid are poor because they are lazy. They don't understand that people with disabilities have no choices, that many of us would like to work but can't because we would lose our necessary funding for attendant and medical care."

"It was great to see so many people with disabilities from across the state there to protest today. The strength in the numbers and the testimonies might have been enough to sway the senators. But just in case it wasn't enough, I'll write some letters to senators tomorrow."

"Do you want to go see a movie?" Bill added, still very tired, but with a slight smile on his face.

"Sure. Let's go." I said delighted to see that my advocate was so quickly able to get back in the saddle.

Johnny Cash had finished his gospel lament, including his need for God's amazing grace. We needed it too, by the bucketful, if we were going to get past this mess.

Out the door we went for a little movie escapism. Sharing some popcorn with Bill would make the movie even more enjoyable.

Endnotes

1. 1. Jason Gertzen, "Citizens Gather to Fight Cuts." *Omaha World Herald* (March 4, 1993).

MEDICAID HEARING *March 4, 1993*

OPPOSITION: More than 150 people pack into the main hearing room of the Legislature's Health and Human Services Committee.

PHIL JOHNSON/THE WORLD-HERALD

Citizens Gather to Fight Cuts

Disabled Man Calls Trims 'Disastrous'

BY JASON GERTZEN
WORLD-HERALD BUREAU

Lincoln — Dozens of disabled Nebraskans pleaded with legislators Wednesday not to take away their dignity and ability to live on their own by eliminating services covered by the state's health-care program for the poor.

"If you make these cuts, they would be disastrous for me and countless others," said Bill Rush of Lincoln. "If you cut the Medicaid budget, you will discourage people from living full lives."

Rush, 37, who has cerebral palsy, said he has depended on services paid for through Medicaid to live on his own for nine years.

More than 150 people, many of whom were in wheelchairs, packed the main hearing room of the Legislature's Health and Human Services Committee. They were there to oppose six bills that would reduce or eliminate healthcare services paid for by Medicaid.

More than 100 disabled and mentally ill Nebraskans and their advocates massed outside the State Capitol before the hearing chanting "no cuts" and "people first."

"We are here to say, 'Don't take our services,'" said J. Rock Johnson, a Lincoln mental health advocate. "Don't take our quality of life."

State Sen. Scott Moore of Seward, a co-chairman of the Legislature's Medicaid task force, said the proposals were offered in response to the fact that the health-care program has been consuming a larger and larger portion of the state budget each year.

Just since 1990, the state's share of

Please turn to Page 12, Col. 2

PROTEST: Howard Kling, standing, and his uncle, Donald Steward, both of Lincoln, attended a rally outside the State Capitol to protest cuts in Medicaid programs assisting disabled Nebraskans.

PHIL JOHNSON/THE WORLD-HERALD

OMAHA WORLD-HERALD Th

Citizens Gather to Fight Medicaid Program Cuts

Continued from Page 1
funding for the program has increased by nearly 90 percent from $126 million to $239 million.

Of 33 medical services, the federal government mandates that states with Medicaid programs provide 11, Moore said. Some of the remaining services — known as optional services — would be eliminated or limited by bills introduced by the Medicaid task force.

"These cuts aren't fun, and I am not saying that I even support all of them," Moore said. "But these are the only things you can cut to have short-term impact on those rising Medicaid costs."

Legislative Bill 793 would save about $4.14 million over two years by eliminating Medicaid coverage for low-income children between the ages of 10 and 21 with incomes above the standard for Aid to Dependent Children.

LB 794 would save about $10 million over two years by eliminating 13 optional services that would result in a cost savings. Among the services affected would be chiropractic care, podiatric care, physical therapy, speech, hearing and language therapy, liver and heart transplants and dental work.

LB 796 would eliminate all optional services.

LB 792 would save about $4.3 million over two years by eliminating coverage of medically needy adult caretaker relatives in Aid to Dependent Children-related households.

Officials in the State Department of Social Services already have eliminated the program targeted by LB 792. Passage of the measure only would endorse the program's elimination, which took effect Monday.

Douglas County officials attended the hearing to protest the cut.

"We at the county level have grave concerns about the shifting of financial responsibilities to counties from the state," said Jan Pelletier, director of Douglas County's Department of General Assistance.

Ms. Pelletier said her office already has been contacted by 50 people no longer receiving state assistance who appear to qualify for county assistance. Each day, between 30 and 40 people call asking questions about the program.

Social services officials now estimate the cut will affect 5,385 people throughout the state. This estimate was raised from an initial projection of 365 people.

Douglas County Commissioner Bernice Labedz told the committee that implementation of the cut left counties little time to plan. It also will leave some Nebraskans without the ability to get medical help.

"The financial impact must be ba-

LIABILITY CAP: Senators again reject a measure that would limit recovery in lawsuits against the state to no more than $1 million. **Midlands, Page 13.**

1993 Legislature
AUDIT: Two legislators plan to fight an outside audit of state senators' telephone records. **Midlands, Page 13.**

MULTICULTURALISM: The fight over multicultural education in schools may be over. **Midlands, Page 15.**

FERTILIZER: Farm groups say fertilizer dealers are trying to rip them off in the name of environmental protection. **Midlands, Page 15.**

lanced by the human impact," Mrs. Labedz said.

Social services officials said they eliminated the program because it has grown too large. More people are using it as a publicly funded insurance program for general health-care services.

Elaine Rich of Norfolk, who testified by satellite from her hometown, said she has received treatment and prescriptions for her mental illness through Medicaid.

"I feel I have a right to stay well and out of the hospital," Ms. Rich said.

More than a dozen disabled Nebraskans said services they receive through Medicaid are critical to allowing them to live independently.

Providing aides and wheelchairs for people living in their own homes is much cheaper than sending disabled people to institutions, they said.

"I'm too young to be sent to a nursing home," said Carolyn Rogers of Omaha. "I don't know what I would do if you cut Medicaid."

Tim Kolb, president of the Nebraska Coalition for Persons With Disabilities, said he wished the state would change regulations to save money rather than cutting programs.

The way the program is designed now traps people in the welfare system, Kolb said.

"If we want to get a job or get married, we find ourselves losing the very foundation of support we need to do those things," Kolb said.

CHAPTER 41

(Chris' Voice)

Mr. Bill Goes to Washington

The protest had been successful. Disaster was averted. Within a few weeks, State senators decided not to push the legislative bill that would eliminate payments for state optional programs such as attendant care.

Bill didn't have to move to a nursing home and we could both breathe, but the institutionalization threat had taken its toll. Bill and I were both emotionally exhausted. Spring was in the air and I was praying for some newness of energy and hope for both of us.

My prayer was answered by showers of acknowledgement for Bill's efforts to create his own life and advocate for people with disabilities, but with an additional unwanted complication.

"Can you get time off work to come to Washington, DC with me in April? The Governor's Office called to say that I am getting a State Victory Award," Bill said. I could hear his footplates clanging because his legs were jumping around, and Bill was doing that moose-call sound that he couldn't help make whenever he was excited. Bill had managed to call me at the school where I was working. The school staff had paged me to the phone.

Bill continued, "I want to go to the Lincoln Memorial this time. Last time I was in DC I only saw the inside of a hotel. I really want to go there and to the Washington Memorial, the Vietnam War Memorial and to the place where Martin Luther King Jr. made his famous "I Have a Dream" Speech", he slowly typed out on his Liberator™, while still jumping around in his wheelchair.

"I have to ask my boss for some time off Bill. It's too bad that you aren't going in June when school is out. I'm going to have a hard time getting some time off to come with you." I said honestly.

"I want you to come with me," Bill insisted, and I understood how much he wanted me to be there. I wanted to go as well but couldn't promise anything.

"I know. I'll work on it. Gotta go," I said and hung up.

Immediately I called my boss. "Like how much time do you need?" he responded when I told him about Bill's award in Washington.

I answered, "Could I have a week off?"

He said something about not being able to get anyone to cover for me, and then reluctantly gave me permission to take the week off.

"Thank you." I responded, delighted that I would be going to Washington with Bill to get a much needed energy boost to keep us fighting for a better situation at the state level before we got married.

Bill wanted to put his best wheel forward when going to the home of the President of the United States. He wanted to take his power wheelchair to be his most capable self when he attended the reception with the Vice President in the Rose Garden. I also wanted Bill to be the person I knew him to be at home- independent and confident. He needed his technology to be all of these things.

In order to get Bill and all of his technology to Washington, we would need some extra strong arms to come along with us. Bill asked a long time attendant. He agreed to come, conditional upon taking his wife.

Needing to get the plane tickets purchased, The National Rehabilitation Hospital, who sponsored the event, ordered two extra tickets in the names of Bill's attendant and his wife. The attendant was required to reimburse the rehabilitation hospital for the spouse's ticket.

The week before we were to fly to Washington the attendant told Bill that he would only come if we paid for his wife's ticket.

Bill was livid! He fired the attendant on the spot.

"He tried to blackmail me, because he knew that I needed the help." Bill said angrily to me. "The relationship is over. I will not be blackmailed. We will find someone else to come along and help us."

"I'll ask my mom if she wants to come," Bill said the next day, and then I heard his Ability Phone start to dial her telephone number.

"If any son of mine is getting an award in Washington, sure, I'll come," Bill's mom responded without hesitation after we explained the situation. She added, "But I'm no spring chicken and I can't help much with the care you need, Bill."

"We'll get another younger person to come too. You can help to feed me," Bill said, delegating his care jobs.

"There is one problem Mom," Bill said. "The tickets are in a man and woman's name."

"I'll say that I'm Mrs. _____ that'll work." Bill's Mom responded confidently. *Pretty clever,* I thought to myself.

"OK, we'll line up someone else who will go as your daughter since you both have the same last name." Bill said, agreeing with how we were going to play this game. I was just hoping that we would be able to pull this off at all.

I recruited a strong female co-worker to come along to help us and act as Bill's mom's daughter but not Bill's sister, at the airport. We were happy that we found two actresses who were confident they could impersonate someone else.

I kept praying that they would not be found guilty of impersonating the people for whom the tickets were created for, and end up in jail – just because we needed some extra help.

Four of us, all with our own luggage, plus all of Bill's technology, arrived, on mass, in front of the airline counter at the Lincoln Airport. The airline clerk tried to keep a professional demeanor, as she visually scanned all the stuff that the airlines would have to load.

"We had better start to label all of these bags and boxes and figure out what to do with the batteries for that wheelchair," the attendant said, and gave us tags for any unlabeled boxes. She came around the counter and started moving the power wheelchair back behind the counter to talk with her colleagues, about how it would be loaded onto the Boeing 737.

Thanks to all of our and Bill's stuff, we took up all of the employees pre-boarding time; they didn't have time to look at the names on the tickets.

"Gore 2000!" Bill's Liberator™ belted out at full volume.

Al Gore, the Democrat Vice President of the United States heard Bill's electronic voice and responded, "Thanks, I'll think about it."

Al Gore had just finished his speech to the forty-seven state, five National, and the ten International Winners of the Victory Awards in the Rose Garden. Bill was excited to be here, at the White House. Always the ardent democrat, my activist couldn't help but put a little politics into the occasion. On this day in April 1993, Bill was suggesting that Gore run for President of the United States in 2000.

Bill had felt honored to be nominated for this award by Nebraska's Governor Ben Nelson, in recognition of his hard work and dedication to create a "regular life" for himself and for other people with disabilities.

However, he did say that he found it ironic that the same personality traits that had caused people to label him obnoxious and pushy in his university days, were now being used to characterize him as being courageous and having integrity. For Bill, there was a bitter sweet quality to this award.

The crowd in the Rose Garden was filled with individuals like Bill who had overcome great adversity and had also contributed greatly to society. Forty-seven states had selected a recipient that year; each state recipient had a solid record of advocacy at the government level and providing support to others in the community with disabilities. It was just the boost that Bill and I needed to be in the midst of a group of such strong and articulate advocates.

The other recipient from Nebraska, Senator Bob Kerrey was receiving a National Victory award. Bob Kerry, a former elite Navy Seal had lost part of his leg during the Vietnam War. A self-made business man, Kerry had served as the Governor of Nebraska, and was currently serving in the US congress.

National Awards were also given to Actor Christopher Burke, who has Down's Syndrome and played Corky in the television series "Life Goes On" and actress and disability rights advocate Patricia Neal, who had had a series of strokes, was honored. Former Detroit Lions player Mike Utley, who was paralyzed during a football game, was awarded for his Foundation that supports research, rehabilitation and education for persons with spinal cord injuries.

After the speeches were finished, Al Gore invited us to enjoy ourselves in the Rose Garden. Bill and I enjoyed a stroll on the President's newly installed $20,000 jogging track. It was very soft to walk on. "I'd like one of these," I said and Bill smiled.

We had visited the sights that Bill wanted to see in Washington. Later that evening we were off to The Gala Reception and Awards Presentation at the Warner Theatre. It was a black tie event and we all dressed up for the occasion.

The National and State Award Recipients were sitting in order of recognition at the front of the theatre. We guests of the recipients sat at the back. Bill was sitting with the group with last names starting in the last half of the alphabet.

We all watched and cheered as Marilyn Hamilton, the internationally known creator of the Quickie Wheelchair, and National Victory Award winner, read the names of the awards to those with the last names starting with the letters A to M. The recipients stayed in their seats.

Then Wonder Woman, Linda Carter stepped forward to read names of the recipients with last names starting from N to Z.

Bill's mom leaned over to me to whisper, "Bill loved Wonder Woman as a teenager."

I looked to her and nodded, thinking, *No Wonder.* Wonder Woman was drop dead gorgeous, and tonight particularly so, dressed in a mermaid looking gold suit. I wondered if Bill who was sitting much closer to her, was drooling.

Sitting on the edge of our seats, we listened as the names were announced, and cheered mightily when Bill's name was read.

At the awards reception following the presentation, we found Bill visiting with one of his fellow honorees Sam from Minnesota.

They were joking about how the second half of the alphabet had it better for once, in that they got their names read by the "Wonder Woman," Linda Carter.

Suddenly, the gold mermaid herself, Linda Carter, approached Bill. She appeared curious about his electronic voice and stopped to look at it. We naively thought that she wanted to talk with Bill.

Bill's mom took a picture of Bill "talking" to his favorite Wonder Woman. We were all mesmerized by stardom up close.

Perhaps she didn't know that Bill was talking to her. Or perhaps she was one of those curious humans who couldn't help but want to look closer at Bill's technology but not meet him. For whatever reason, she left as soon as she had arrived.

Bill finished typing and looked up to find her gone. The look on his face said that he was no longer that impressed with his Wonder Woman.

"*Beauty is as Beauty Does*," I thought to myself smugly, not allowing for any rational reason for her dismissal of Bill.

CHAPTER 42

(Chris' Voice)

Mr. Bill, My Green Card Lawyer

It was the summer of 1993 and I was running out of free trade work permits to allow me to stay and work in the US. The Immigration and Naturalization Service agent told me, in no uncertain terms, when I had recently renewed my permit at the border, that I had better get a permanent resident Green Card, or be prepared to leave the country.

Bill and I were thinking about our options.

"Because I am minimally employed, I would not be able to sponsor you for a marriage Green Card. And besides that, we are not ready to do that yet. Maybe this is the next piece of the puzzle for us Chris." Bill thought out loud.

He continued, "Let's make you a permanent resident and then we can begin to fill in some of the other stuff. It makes the most sense for you to get a work-sponsored green card. You like your work and your boss might be willing to help you to get it. Why don't you try that?"

"Sounds like a good plan." I said.

I asked my employer about it the next day at work.

"Sure. Get yourself an immigration lawyer to help with this and I'll sign whatever. Chris, it might be easier if you just went to California and bought one off the street. They cost like $25 for a fake one," my boss teased.

"Uhhh, I don't think so." I responded, thinking how fast my life with Bill would end, should I get caught. I'd be deported immediately. We had worked too hard to get this far.

"We had someone else working for us a few years ago who used an immigration lawyer in Lincoln. We could get you that person's name," the boss offered more seriously.

"Thanks! That would be a good start," I said, relieved and also very thankful that I had an employer willing to sponsor me to get a Green Card.

Later that day I called the attorney's office and listened to the lawyer tell me that it would cost me up to $5000 and might take three years to get my Green Card. Thanking her for her time, I hung up.

I had worm out the welcome mat of Free Trade permits. I needed a Green Card yesterday and I didn't have $5000. So I went home and hired Bill to be my attorney.

He had a lot more at stake than any lawyer in helping me to get my Green Card. He was thorough and would put his terrier teeth into this. I knew that he would be relentless until it was done.

Plus the regional office of the INS just "happened" to be within rolling distance of Bill's apartment. Another God-sighting that I couldn't deny. Our journey to get this far together had been difficult, but I was seeing again and again, in very practical ways, God leading us forward, one step at a time.

I went home and offered Bill the job. He accepted it on the spot.

Bill put his writing and disability rights work aside to work for me. He rolled around town, making trips to the INS office at the Federal building and to the library, gathering everything he could find to learn the process and paperwork that I needed to get a work-sponsored Green Card.

Bill loved being the heavy for me, using his powers of persuasion to help get what I needed. By seating himself in some officials office at the INS, and pressing my case, Bill managed to clear the way for my most recent free trade permit to be renewed (despite that fact that it shouldn't have been) to allow for some extra time for us to get this process underway.

By the beginning of 1994, my lawyer Bill and I were working with my employer to apply for an Alien Employment Certification for me. This was the part of the process whereby the Department of Labor had to certify that I was not taking a skilled job from a capable American.

In order to prove this, my job would have to be advertised in local papers for 30 days, while I continued to work as though I was not asking if anyone would like to take my job from me.

I immediately thought of an Occupational Therapist colleague I knew who lived close to my work and travelled some distance to her job. She could very easily take my job and I would be moving back to Canada because I was all out of free trade permits. Praying what to do about this situation, I decided to call her and tell her the truth.

"Hi Sue," I said, trying to sound as nonchalant as I possibly could. "I'm wondering if you have seen my job advertised in the newspaper."

"Yes. I did. Why? Are you leaving Chris?" she asked.

"I'm not or rather I don't want to. I'm applying for a Green Card. In order to get one, the Department of Labor has to advertise my job for 30 days to prove that I am not taking it from an American citizen."

"Oh that sounds pretty scary Chris. Wow! I had no idea." Sue responded sounding shocked to hear that I was in this position.

"You have the right to take it from me, but then I will have to leave the country because I will no longer have status to work here," I said, feeling guilty that I was begging this professional colleague to not apply for my job. But then I thought, at least if she knows the circumstances, maybe she won't apply. I held my breath and waited for her reply.

"I was thinking about applying for it but I owe my current employer some time because I went on maternity leave and also to an expensive course. It's not the right time for me to apply for your job." Sue confessed.

"Thank you for your honesty, Sue. I'm sorry to bother you but I wanted to let you know." I said and we finished the call.

How many others could possibly want my job? I questioned to myself.

I couldn't think of anyone else to call and beg so I begged God to keep eligible people ignorant of the advertisement.

The slowest thirty days of my life with Bill finally passed by. A few days after the deadline, my boss asked me to come visit with him.

With trepidation I walked into my boss's office. There sitting on his desk were two applications.

"Chris, it doesn't look like either of these applicants have the skills we are looking for. Looks like you're staying and might get that Green Card." my boss said and smiled at me.

"Great news!" I said feeling like a hundred pounds had been lifted off my shoulders.

"I'll go ahead and get them sent in to the Department of Labor with the paperwork that says we need you because no American can do your job. Welcome to America!" he said.

I left the office and immediately called Bill to give him the news. He didn't need his communication device to let me know how pleased he was to hear the news. He hollered and I could hear his wheelchair clanging as he jumped up and down in excitement.

"One step closer Chris." Bill, my lawyer finally said with his Liberator™, "We've almost got you permanently Stateside."

CHAPTER 43

(Bill's Voice)
Next Piece of Our Puzzle

"Bill, why is my Green Card pink?" Chris said with a laugh as she looked at the card that had just arrived in the mail. She was holding her brand new pink colored United Stated Permanent Resident Alien Card, known as a "Green Card".

"Just as long as says it's your Green Card, Chris, that'll do," I responded with total relief to see it finally in her hands. Chris was safe from the Immigration and Naturalization Service. They could no longer tell her that she had to move back to Canada because she didn't have the required visa paperwork.

God, Chris and I were a good team. It was February 1995, eighteen months into the process of working on getting her a Green Card, and a little more than four years since Chris' arrival in Nebraska. Four years to permanent status was an achievement. I was proud of what our team had succeeded in doing.

We celebrated Chris' "Green Card' status with a dinner at her favorite Indian restaurant in our fun neighborhood. I ate at home while Chris was coming home from work. At the restaurant I was free to chat while she got her fill of spicy food that my stomach could not handle.

"I'm so happy that you can stay here permanently. No more trying to outfox the INS." I said, and added, "I have a little present for you in my backpack."

Chris opened the small bag that was in my backpack. In it, I had a bookmark that I had bought for her. It said all that I needed and wanted to say far better than I could. Chris read the bookmark and looked at me and smiled. I had tears in my eyes.

I ask myself why have I been blessed with someone so understanding and caring? Perhaps it's because I can truly appreciate you or maybe it's because God knew I needed you so much – Jean Therese

"Thanks Bill. This is beautiful." Chris said, taking time to let the words sink in.

She laid the bookmark aside and took another bite of her favorite curry flavored dish. She looked back up at me and said, "Mmmm, this is so good!"

I just sat there, marveling at my gift from God, who loved to eat spicy Indian food and savouring our "Green Card" victory.

During the next week, I started to think and pray about the next piece of the puzzle of our lives that we should complete. God had helped us to chart our course so far. Surely He would guide us to what would come next.

The disability rights network was suggesting that we should push for legislation for people with disabilities to be able to work and not lose their necessary Medicaid-funded medical and attendant care services. We were envisioning a buy-in provision within Medicaid, much like any other medical insurance. This would be helpful should I try to get employment. And, it might provide a back-up plan to the Waiver and Spousal Impoverishment program option for us.

I began to think about our current options for transportation and how it was impacting our lifestyle and also our relationship.

We were living basically within a 12-block radius around our apartment building. This was the distance that I could travel in my power wheelchair without having to recharge its' battery. We had a really fun neighborhood but we wanted and needed to travel beyond one charge of my wheelchair.

If I needed to give a speech or to conduct a work-related interview for some writing that I was doing Chris would have to get me into my manual wheelchair, push me downstairs to her compact car (which was always cluttered with things from her work), clear spots for my wheelchair, lap tray, computerized communication device and my body. Then she would have to help me to stand and transfer into her passenger seat.

When I sat in Chris' passenger seat, I felt like we were cramming my six foot two inch height frame into a space made for someone of Chris' height or about eight inches less than my own. It was much too small and uncomfortable for me. Without my wheelchair side supports, I easily fell over and often hit my head on the door. Once we arrived at our destination, Chris would have to reverse the process and do the entire procedure over again to get me home.

It was too much work to ask of Chris. I was afraid that her back was going to suffer from doing this for me, even if we only did this very occasionally.

My experience many years earlier when my date had said that she forgot me when she transferred me to and from a car still resonated in my mind. Even though Chris and I had a profound relationship, communicating in an amazing way non-verbally and unconsciously, without audible speech, the voices from the past still spoke to me. I was concerned that she might begin to "forget" me or get tired of me, because of the work involved.

Sometimes we would borrow a friend's wheelchair accessible van. This helped somewhat, but a borrowed van, like Chris' car, was too small for my tall build when sitting in my power wheelchair.

In order to get into a regular sized van that had been adapted for a wheelchair I had to tilt back like when lying in a recliner, to keep from getting decapitated by the top of the door frame when I rolled off the ramp and into the van. Times when we did this I trusted Chris to help me to drive into the van while I looked at the sky. I had to remain tilted throughout the ride and this made me nauseous.

Grateful and excited that the ADA required that regular busses begin to have wheelchair accessible ramps, we tried to use the newly accessible route buses in Lincoln.

Unfortunately, the bus drivers did not have extra time allotted in their scheduled to accommodate for the time it would take for someone in a wheelchair to get safely on the bus and secured into the designated place. Their body language clearly communicated that I was not welcome.

There was also one particularly charged episode with a passenger that quickly extinguished any interest we might have in using regular buses. Chris, working as fast as she could to get me secured into place on the bus, had to deal with a complaining passenger. She lost her patience with the woman and told her to be quiet. Needless-to-say our nerves were raw by the time we got to our destination. Neither of us ever again suggested that we use the local regular bus for transportation.

Clearly, we needed mobility freedom. This was the next piece of the puzzle to create our lives together. I suggested to Chris that it was time to look into getting a wheelchair accessible van that would meet our needs. She loved the idea.

The only detail that I didn't have figured out was how to get money to pay for a wheelchair accessible van.

CHAPTER 44

(Chris' Voice)

Planning a Surprise

In six months Bill would reach the significant milestone of his fortieth birthday. I thought that like lots of people, he might be having some uneasy feelings about turning the big 4-0. But I had no idea how scared he was, until he talked openly about it.

"I was told that I would never live to see forty years of age, Chris."

"Really?" I responded, stunned that any health care professional would set a specific limit to someone's lifespan, given that many factors determined longevity. Bill had lots of things going for him that would encourage a longer life including a grandfather who was living and in his nineties, good health care, weekly exercise, positive relationships, and a strong faith supported by a robust church family.

"That's what doctors told my parents when I was a child," Bill said and added, "So I'm scared to have my birthday."

"Do you know anyone who can get you some information about what happens to people who have cerebral palsy as they age?" I asked, concerned that Bill's limited knowledge on this subject was increasing his anxiety. It was important that he gets some better facts from reliable sources.

"I'll write to the United Cerebral Palsy Associations in New York and see what they have to say about how long I will live," Bill said, and appeared to relax a little because he was back in control of his own thoughts.

A couple of weeks later Bill showed me a letter that he had received from the United Cerebral Palsy Association's, medical director's office. I was delighted to see that this letter spoke very directly to Bill, disputing what he had been told about a short lifespan.

> *Dear Mr. Rush,*
>
> *This is in response to your letter of March 9th. Your information on life expectancy of a person who has cerebral palsy is not correct. The life expectancy of a person with cerebral palsy is not significantly different than that of the general population. If the person is institutionalized, then it would be shorter.*
>
> *I've checked with the Medical Director regarding some of your questions. Exercise such as swimming would be good. You should have a checkup regularly.*
>
> *Please find attached more information about aging for persons who have cerebral palsy.*
>
> *Sincerely,*
> *Irene Bundziad*
> *Administrative Assistant to*
> *Medical Director.*
>
> *(Bill Rush Personal Communications)*

"I guess that I'm going to be around for a while," Bill said with his Liberator™ and then looked at me with a smile.

"I'm counting on it," I responded, with absolute delight that someone with authority had set the record straight. Then I had another thought.

"Hey Bill, do you want to visit with your doctor before your birthday to see what he says about your health?" I asked, thinking that I wanted him to have the most accurate information about the state of his own health as his scary birthday approached.

"I'll get an appointment and see what he says," Bill responded.

A couple of weeks later Bill was excitedly telling me what the doctor found during his medical check-up. His worst fears were being averted.

"On a scale of 1 to 10, the doctor says my heart is a 10. He said that I should expect to live for a lot more years."

Bill was feeling much better about his approaching birthday. He was growing more confident that his health really was good.

However, since he had lived his life not expecting to live this long, I decided that I would make a big deal of celebrating this birthday. We would make this the best birthday ever for him!

It was time to take a break from all of the work that we were doing to create a married life together and celebrate what we had; a secure and growing relationship, in the context of lots of people who loved us. A surprise birthday celebration would give us the opportunity to press the pause button and savor all that we had.

When planning this surprise birthday event, I found myself thinking about a conversation that we had had about a year before when I had received an invitation to my high school class's 10th reunion in Canada. I asked Bill if he had ever been to a reunion.

"I never really belonged to a group, outside my family, until I went to Journalism school," he said.

"It's really hard to have a reunion when you are a class of one. I was a class of one in high school, because I did my work via correspondence with the UNL's high school program. I liked the able-bodied kids who were brought over from Westside High to interact with me, but I never belonged with them. They had their own school." Bill lamented.

Later, Bill, who had been thinking about the concept of belonging added, "My church family at First Baptist is the first place in my life where I have felt a sense of belonging outside of my family."

Bill's reminiscing got me reflecting about how different and positive my own experience of belonging had been during high school. I remembered in particular, a surprise birthday party that friends had thrown for me in my last year of school for me. I enjoyed reminiscing about how delighted I was to find that my friends cared enough to organize the event for me, and to pick out a special group gift of a necklace with my name on one side and the class year on the other. As an adult, I continued to treasure this gift. The party had created for me a real sense of belonging to my group of friends and to my graduating class.

I asked Bill, "Has anyone ever given you a surprise party?"

"No, my family always did stuff for my birthday but it wasn't a surprise," he said.

His response led to my decision to organize a surprise party for Bill's 40th. I had about six months to plan something wonderful for him.

I would invite people from all facets of Bill's life, present and past, to come and show him how he much he belonged and was treasured in their lives. I started to think about a guest list. Then I thought about a group gift for Bill.

I can ask people to give money towards a van that we desperately needed, in lieu of a gift for Bill. Oh this is going to be Perfect! I thought to myself.

CHAPTER 45

(Bill's Voice)
A Sense of Belonging

There was a knock on my apartment door. I opened it, assuming that it was my attendant who had been let into the building by someone entering the locked door, bypassing the intercom system to let me know that he was coming up.

A parade of people, led by Chris entered my living room with a chorus of "Surprise!" and singing of "Happy Birthday!"

I sat, totally mesmerized by what I was looking at, trying to take it all in. I watched as my favorite people from my past and present quickly filled my apartment living room and kitchen area. How could this be happening?

Chris was smiling from ear to ear, obviously pleased that she had managed to keep this secret from me. There was my mom enjoying my stunned reaction. Friends and my two older aunts from Omaha were there. A friend, who was a counselor of mine at Easter Seals camp when I was a teenager, had driven from Kansas and brought his boys. Jeff, my former neighbor was in the crowd with his wife and their first child. A few of the families from church were there too. One of them was carrying a cake, covered with candles. And Marlene entered with a bright smile on her face. More people came later including my older brother Jim and his wife.

It felt so good to have all these people with me in my apartment.

This must be what heaven is like, I thought. *It's everyone you love in one place.*

They all gave me cards and balloons and cake and celebrated my life and my birthday with me.

I soaked it all in, like a cactus in the rain.

Later, I was talking with Chris about this experience.

"The party and cards were wonderful and affirming." I said. "I felt loved and that I belonged. People gave me compliments because I belonged to and contributed to their community." [1]

Chris waited for me to go on. She sensed that there was more. She had a way of waiting for the truth to emerge. And out it came.

"I don't know how to take compliments because people with disabilities, seldom get complimented sincerely. We get compliments such as, "You're so brave to live with a disability. I'd kill myself if I were you.'"[2]

"Oh Bill! That is just awful! Why would people say such things to you?" Chris said with absolute horror. "I didn't know that you had experienced that kind of thing. No wonder it is so hard for you to learn to take a compliment."

"I know that those kind of "compliments" say much more about the person saying them then they do about me."

"No kidding," Chris agreed.

"They are really saying that they are terrified about the unknown of living with a disability. I was always able to accept my disability so I let those so called "compliments" go in one ear and out the other. But now I don't know what to do with real genuine compliments."

"Bill, the people at your party really love you and want you to know what you mean to them. It's time for you to learn how to take real compliments. You just say 'thank you'. That's all you need to do. You won't become conceited because of sincere compliments. We all need affirmation."

I sat thinking about my party and what Chris had just said. I felt loved and good about my value to my various communities-. family, church, neighborhood and disability rights.

I also thought about the overwhelming response to Chris' request for money for a van as a gift for me. We had received so much gift money that we were ready to start to look for a van to modify for my needs.

This had been the best birthday ever. And turning forty wasn't so scary after all.

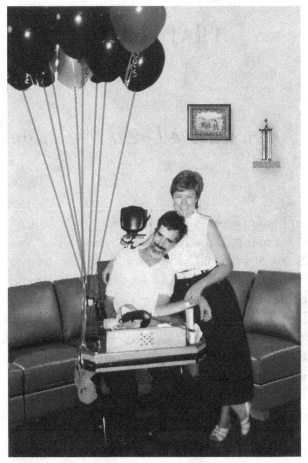

Photo of Bill and Chris at Bill's 40th birthday party.

Endnotes

1.   Bill Rush, "Belonging and Compliments: Both are Necessary" *Nebraska Rehabilitation and Community Newsletter*, Vocational Rehabilitation, Nebraska Department of Education, (October 1995). Reprinted with permission from the publisher.

2.   Ibid.

CHAPTER 46

(Chris' Voice)

An Accessible Dream Vacation

But what would I give to Bill as my special gift for his *40*th? I thought long and hard to myself. I wanted it to be really fun. It also needed to be a validation of what Bill had done with his life so far, while offering a glimpse of wonderful things yet to come for people, like him, with a significant disability.

Sudden, I knew what my present would be. And it was perfect!

I would take Bill to the National Disability Rights Center in Denver, CO. It was a Mecca of sorts for people in the disability rights community. Bill would love it.

If I could make the trip to Colorado a surprise, that would be even more fun for Bill. But I would need help from a lot of people to pull it off.

With a little research I learned that we could fly to Denver direct from Lincoln and get an accessible over-the-highway bus from the airport into the city of Denver. We could link to Denver's accessible city buses to get to the Disability Rights Center. And we could get a hotel near the center.

The Disability Rights Center would help with coordinating attendant care at that end. It took some work with the state of Nebraska to get the payment for Bill's attendant care shifted to this organization in Colorado, but it was well worth the effort to create this 'futuristic' experience for Bill.

Even the most visionary among the disability rights community were not then thinking in terms of 'vacation' and 'portable attendant care' to make a vacation possible. Our trip would be a taste of what life might be like for future generations of Americans with disabilities!

Friends of ours from Boulder, Colorado of ours would meet me at Denver's airport to help me to reassemble Bill's power chair. One of the friends was an engineer: the perfect person to have on our team when faced with reassembly of a huge, complex power wheelchair.

I was feeling like God was helping me to pull this off, opening doors to portable attendant care, and providing engineering support at the Denver International Airport. So far, so good.

At home in Lincoln, I still needed help from Bill's home health agency to keep this trip a secret from him and also help from his power wheelchair dealer to learn how to transport his big, approximately 200-pound power wheelchair.

I called the home health agency scheduler first.

"Hello this is Chris. I'm calling to ask if you will help me with a surprise for Bill's birthday that's coming up in August."

"Sure. Birthday surprises are always fun." said the scheduler, "What do you need?"

"I'm going to take Bill to Colorado for a week. I don't want him to know that he is going but he will be worried if he doesn't see an aide schedule arrive in the mail the week before we go." I said.

"We can send out a fake schedule for Bill. That will be no problem. We'd love to do it. Very rarely do we have any clients who go on vacation, let alone a surprise one. I will tell the aides not to say anything and we will help you to keep it a secret," the scheduler said with much pleasure in her voice.

Yeah, not much gets past Bill, I thought to myself. *The home health agency will really enjoy playing this game for him. This is going to be fun for them too.*

"Thanks so much," I said with excitement because my birthday plans for Bill were coming together piece by piece.

Next I called Leon to ask about transporting Bill's new power wheelchair on the airplane.

"Glad to hear that you are taking Bill over to Colorado," Leon said and then added. "You'll have to protect all the electronics and carry them inside the cabin. The batteries are gel batteries and not lead acid so they will be OK to travel in the luggage compartment."

"OK. Thanks," I said and hung up the phone, feeling overwhelmed because I didn't know which parts of Bill's chair needed to be protected and how to disassemble those parts. We had taken Bill's power wheelchair to Washington, DC in 1993, but since then he had upgraded to a newer power wheelchair, from a different manufacturer with very different parts.

I needed practice taking Bill's wheelchair apart but I had a big problem. He was in it all day. He was only out of it at the pool or when he slept beside it at night. *How was I going to create an opportunity to practice taking the chair apart to pack the electronics, without Bill knowing?* I couldn't figure out how to do this.

We were down to the week before the trip and Bill's home health agency sent him a fake schedule. All the attendants managed to keep the secret from Bill. *What fun!*

But I was also getting anxious because I had still not had a chance to practice taking the chair apart and packing the electronics and tools we might need to reassemble it in the Denver airport.

I kept the secret too, until I felt desperate and had to say something.

Bill was playing chess in the Cornhusker state games during that last week before we were to fly. I met him for lunch with his attendant at the Cornhusker Hotel in downtown Lincoln between games. Bill was busy chewing on his sandwich and the aide and I were chatting. He had finished his bite and was waiting for the aide to give him another bit of his sandwich.

All of a sudden I blurted, "Bill, you are going to Colorado next week and I have to practice taking your power wheelchair apart and I need your help to do it."

The aide stopped feeding Bill, and looked at me in dismay, as if to say, *Why are you telling him?* Bill looked at me as if he didn't hear or believe what I was saying! So I said it again.

He sat upright and typed, "But I have an attendant schedule for next week. We need to cancel them."

"Bill that's a fake schedule," I said, "Your home health agency and all your attendants have done such a great job of keeping this a secret for weeks. Now I've blown it because I'm getting anxious about your power wheelchair that is coming with us," I said with tears rolling down my face because I felt so badly that I couldn't keep it a secret until the last minute. I needed to know how to get the chair on board the airplane. And I needed to know if I should get Leon to come over to help me, before we left for the airport.

"I wanted it to be a surprise until the day we leave but I can't do this part without your help. We're going to visit ADAPT and you will have attendant care there."

"It's OK. We'll figure out the wheelchair," Bill said and then added, "Wow, a vacation to Colorado to the Disability Rights Center with portable attendant care! That's Disability Cool Chris!"

And then I heard Bill make his Liberator™ say, "Thank you. Thank You. Thank you!"

CHAPTER 47

(Bill's Voice)

ADAPT

"Want to come meet us in Washington DC to protest at the United States Capitol for Universal Attendant care Bill? We have planned an action there next month. We chain our wheelchairs to the pillars in the building. Then we all share the food, water and wine that we have brought in our backpacks for the sit-in, and party until we get some response from the congress or get arrested, whichever comes first. I have been arrested 34 times," the cool guy in the power wheelchair bragged with a big grin.

I can't believe that I am even contemplating this idea, I thought to myself. I looked at Chris to get her response to this offer.

"Count me out Bill. If I get caught, I could get deported and it's not worth that." Chris said with a nervous laugh and a look on her face that said she was stunned that I would even think about such an act of civil disobedience.

Chris and I were visiting the National Disability Rights Center in Denver, Colorado, the home of ADAPT, formerly known as Americans Disabled for Accessible Public Transportation, and more recently known as Americans Disabled for Attendant Programs Today. Being a sort of Mecca to the disability rights community, it was one of several places that I had always wanted to visit. Now in the summer of 1995, I was excited to be here talking with these disability rights advocates, learning from their experience and sharing from mine.

I, like many others, had labeled this group as militant extremists in the Disability Rights Community. "[Back in Lincoln Nebraska,] I had heard how ADAPT members had chained themselves in their wheelchairs to the bumpers of Denver's fixed route buses, chanting, "We will ride! We will ride!" I didn't think this was the way that nice people with disabilities should act." [1]

And yet, here I sat, talking to one of their staff, considering joining them for one of their events. *You are unbelievable*, I thought to myself.

"Sounds like a crazy time. What do you do about your attendant care needs while you are chained up?" I asked, realizing that I was getting excited enough to consider chaining myself to something at the Capitol in DC and then getting my behind, sitting in my approximately 200-pound power wheelchair, hauled off to jail.

"We have our own ADAPT volunteer attendants Bill. They come with us to the protests, to help with whatever is needed. They even party with us when we are chained up, helping to pass around the wine and food. After we get arrested, the police often hold us for 24 hours. We need attendant care for that time as well and the police let them come along."

Wow! I wouldn't starve to death, or be denied the bathroom in a 24 hour chained-up protest, I thought, while also admiring this group's ability to manage taking care of everyone's personal needs while also executing their protest "actions."

The energy of this militant disabled rights advocate guy was contagious and I was getting pretty close to signing up.

Then I remembered where I come from, and that I had my reputation to keep as a rational, articulate advocate for persons with disabilities. Going off half-cocked to chain myself in DC would get me some notoriety as a nutcase, but would also tarnish my name forever at home. Nebraskans had long memories.

In Nebraska, people with disabilities had walked, and rolled around the capitol and shouted protest messages when we faced the Medicaid Budget cuts in 1993. Many of us filled the hearing room and gave testimonies. Many, including myself, wrote letters and talked to the state senators, one-on-one about the impact, should the bill pass. But no one thought of chaining themselves and their wheelchairs to the state capitol as an act of protest. They would have lost respect in the eyes of the senators and the public. And they could have been hauled away to a mental institution or a jail. Nebraska did not have much tolerance for that kind of protest.

At the ADAPT headquarters, I was [learning] that this was not a radical camp, wanting to overthrow the United States government. Rather they were a group of [committed] people [with disabilities] with a fierce pride in who they are and what they have accomplished. News clippings on their walls told how they fought for and finally won accessible public transportation in major centers across the nation...

I learned how they had trained, developed and empowered disabled activists to win access to public transit nationally. ADAPT staff serving as volunteer trainers and attendants. In seminars, the novices [people with disabilities] were taught the basics of community organizing along with training in nonviolent civil disobedience and disability rights. [2]

They also had many clippings from their most current fight to get attendant care available for all Americans who needed it, especially those who were trapped in institutions because of no attendant care if they moved out. This latest campaign involved pushing for Universal Attendant Care for all Americans by lobbying for the Medicaid Community Attendant Service Act (MICASA) to pass in Washington DC. This national legislation would amend the Social Security Act, by creating a new Medicaid service called "Qualified Community-Based Attendant Services." It would allow individuals in any state of the nation, who received care in a nursing facility or a care facility for persons with mental retardation to use the same dollars for a "Qualified Community-based Attendant Care service."

I wanted other Americans with disabilities to have the choice, as I did, to be able to live outside of an institution and in the community. I just wanted to get it in a different way.

After spending some time visiting the center with Chris, while thinking about the differences in disability rights advocacy between Nebraska and Colorado, and my good reputation at home, I finally spoke to the guy who asked me to join the MICASSA protest party in Washington DC.

"Thanks but no thanks for the offer to come to DC to protest with you. In Nebraska, we do advocacy one-on-one. I can go and visit with the Governor and state officials whenever I need to, because I have a good relationship with them. Nebraska might be boring by your standards, but it works for me."

"Well Bill, if you have the ear of the Governor, you don't need to chain yourself to your state capitol or the US Capitol, do you." the guy responded, sounding very impressed with my network. He continued, "Sounds like you Cornhuskers have set yourselves up a pretty nice system of advocacy. I'm surprised because we don't hear much about you. But I guess you just get it done there, without any fanfare, in a nice Nebraska way." he concluded with a broad acknowledging smile.

"Thanks for giving us a tour today," I said to the guy and then added, "If I ever get an itch to go chain myself to something in protest I won't hesitate to contact you."

"Sure Bill. We're always here if you need to get out of the cornfields and add some excitement to your life," the guy teased.

Yes, we Nebraskans and Coloradans, even if we were neighbors, had very different tactics in our disability advocacy work. But we were working for the same things. All of us in the disability rights community were fighting for people with disabilities to have the opportunity to live regular lives.

The trip taught me that there is room for different strategies in our disability rights movement.

On the flight home, I felt affirmed that our relationship-based strategy in Nebraska, although not as exciting as those in Colorado, had gotten us this far.

Going forward, I would hold my head high. I was proud to be a Cornhusker who was part of the civil but effective disability rights movement in Nebraska.

Endnotes

1. Bill Rush, "ADAPT." *Nebraska Rehabilitation and Community Newsletter,* Vocational Rehabilitation, Nebraska Department of Education, (September 1995). Reprinted by permission of the publisher.
2. Ibid.

CHAPTER 48

(Bill's Voice)

On The Road- Finally

[It was the spring of 1996 and] I was in love with our new candy-red, lift-equipped cargo van. Chris didn't mind because she was in love with it too.

To us, the van symbolized the "system" working as it should. That is, we were able to set our own goals, and with help from knowledgeable government bureaucrats, get the support we needed to meet our goals.[1]

Of course, before we accessed the "system" for money to modify a van for my wheelchair needs we had to have money for the purchase of a brand new van in which to make the modifications. Thanks to the money that had been given me for my birthday, Chris and I had sufficient funds to purchase a new van.

I contacted my Vocational Rehabilitation Counselor, who agreed that helping me modify a van fell within my goal of getting a job. We were directed to Kathy Burger, an independent living specialist, who helped us to figure out what we wanted.[2]

With Kathy's help we decided that we needed a bare bones cargo van, one without flooring, insulation or seats, except for Chris' driver seat. We would then need to have both the floor lowered and the ceiling and rear door raised to accommodate my six foot two inch height, sitting in a large power wheelchair. We would also need a bus-sized long automatic lift that would be long enough for my large power wheelchair and extending footrests that held my long legs.

Kathy directed us to Bill Siebert, a van conversion specialist in Glenwood, Iowa. Bill listened to what we needed and wanted.

We wanted a van where I could sit up front so that Chris could talk to me while she drives. We wanted to have my power chair secured so that it would not move-something that seemed impossible [given the approximately three hundred pound weight total of my body and my wheelchair that had come loose easily when we used regular tie-downs in borrowed vehicles. This would leave me ricocheting around –really dangerous. And I wanted to be able to get in and out of the van by myself, staying upright and driving into a lock-down mechanism independently]. [3]

Siebert bought a new cargo van that he got off the factory assembly line in Michigan for us and then did the modifications, exceeding our expectations. In April, 1996, after eight months of work to create what we needed, we drove "Candy" home.

Going from having access to 12 blocks around our apartment to having access to anywhere in North America took some adjustment.

A couple of weeks after we got the van, Chris said that she wanted to go get something to eat and started to list places near our apartment building. I reminded her that we had a van. She could pick a street, and we could go there and see what restaurants were on that street. North America was suddenly our oyster! [4]

Different groups started asking me to do presentations and Chris and I accommodated them when we were able. I enjoyed teaching "helping" professionals from my personal experience.

I spoke to school teachers about why inclusion is logical. In one session, I asked that some Speech Language Pathologists volunteer to limit their speaking to the kinds of preprogrammed devices that they give to their students, in order for them to experience what it is like to talk a while in my shoes. I also talked with college students studying health sciences about what dignity really means and how to make sure that they treat all their clients with dignity.

Now that we had Candy, I could accompany Chris to her continuing education conferences. One in particular stands out from the rest.

We drove our accessible van to Colorado Springs in the summer of 1996, enjoying every moment of our new mobility freedom.

I found out that I couldn't control my headstick to use my Libby while we were driving. So Chris and I decided to enjoy our time together on trips by listening to audio books.

For this trip we chose the latest John Grisham novel for the ten hour trip there and to the latest Robert Parker Spencer mystery for the ten hour trip back. The long Grisham tale helped to make the miles pass as we travelled across the entire state of Nebraska and down into Colorado.

Assuming that Colorado Springs would be as accessible as Denver had been during my birthday trip the previous year, I thought that I might roll around the street a bit and then come back to do some writing on my Liberator™ while Chris was in session. But Colorado Springs, at least where we were staying, was not Denver.

I couldn't even leave the hotel parking lot to get some air. The curb cuts in front of the hotel and on that street were non-existent, similar to how they had been in Lincoln fifteen years past, before we in the movement, including myself had gotten after the city fathers.

I remembered how I had taken one of the city managers with me for a walkabout to experience the dangerousness of just rolling around town. More curb cuts had suddenly appeared. *This part of Colorado Springs needed some ADAPT people to come and protest these inaccessible streets,* I thought.

I felt trapped. At home in Lincoln, I could come and go from my apartment as I pleased, to go on errands or even to take a stroll if I needed it to clear my head. Now I couldn't even leave the hotel grounds.

I was relieved when I saw that Chris was finished with her session on the first day. She could tell that I was going a little stir-crazy.

"Bill why don't we go check out the Garden of the Gods tomorrow when I'm done," she offered.

"Sure. If it's God's garden, it's got to be more accessible that this place." I said in response, feeling pretty grumpy.

To keep from becoming overwhelmed by my feelings of being trapped, while Chris finished the second and last day of her continuing education, I focused my thoughts on writing something for a presentation that I was going to give to family members of persons with disabilities as part of a program called Partners in Policy Making sponsored by the ARC, the Association for Retarded Citizens of Nebraska.

I thought about how Chris and I had taken this course a couple of years before, even though I didn't have mental retardation. The ARC offered the course to empower individuals with any type of disability and their family members to become grassroots disability rights advocates. I already knew most of the material, but I wanted Chris to get some training in political advocacy and they welcomed her. Chris had been the first ever significant other to take the course. The ARC and I were both proud of that.

Finally Chris came out of the conference room, having finished her continuing education, and we could get away from this inaccessible place. Off we went to find the "Garden of God."

Chris easily found the tourist attraction we were looking for and parked Candy in a large van-accessible parking space. She got the van lift out to allow me to independently drive out of the van.

I rolled out onto the lift and looked at another world, a land of wheelchair accessibility.

My heart was instantly lifted in praise to the God of this garden when I looked out on the park and the mountains in the distance. Hooray! *Colorado Springs is not totally a wasteland of inaccessibility after all*, I thought to myself. This really *was* God's garden.

Right in front of me was a six foot wide cement pathway available for walking, running or bicycling, designed to be the same color of the stone around it, so as to keep the stunning natural look of this place. Pine trees lined the sides of the wide pathways. Mountains beckoned me to come and explore.

Chris powered the lift down so I could roll off the lift and onto the ground. Instantly, I put my power wheelchair into warp speed, my fastest speed of eight miles an hour, and I took off driving with my head control down the wide pathway toward the mountains.

I could feel my body, tense from the sense of being trapped at the hotel, start to relaxed. Taking deep breaths of clear fresh mountain air, I roamed and roamed until I was finally done. Then I came back to find Chris.

She had taken my picture while I was driving away from her on the pathway, because she was so struck by how my body language had changed from a sense of tight entrapment to being free and relaxed. I told her that I wished that she had been with me but that I had felt a need for some speed and movement. Chris already knew this and was fine with it.

She rejoiced that she had been able to take my picture. She loved watching how God had used a beautiful accessible garden, where I could roam as far as my wheelchair battery would go, to instantly transform my emotions and body.

In the Garden with God, I was happy to also be with Chris. I felt free, free, free at last!

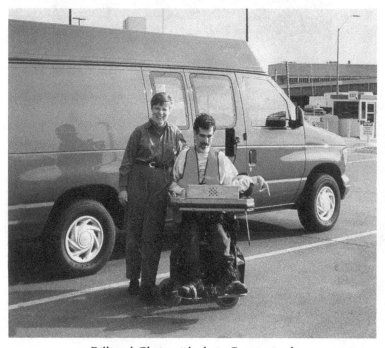

Bill and Chris with their Customized
Wheelchair Accessible Van, April 1996.

Bill driving in the Garden of the Gods (our Garden
of God) Colorado Springs, Colorado.

Endnotes

1. Bill Rush, "On the Road-Finally." *Nebraska Rehabilitation and Community Newsletter*, Vocational Rehabilitation, Nebraska Department of Education, (July/August 1996.) Reprinted with permission of the publisher.

2. Ibid.

3. Ibid.

4. Ibid.

CHAPTER 49

(Chris' Voice)

Active Waiting

"Chris, I got a letter from a friend, offering to help us create a bonding ceremony. People sometimes do this when they can't get or stay legally married because of problems with insurance coverage. What do you think of that idea?" Bill asked.

"You mean like a fake wedding?" I responded with some amazement. Then I added, "I wouldn't settle for a bonding ceremony, whatever that is, with any guy who was able-bodied, so why would I settle for it with you?"

"True. Bill responded. "I didn't like the idea either. It's got to be the real legal thing or we haven't gained anything."

"Are we ever going to get a back-up plan?" I asked Bill. I was beginning to feel like we were getting stuck. It seemed like marriage was very much out of reach. I now had my Green Card and we had purchased a van. What was I supposed to do next in creating our life together?

"Maybe we should just take the exemption route at the state and be done with it." I lamented.

But my terrier was not giving up his bone.

"We can't stop now, Chris." Bill said. "I have a wedge in the door at the state and I need to use it to push the door open for people with disabilities. I have to look after others too and not just myself. I know that a waiver exemption could lead to system change, and maybe we could get more exemptions. But I won't settle until we get ourselves a back-up plan. People with disabilities can't get jobs or have families because of the cost of their attendant and healthcare. We are all being denied access to the mainstream of American life. The current system demands that we stay poor in order to get our necessary care paid for by the state. The unfairness has got to stop."

And he added, "I have written a piece for the Lincoln Journal Star about this." (Bill's article, *It's time to Deliver on Promises to Americans with Disabilities,* April 27, 1996, is included at the end of this chapter.)

"It's great that you are working on this Bill." I said, half-heartedly.

Then I complained, "I remember you saying it would take ten years. It's 1996 and I've been in Nebraska over five years. We met almost eight years ago. I'm getting really tired of waiting, Bill."

Bill's response was unequivocal. "We have lots to do. We need to start thinking about a place to live. We'll be the first to ever do this with your comfortable assets so we will have to make sure that we protect them from the state's coffers when we get our license. It's going to take some work to do that. But it'll be worth it. Hang in there, Chris."

"OK." I said, still feeling pretty frustrated, but nonetheless fully assured that Bill knew what he was talking about.

"Besides Chris, God is on our side. He wants His people to be in families and to be productive for Him. He will help us," Bill added with a confident smile.

I was feeling selfish. I didn't really care about others with disabilities. Couldn't they take care of themselves? Creating our own life was enough for me, thank you very much.

But I knew that Bill would always be thinking of how he could support others with disabilities at the same time. He had learned this from the Disability Rights Movement. It was the essence of who Bill was and I would not be able to, nor would I want to change it.

Within days there were signs of another writing campaign underway at Bill's place. His dot matrix printer was clicking and squealing and a realm of paper was growing on the floor in front of it.

Bill was joining a growing national chorus in the disability rights community. He was petitioning members of both state and federal governments to support a Medicaid Buy-in option for workers with disabilities.

I folded his letters and stuffed them into their corresponding envelopes. It helped to have something concrete to do to support Bill's efforts on our behalf.

We had been very busy for the last five years since I had moved to Nebraska, working hard with people and agencies to push our lives forward. Bill and I had managed to get me a Green Card. I had gathered money for a van and then worked with Bill to get one to meet our needs. We had travelled and Bill was doing some speaking work.

Now I had run out of jobs to do to help us to create our life together. My day job as an occupational therapist continued with its normal ups and downs. As I began to realize that in order for us to be able to get married we would need something that we could not get by our efforts alone, I was feeling depressed.

My self-sufficiency had run its course. It was time for me to turn to God for a piece of legislation that I didn't know would ever be created.

Looking back, I can see that this period of 'active waiting' I was now entering was necessary for my relationship to God to grow. But like any kind of growth, it involved lots of growing pains.

I would eventually figure out that my 'job' was to wait for the legislation we needed in a state of obedience to God. "My job" wasn't to be in a state of resignation. Rather, it was the work of watching and praying for strength, hope and courage, for Bill and others, as God orchestrated the process through them.

Yes, I would get frustrated and angry at times, but ultimately I knew that our current difficult situation was not just about me. My feelings could not be indulged. My job was to walk by faith -not by my feelings. God would, as he had done throughout our journey, tell us what to do next when it was time, and not a minute too early.

For the eighteen months that we waited for some legislation to be proposed, I asked God daily for sufficient hope for that day. Then I simply got out of bed every morning and went about my day, awaiting a word from my God.

I also prayed for specific ways to help Bill. And I asked for the ability to stay out of his way so that he could do what he needed to do. I didn't want to nag him because he had enough on his plate.

Bill was going to see this through; I could choose to be a help-mate or a hindrance. I chose to embrace the privilege of being of help to him and others with disabilities.

I also prayed for encouragement to rain down on me to help me to stay the course. Some of the encouragement that I desperately needed, came through letters from state Senator Wesely to Bill that were written in response to his petition for a Medicaid Buy-In. Senator Wesely was most supportive of what he referred to as "Bill's idea".

Senator Wesely showed his support for Bill in concrete ways. He made it possible for Bill to communicate with the Head of the Department of Social Services about a possible Medicaid buy-In program. Senator Wesely would be a key person throughout this endeavor.

These letters showed me that Bill *was* having an impact on a governmental level. Senator Wesely was responding to Bill's determination and steadfastness and his ability to clearly and consistently explain what he and others with disabilities needed by helping him to push the idea forward.

God helped me to hang in and wait. He told me to watch and wait for Bill to direct our path forward thru the maze.

Reprinted with Permission of Lincoln Journal Star, Lincoln, Nebraska.

CHAPTER 50

(Chris' Voice)

Chris' Adult Baptism

While waiting on God to get us some back-up legislation, I had periods of real doubt that He would help us with this specific thing that we were asking for. After all, why would God care enough about our concerns when He had a universe to look after? Perhaps our need for more financial and political security before getting married, wasn't of concern relative to God's Kingdom anyway.

At these times I listened to and learn much from Bill.

He taught me how to grow closer to God. I saw Bill go to great lengths to go to worship, fellowship and to benefit from the teaching at First Baptist. In every kind of Nebraska weather, he was there to learn from them, and to grow closer to Jesus by hanging out with and letting those who were closer to Jesus rub off on him. Bill would organize his attendants to meet him all over town to be with some of the men from church, for breakfast.

Growing so close to God, on one occasion, Bill was admonished by the League of Human Dignity for putting "God" into a secular article that he had written for them, without even noticing. Laughingly, he told me about this, saying that he was becoming such a Follower of Jesus that He was naturally included in his writing. With an apology, Bill took God's name out of the article, so as not to offend anyone in the secular world, even though it had flowed so naturally into his story.

While Bill was growing closer to Jesus by the day, I was hiding behind all of my reasons for not going deeper. Rationalizing that I had been baptized as a child and raised in a mainline church, I told myself that I was already in the kingdom of God. I went to church and even Sunday school. Was that not enough for Jesus?

But something was missing. Bill's growing faith had energy and delight. My faith, if I had been honest with myself at the time, would have been described as being superficial and stagnant.

Bill had been raised in what I saw to be a 'bold revolutionary' Christian culture in the United States. He had no difficulty going straight to the King of the Universe to petition his case. Bolstered by his study of and indoctrination in civil rights, he was confident in his belief that God created all people to be equal and that therefore, God would support his efforts to free people with disabilities to become full members of society. Bill knew that his part of the plan was to do his work. And that God would enable him to do it.

Similarly, Pastor Lee, a converted Jew, and the current pastor at First Baptist in Lincoln was also bold in his faith practices. He believed that Christians could benefit from the Hebrew tradition of asking questions as a part of the learning process, even asking questions to God. He suggested that it was good practice to lay our questions at the Throne, as long as our attitude was one of reverence and respect.

Surprising to me at the time, but so clearly seen in hindsight, God's next step was to orchestrate a plan to get me to go straight to Him with my rationalizations.

It all started as a joke, I would later learn. Pastor Lee had asked if I would like to be baptized with another woman candidate Beth, and do it in bungee jumping style. I would later learn that he had assumed that I had already been baptized as an adult. The comment about bungee jumping into the baptismal tank was just banter. We had all laughed about it.

But, after this conversation with Pastor Lee, I started to think again about adult baptism. Attending an American Baptist church with Bill for several years now, I had contemplated adult baptism many times.

I was still struggling with whether I needed to be baptized as a necessary part of my growing faith and trust in God. I had been baptized as a child and later had been confirmed at the age of thirteen into a protestant church in Canada by a profession of faith. I had known Jesus for as long as I could remember. Was that not enough?

I started sharing my rationalizations with Bill, my teacher.

"Bill, I thought that there has to be a need to be baptized as an adult, such as repenting from some wayward lifestyle. We are not living a wayward lifestyle. We are both trying to live as God would have us live, even in this difficult situation."

"I respect the meaning of adult baptism as practiced in the Baptist church. But just because I am worshipping in a Baptist church doesn't feel like enough of a reason for me to be baptized again. It has to have more meaning than that," I concluded, thinking that I had made my case to Bill and to God.

Bill's response was, as usual very wise. He didn't rip at my sinful pride disguised as rationalization.

After all, Bill knew what it was like to have your own "reasons" for not going deeper with God. His had been anger and disappointment because of the discrimination that he had experienced in his life, before God had set him straight. Mine turned out to be simply ugly pride, disguised as intellectualizing.

Ultimately, I recognized there would be no rational reason for me not to do as Jesus had commanded in the great commission. That is, to be baptized in the name of the Father, Son and Holy Spirit, as a part of turning my life over to Him. Jesus knew that to do something so embodied (my words) would provide me with a meaningful experience of how much He loved me. Going down into the water and coming back up would remind me, in my body and my mind, that Jesus had come to die for me, to pay the price required for unlimited access to God NOW as well as eternal life with Him in heaven. No better deal could be found on earth.

Back to my conversation with Bill about adult baptism... Bill had stayed silent while I had outlined my reasons. My assumption is that he was turning my reluctance over to Jesus.

'Pray and see what the Holy Spirit would have you do" was Bill's response, said in all seriousness. And then he added with a howl of delight, "But if you do decide to be baptized, I will personally fill the tank for you!" He was laughing at the shear ridiculousness of his comment; Bill did not have the physical skills needed to fill a cup with water, let alone a baptismal tank.

This was a typical Bill response to anything that I would discuss with him. He put much thought into his responses, always concerned for my personal wellbeing and growth, and also what was best for me in relationship with him and with God.

And his trademark oddball comments disarmed people, including me. Without knowing it, we were laughing at the exclamation mark that he often added, via humor, at the end of his thought.

I decided that it was time to test out some of Bill's and Pastor Lee's boldness at the foot of the Throne. I asked God, "Why should I be baptized?" and added, "I don't want to do it just because I am worshipping in a Baptist church."

The next day I told Bill what had happened after I had asked God my question. "Wow Bill! Did I ever get answers to asking God why I should be baptized! I'm really amazed. Being bold really worked!"

"What did God tell you?" Bill asked with a big grin.

"He said that I could be baptized to publicly declare my desire to repent from my sins and to follow Him as an adult. He reminded me that I have sins, just like everyone else. He also said that it is a witness for Him, reminding us of what He has done for us through Jesus Christ. He also said that He knows that I am grateful for my upbringing and baptism as a child but that this is a different issue."

"So is that a good enough reason, Chris?" Bill asked, hopefulness displayed all over his face.

"Oh yes! Do you know what today is, Bill?" I responded.

"Of course, it's Canadian Thanksgiving."

"And do you know when the next baptism is going to be at church?" I asked.

"American Thanksgiving in November," Bill said.

"It's perfect," I said. "I can give thanks to God on American Thanksgiving for a church home in the United States. I will thank God for the timing of truly crystalizing my desire to be baptized on Canadian Thanksgiving, that has allowed me to consciously further my growth in Him and join First Baptist church on a holiday set aside for giving thanks to God in America."

Seven weeks later, on December 1st, 1996, I walked into the baptismal tank at First Baptist with Pastor Lee and. turned to face him. He asked me to answer questions that would attest to my faith and I was told to answer each question with an affirmation of my belief.

"Chris, do you proclaim Jesus Christ as your Lord and Savior? Do you believe that He has forgiven all your sins and prepared a place in heaven for you for all eternity? Do you agree to use your spiritual gifts to the benefit of this church and agree to be ministered to by the members of this church?" It was felt wonderful to answer each question, with a simple "Yes, I do."

Pastor Lee then moved to my side to get ready to dunk me. He said, "By the authority granted to me as a minister of the gospel of Christ and according to your own faith testimony, I baptize you in the name of the Father, Son and Holy Spirit."

With my hands on my chest, I was gently lowered by Pastor Lee backwards under the water, and then was supported by him to lift myself upright again, symbolizing my desire to die with Christ and be born again with Him as my Lord and my Savior.

Friends and Bill's mom who had come especially for this occasion, greeted me at the end of the church service. I was delighted to have these important people come to witness my spiritual milestone.

"So what did you think of the dunking?" Bill asked me later that day with a smile.

"I got water up my nose but in spite of that, the experience was very profound," I said. "Christ knew what He was doing, I guess. The whole dunking thing, representing dying to self and then getting a new life in Christ, similar to how Christ had died for me and then was resurrected, is a very cool experience. Taking on accountability for my belief in Christ as an adult feels really good too." I responded with a big smile.

CHAPTER 51

(Chris' Voice)

A Back-Up Plan on the Horizon

"Our back-up plan is on the horizon, Chris. I can see it from here but we don't have it quite yet." Bill said, showing me a newspaper article with a look of excitement and anticipation on his face.

I read the local section of the *Lincoln Journal Star* for Jan 12, 1998. The title of the article was, "Proposal could prevent Medicaid loss."

Bill's voice was again speaking on behalf of Nebraskans with disabilities, for both present and future generations:

> "*Wednesday, Rush urged members of the Health and Human Services committee to support LB1078 so others don't have to face the same struggles.*
>
> *We deserve to be treated, not as an exception, but as the norm," he said. "Now that (people with disabilities) are out of the closet, we want families, home and jobs, not necessarily in that order."*
>
> *But many disabled Nebraskans can't have families or jobs without losing their Medicaid coverage, Rush said.*
>
> "*And that can mean going without health coverage, having to pay high premiums or copayments*

on low wages or having coverage which doesn't pay for the care people need, such as home care aides."

LB1078, introduced by Sen. Don Wesely of Lincoln, aims to remedy the situation by allowing disabled Nebraskans to maintain Medicaid coverage at higher incomes. But it would require people to pay premiums to the state at higher income levels.

Current law allows coverage only for people whose household incomes are at 100 percent of the poverty level or below.

Wesely's proposal would raise the cutoff to 500 percent of poverty, if the federal government agrees, or 250 percent without federal approval. Those covered would have to pay premiums that increase with the family income.

Nebraska health and Human Services System officials estimated the plan would add 1,000 people to the Medicaid rolls, at a cost to the state of $4 million a year. But Wesely estimated that only 300 to 500 people actually would take advantage of the plan.

The proposal could actually save the state money, said Tim Kolb of Franklin (another Nebraskan with a disability). Many people with disabilities choose to remain on welfare, using tax dollars instead of paying them. They also choose to live together rather instead of getting married.

The proposal would make it easier for disabled people to find work, Rush said. It would ease the fears of employers about rising health care premiums. It would provide coverage for medication, attendant care and other care that some disabled people need to get to work." [1]

"Sure looks like we are getting really close, Bill!' I exclaimed with amazement after I finished reading the article.

The rescue airplane is on the radar. The Calvary is coming! I thought to myself.

With God's help, Bill and many other persons with disabilities had fought courageously to get this radical idea of a Medicaid Buy-In proposed after what Bill had said was a total of five years of serious collective work. The notion that people with disabilities wanted to work was progressive enough. The idea that this minority group would want to help to pay for their own health and attendant care needs, in order to allow them to join the mainstream of the American workforce, was downright futuristic.

Bill had shared with me that the Disability Rights movement was believed to be the fastest social movement in history. In less that 50 years, individuals with disabilities had moved from being hidden in family homes and institutions in the 1950's, with limited opportunities in the social, educational and vocational aspects of American life, to pushing open doors to the beginning of full participation for some in the mainstream by the end of the 20th century.

And, given that so many people with disabilities could not get to or access voting stations until the 1984 Federal Voting Accessibility legislation for the elderly and handicapped was passed, disability rights advocacy, I surmised, must have been happening at the grass roots level, unnoticed for a many decades. Parents of individuals with disabilities, like Bill's mom and dad, had in fact, begun this movement, in their own communities, by asking for what their children needed to attend schools and advocating for them to be a part of their local communities. Children of the 50's and 60's were merely taking their parent's work to the next level, pushing for access to be able to have full lives as adults. It would take decades of additional work to see the fullness of this dream come true, but a course was being set for future generations of Americans with disabilities.

I was learning about so many noteworthy aspects of the distinctiveness of the disability rights movement. For example, unlike other minority groups, financial resources were required by this minority group in order for them to take their rightful place in society. The business lobby, because of the enormous costs to retroactively making retail spaces accessible had, fiercely opposed the passage of the Americans with Disabilities Act of 1990.

Depending upon the disability that the individual had, expensive resources might be needed, in order to engage minimally if not fully in the world. For example, I once calculated, when driving with Bill in our vehicle that I was driving around with approximately $100,000 worth of adaptive equipment. Bill's attendant care costs ran upwards of $40,000 USD per year in 1998.

Bill had fought throughout his adult life to push the boundaries of outdated and archaic programs set by limited mindset bureaucrats in order for him to have a meaningful life outside of an institution. When I entered a relationship with Bill, I became a tag-along in the next steps of his advocacy work towards marriage and possibility for productive and paid work, with more than one state programming option to do so. Our stubborn refusal to live together in poverty in order to access whatever the state might dole out to us, had pitted us against the government.

Furthermore, the threat of institutionalization had taken its toll. We would not put all of our eggs in one basket and watch the state, when under political pressure to cut funds, take them all away from us.

I would later learn that the Nebraska legislative bill LB 1078 was written in response to what the federal government had offered in the Balanced Budget of 1997, section 4733, Disabled Worker Buy-In Option. This similar legislation, offered at the federal level, was written to support individual state legislatures in their efforts to provide health care coverage, for Americans with Disabilities wanting to go to work. (A copy of this legislation is included with this chapter.)

A much later piece of legislation, Bill 261, passed January 16, 2013 would take this work even further, for future generations. (A copy of this legislation is included with this chapter.)

Bill told me how grateful he was for state Senator Wesely's support.

"He has been with us all the way. He was willing to propose this landmark legislation in the legislature. We're calling it the Medicaid

Buy-In legislation. It probably won't pass this time because of the fiscal note attached to it. But we will get a scaled down version, sooner rather than later."

I found myself thinking about the two years of waiting for this legislation and the many things that I had learned during that time.

When I didn't always *feel* calm or peaceful during the extended period of waiting for the unknown, I acted like I did and my feelings eventually caught up with my behavior. Copying my British ancestors' history of having a "stiff upper lip" had worked. I had merely acted the way that had been modeled for me by my parents and grandparents. These emotionally stable people believed that if you acted a certain way, then you would eventually come to feel that way.

I found that God had used this time to strengthen my 'trust in Him muscle'. Trained as an occupational therapist I knew that unused muscles would atrophy and that specific types of resistance applied to muscles would strengthen them. My "trust in God muscle" had been pretty weak at the beginning of the time of waiting, and now it was strong because of the work required to not give in to doubt that Bill would get the legislation that he wanted as his "back up plan" and push disability rights forward.

I also believed that my upbringing in a constitutional monarchy had been good preparation for this time of learning about and trusting God's sovereignty over my life. God would deliver what was needed according to His timing and not mine. He taught me that He is not a vending machine. He would not dispense candy bars or blessing just because I gave Him praise or a prayer.

I might not like His timing, but He could be trusted with my life, both on earth and for eternity, because He knew what was best for me.

My obedience in waiting was thankfully, being rewarded, not only with the proposal of this specific legislation but also with spiritual fruits of patience, faithfulness and peace, traits that can only be developed under consistently applied pressure.

God had heard the cry of my heart and Bill's heart for this legislation to be moving forward. He had deemed it right and just to help Bill and others to achieve what they were willing to work for. God had honored the work of Bill and others with disabilities because they had done it for the benefit of many people with disabilities.

They had done their hard work but God had enabled them. And I had had the privilege of being able to watch all of this unfold.

Back in our conversation, I heard Bill say, "We're getting close enough to the legislation we need, Chris. It's time to take the next step. Let's start talking to anyone and everyone about getting us a house." Bill said.

"Oh yes!" I said, with relief and excitement that we were finally moving forward again.

LOCAL

Page design: George Wright

Proposal could prevent Medicaid loss

BY MARTHA STODDARD
Lincoln Journal Star

Bill Rush of Lincoln had to seek special permission from state officials to get married.

If he hadn't — or if he and his fiancee had been unsuccessful in their campaign for permission — he would have lost the Medicaid coverage that pays for aides to help him get up and get through his day.

Wednesday, Rush urged members of the Health and Human Services Committee to support LB1078 so others don't have to face the same struggles.

"We deserve to be treated, not as an exception, but as the norm," he said. "Now that (disabled people) are out of the closet, we want families, homes and jobs, not necessarily in that order."

But many disabled Nebraskans can't get families or jobs without losing their Medicaid coverage, Rush said.

And that can mean going without health coverage, having to pay high premiums or copayments on low wages or having coverage which doesn't pay for the care people need, such as home care aides.

LB1078, introduced by Sen. Don Wesely of Lincoln, aims to remedy the situation by allowing disabled Nebraskans to maintain Medicaid coverage at higher incomes. But it would require people to pay premiums to the state at higher income levels.

Current law allows coverage only for people whose household incomes are at 100 percent of the poverty level or below.

Wesely's proposal would raise the cutoff point to 500 percent of poverty, if the federal government agrees, or 250 percent without federal approval. Those covered would have to

pay premiums that increase with the family income.

Nebraska Health and Human Services System officials estimated the plan would add 1,000 people to the Medicaid rolls, at a cost to the state of $4 million a year. But Wesely estimated that only 300 to 500 people actually would take advantage of the plan.

The proposal actually could save the state money, said Tim Kolb of Franklin. Many people with disabilities choose to remain on welfare — using tax dollars instead of paying them. They also choose to live together instead of getting married.

"I, like many of my colleagues, want to be married and employed but what's normal and anticipated for the nondisabled is beyond the boards of what's accepted for the disabled," Kolb said.

The proposal would make it easier for disabled people to find work, Rush said. It would ease the fears of

employers about rising health care premiums. It would provide coverage for the medications, aides and other care that some disabled people need to get to work.

Reprinted with permission of Lincoln Journal Star, Lincoln Nebraska.

LB 1078 LB 1078

LEGISLATURE OF NEBRASKA

NINETY-FIFTH LEGISLATURE

SECOND SESSION

LEGISLATIVE BILL 1078

Introduced by Wesely, 26

Read first time January 12, 1998

Committee: Health and Human Services

A BILL

1 FOR AN ACT relating to medical assistance; to amend section
2   68-1020, Reissue Revised Statutes of Nebraska; to change
3   provisions relating to eligibility; and to repeal the
4   original section.
5 Be it enacted by the people of the State of Nebraska,

-1-

1   Section 1. Section 68-1020, Reissue Revised Statutes of

2   Nebraska, is amended to read:

3   68-1020. (1) Medical assistance shall be paid on behalf

4   of dependent children, aged persons, blind individuals, and

5   disabled individuals, as defined in sections 43-504 and 68-1002 to

6   68-1005, and on behalf of all individuals less than twenty-one

7   years of age who are eligible under section 1905(a) of the federal

8   Social Security Act, as amended.

9   (2) The Director of Finance and Support shall adopt and

10   promulgate rules and regulations governing provision of such

11   medical assistance benefits to qualified individuals:

12   (a) Who are presumptively eligible as allowed under 42

13   U.S.C. 1396a, as amended; or

14   (b) Who have income at or below one hundred fifty percent

15   of the Office of Management and Budget income poverty guidelines,

16   without regard to resources, including children up to such age as

17   allowed under 42 U.S.C. 1396a, as amended.

18   (3) Medical assistance shall be paid on behalf of

19   disabled persons as defined in section 68-1005 who are in families

20   whose income is less than five hundred percent of the income

21   official poverty line applicable to a family of the size involved

22   and who but for earnings in excess of the limit established under

23   42 U.S.C. 1396d(g)(2)(B) of the federal Social Security Act, as

24   amended, would be considered to be receiving federal Supplemental

25   Security Income. Such disabled persons shall be subject to payment

26   of premiums as a percentage of the family's gross income. The

27   premium payment shall be the percentage of family income in Column

28   B which corresponds with the family's income as a percentage of the

-2-

276

1 official poverty line in Column A:

2   Column A   Column B

3   Income as a   Premium as

4   percentage of   percentage

5   official poverty   of the family's

6   line   gross income

7   101% to 199%   3%

8   200% to 299%   6%

9   300% to 399%   9%

10   400% to 500%   12%

11 If the federal Health Care Financing Administration does not

12 approve the higher income limit for persons described in this

13 subdivision, the premium payment shall be the percentage of family

14 income in Column B which corresponds with the family's income as a

15 percentage of the official poverty line in Column A:

16   Column A   Column B

17   Income as a   Premium as

18   percentage of   percentage

19   official poverty   of the family's

20   line   gross income

21   101% to 199%   3%

22   200% to 250%   6%

23   Sec. 2.   Original section 68-1020, Reissue Revised

24 Statutes of Nebraska, is repealed.

-3-

277

LB 261   LB 261

LEGISLATURE OF NEBRASKA

ONE HUNDRED THIRD LEGISLATURE

FIRST SESSION

LEGISLATIVE BILL 261

Introduced by Gloor, 35.

Read first time January 16, 2013

Committee:

A BILL

1   FOR AN ACT relating to public health and welfare; to adopt the

2   Medicaid Insurance for Workers with Disabilities Act; and

3   to create an advisory committee.

4   Be it enacted by the people of the State of Nebraska,

-1-

278

1   Section 1. Sections 1 to 6 of this act shall be known and

2   may be cited as the Medicaid Insurance for Workers with Disabilities

3   Act.

4   Sec. 2. The Legislature finds and declares that:

5   (1) The federal Ticket to Work and Work Incentives

6   Improvement Act of 1999, updated in 2008, is designed to provide

7   clear criteria for Social Security Disability Insurance and

8   Supplemental Security Income beneficiaries to remove employment

9   disincentives and to support their financial independence through

10 work; and

11   (2) Updating Nebraska's current Medicaid Insurance for

12 Workers with Disabilities program to utilize the federal Ticket to

13 Work and Work Incentives Act of 1999 would encourage the following

14 stated purposes of the federal act: (a) To provide health care and

15 employment services to individuals with disabilities that will enable

16 those individuals to reduce their dependency on cash benefit

17 programs; and (b) to encourage states to adopt the option of allowing

18 individuals with disabilities to purchase medicaid coverage that is

19 necessary to enable such individuals to maintain employment.

20   Sec. 3. For purposes of the Medicaid Insurance for

21 Workers with Disabilities Act:

22   (1) Department means the Department of Health and Human

23 Services;

24   (2) Employed individual with a medically improved

25 condition means a person who (a) is at least sixteen but less than

-2-

1 sixty-five years of age, (b) ceases to be eligible for medical

2 assistance under the medical assistance program established in

3 section 68-903 because the individual, by reason of medical

4 improvement, is determined at the time of a disability determination

5 service or regularly scheduled continuing disability review to no

6 longer be eligible for benefits, (c) continues to have a severe

7 medically determinable impairment, and (d)(i) is earning at least the

8 applicable minimum wage and working at least forty hours per month or

9 (ii) is engaged in a work effort that meets substantial and

10 reasonable threshold criteria for hours of work, wages, or other

11 measures; and

12   (3) Person with a disability who is employed means a

13 person who is at least sixteen years of age but less than sixty-five

14 years of age and who (a) is disabled under 42 U.S.C., as it existed

15 on January 1, 2013, or (b) has been determined to be disabled by the

16 department.

17   Sec. 4. (1) Medical assistance from the medical

18 assistance program established in section 68-903 shall continue to be

19 paid on behalf of a person with a disability who is employed,

20 including an employed individual with a medically improved condition,

21 whose countable family income is less than two-hundred-fifty percent

22 of the Office of Management and Budget income poverty guideline for

23 the size of family involved. Countable family income shall equal the

24 sum of all unearned and earned income minus the allowable standard

25 Supplemental Security Income Exclusions as specified in 42 U.S.C.

OUR LIFE OUR WAY

1   1382a, as it existed on January 1, 2013, and, if the participant is

2   in a designated trial work period or extended period of eligibility,

3   minus his or her Social Security Disability Insurance unearned

4   income. Allowable assets limits shall be determined by counting the

5   number of individuals in the family, with limits of (a) ten thousand

6   dollars for a family of one, (b) fifteen thousand dollars for a

7   family of two, and (c) fifteen thousand dollars for a family of three

8   plus an additional twenty-five dollars per additional individual. All

9   assets and resources specified in 42 U.S.C. 1382b, as it existed on

10 January 1, 2013, and eligible retirement accounts shall not be

11 considered as part of these allowable asset limits.

12   (2) Such recipients of medical assistance whose countable

13 family income is one hundred percent or more of the income poverty

14 guideline may be required to pay a premium in an amount established

15 by the department in rules and regulations using a sliding-fee or

16 tiered-fee approach, but the premium shall not exceed seven percent

17 of the recipient family's countable unearned income plus three

18 percent of the recipient family's countable earned income.

19   (3) Such recipients of medical assistance who

20 subsequently lose employment shall be able to continue to be eligible

21 for medical assistance for up to six months if (a) they demonstrate

22 that they are (i) currently looking for employment if the loss of

23 employment was due to involuntary job loss or (ii) unfit to work

24 because of a medical necessity and (b) they continue to pay any

25 premiums as required in subsection (2) of this section.

-4-

281

1   Sec. 5. In order to increase the utilization and

2   effectiveness of the program under section 4 of this act, the

3   department shall:

4   (1) Provide education and training about the program to

5   all appropriate staff of the department;

6   (2) Conduct outreach and education about the availability

7   and benefits of the program focused on the populations that can

8   benefit from the program;

9   (3) Submit a report to the Legislature and Governor, on a

10   biennial basis, to show the effectiveness of the program. The report

11   shall contain the following information: (a) The number of

12   individuals enrolled in the program, (b) demographic information

13   about the recipients, including age, gender, disability type,

14   ethnicity, educational level, county of residence, Title II or Title

15   XVI eligibility, earned income, and amount of premium payment, (c)

16   internal and external educational activities about the availability

17   and purpose of the program, (d) outreach activities to increase the

18   utilization of the program, (e) the costs and benefits of the medical

19   assistance provided pursuant to section 4 of this act, and (f) the

20   number of people who are classified as medically needy, and specific

21   goals as to how to increase participation in the program; and

22   (4) Develop a plan to designate nonprofit employment

23   networks that have benefit specialists, to work as work-incentive

24   specialists, as specified in 42 U.S.C. 1320b-20, as it existed on

25   January 1, 2013. The benefit specialists shall work with program

-5-

LB 261   LB 261

1   participants and potential program participants to (a) meet the

2   stated   purpose   of   the   Medicaid   Insurance   for   Workers   with

3   Disabilities Act, (b) increase participation in the program, and (c)

4   achieve greater self sufficiency.

5   Sec. 6. The department may adopt and promulgate rules and

6   regulations to carry out the Medicaid Insurance for Workers with

7   Disabilities Act.

-6-

Endnotes

[1]   Rush, William, 1998. "Proposal Could Prevent Medicaid Loss." Lincoln Journal Star, January 12.

CHAPTER 52

(Bill's Voice)

Building A Home for Us

"Bill and Chris, even though you don't financially qualify for the housing program that we offer, perhaps we can find a way for you to be able to speak with the builder and the architect that we use," the coordinator offered.

Using my journalism technique of following all possible leads I found this seminar for us to attend, entitled, "How to buy your own house" offered by Neighborhoods Inc., a non-profit housing development agency committed to redeveloping rundown areas of the city of Lincoln by offering affordable housing to people with low incomes.

I knew that we didn't meet the income guidelines for this program. But I was hoping that we might make some connections through this agency to builders and /or architects who might work with us.

The problem was not a lack of information regarding accessible housing. The League of Human Dignity, Lincoln's Independent Living Center had access to much information regarding accessible housing designs.

Passage of some key pieces of national legislation had set the stage for the development of accessible housing designs. We were, as usual, ahead of the national curve. We wanted to build our own home, independent from any low income program, typically used by people with disabilities.

The Fair Housing Act of 1988, enacted by President Regan started accessible housing, in that disability was added to the list of people for whom it was illegal to discriminate in the renting or selling of property. It was an update to the Fair Housing Act of 1968 that prohibited discrimination in renting or selling to people because of color, sex, race, national origin or religion. As a result of the 1988 legislation, the US department of Housing and Urban Development was required to make accessible housing available to low income persons with disabilities, and information about how to build accessible housing was available starting in the early 90's.

With the passage of the Americans with Disabilities Act, one could easily find Universal Accessibility Standards to be used for construction of public buildings. For example The Center for Universal Design at North Carolina State University had created many resources to assist us. [1]

Our problem was one of trying to figure out who would work with us in Lincoln to put the knowledge of accessible housing into practice to build a home especially made for us. We didn't fit any of the programs or options available for poor people. And we couldn't afford a custom builder that someone who was rich could use to build them a one-of-a kind accessible home.

In addition to being difficult to figure out how to physically construct it, building a house before we got married felt to us like we were putting the cart before the horse, even perhaps doing things backwards. As Christian believers, Chris and I both believed in the sanctity of marriage, meaning that we believed that God wanted us to getting married before living together. But here we were, building a house together before we were married!

We didn't have the luxury of doing things the way that other Christian couples did. Nothing about our situation was "typical."

So while we built a house we continued to live in two different apartments. Chris spent lots of time at my place, eating there and hanging with me a lot, sharing our life together and caring about each other, but she would sleep in her own place downstairs. Sometimes

Chris would crash on my couch and stay overnight with me. It felt so good to have her with me at my place. But my couch did not provide a comfortable sleep for her. She would need to get back to her bed for some good rest.

We planned to move Chris into the house once it was built. I would move in after we married. Yes, it was odd, but workable.

Throughout the long process of working on the back-up plan and getting a house, I kept remembering what my mom and dad had said to me after they both met Chris. Mom thought that Chris was my soul mate. Dad said that he thought that I could make this work. But he cautioned me to take care of Chris and above all to not hurt her. My dad was a smart man and he liked Chris. I was determined to follow my dad's instructions and to take care of Chris.

Call me old fashioned, I don't care. I took my dad's words about taking care of Chris to include honoring her emotionally and sexually.

I would do anything to honor Chris. I loved her more than life itself. She was the dream that came true, the miracle that God sent me. I wanted us to feel good about what we had together. I would not demand or manipulate her emotionally or sexually because love does not do those things.

When we first met, God was a part of our lives but not prominent, and therefore, not surprisingly He was not in the center of our relationship. As a result, our physical relationship at the beginning was not following what God would have wanted for us. After all, disability or no disability, we were young and very much in love with each other from the first day we met. And we both came from cultures that claimed that sex outside of marriage was both normal and natural.

But after spending time together and with our church family, we grew closer to each other and to God. When we learned and also saw modeled for us, Christians marriages, where sex is to be kept within the confines of marriage, we made a commitment to God as a couple to honor this. We struggled mightily from that point forward to keep our physical relationship for our marriage but we did succeed.

At this point in time, taking care of Chris also meant that I was determined to protect her assets. In order to protect Chris' assets we had to spend them down before we got married. Otherwise, if we signed up for the Spousal Impoverishment Program at this stage of the game, the state bureaucrats would help themselves to Chris' savings account.

It made the most sense to spend down Chris' assets by buying a house, something that we would need after we were married and wasn't on the list for confiscation. This seemed to be the best creative solution to our latest problem with the state. But we just had to accept and live with the fact that it seemed backwards.

Like everything else we did, we went about figuring out how to get a house that would meet our needs in a painfully meticulous way.

We wrestled with the decision of whether to buy an existing house and remodel it or to build a new house from scratch. I wanted to build a new house because I had seen too many buildings that had been remodeled to make them accessible. Too often, builders had to make too many compromises. I didn't want to have to make compromises in our home.

Chris wanted to remodel an existing house. She thought that it would be cheaper and easier, but after seeing how expensive remodeling was, she agreed with me that building from scratch was the way to go." [2]

The low-income program's architect agreed to meet with us and he was particularly helpful. He even went along with our crazy ideas.

"When we rejected all his floor plans, he slapped a blank piece of onionskin paper down and asked, "What do you want? We have to keep the outside pretty much as is. But, you can have the inside however you want." [3]

Delighted by the architect's willingness to work with us, we set about applying what we knew about universal design to our housing plan.

"Chris and I were firm believers (fanatics, actually) in universal design. Universal design is making products and environments to be usable by all people, to the greatest extent possible, without the need for adaptation or specialized design. We could see that universal design benefits people of all ages and abilities. This meant that while we supposedly built our house to accommodate my needs, it would also accommodate Chris' needs as she grows older and loses some of her functioning.

We knew that we wanted and needed large rooms, 48-inch doorways, no hallways, no 90- degree turns, more electrical outlets and a skylight for extra lighting." [4]

We wanted both shower and bath options in the bathroom, and also wanted a raised toilet seat with a place for handrails should Chris need them at some point in the future. We wanted everything that we might possibly need to be located on one level, with ramps rather than stairs to get into the house entrances. Because of where we lived, we wanted a cement brick utility room made on the first floor to function as a tornado shelter. I planned to use door openers that I could activate with my feet and that didn't need a power source to get into the tornado room when I was home alone. We would add electronic door openers to at least one exterior door in the house. By asking for these accommodations to be built right into our home, we assumed that we would be able to live comfortably in it for many years.

Our home would need remote controlled lights and appliances so that I could access them when Chris was not around. Chris could also make use of the electronics when she was home. We planned to use the X-10 system, because of its simplicity. We could use the X-10 appliance modules, plugged into wall sockets or replace the wall socket with an X-10 switch. I knew that my friend Mark would help with any necessary wiring.

Neighborhoods Inc. continued to support us, even if we weren't their official clients, typical or otherwise. They contacted their builder, Ken Inness to see if he would work with us to build our one of a kind house in one of the target areas. He agreed. Neighborhoods Inc. also helped us make connections with the city to help us to buy a piece of land in a target area of the city that would best meet our needs. The city offered us a forgivable loan in return for living in our home in the target area for a few years.

The bank gave Chris a loan to supplement her savings to pay for the building of our house.

By July of 1998, our small piece of land was being converted into the home of our dreams!

Chris and I drove our Candy Red van from our apartment complex over to the construction site several times a week. We delighted in watching each and every phase of our one of a kind home being built.

I believe that God smiled at the creativity we used while being obedient to what we believed was His plan for us, in terms of not living together until we were married.

Endnotes

1. Center for Universal Design, North Carolina State University
2. Bill Rush, "The Making of a Square Hole." *On The Level,* the Newsletter of The League of Human Dignity, Nebraska's Independent Living Center, (November/December 1999)
3. Ibid.
4. Ibid.

CHAPTER 53

(Chris' Voice)

Spousal Impoverishment Dry Run

Some bureaucrat was going through my financial papers, listing all of my assets on a large marker board and I was feeling sick to my stomach.

Bill had set up this "Spousal Impoverishment Dry Run" with the state in August of 1998. We needed this meeting so that we would have time to figure out how to deal with my side of the problems with the government before we got married.

Bill's side of the problems with the state involved making sure that he was still able to get his necessary and very expensive home health care coordinated attendant care services covered by the state funded system even once we were married and his wife had a regular salary. Bill would have to remain poor in order to qualify for the Medicaid Waiver program. (Fig. 1 Home and Community Waver Services, Nebraska Department of Social Services) He would be required to keep a separate bank account from mine and demonstrate that his earnings were below a certain amount.

On the other hand, my side of our problem with the state involved making sure that I would be allowed to keep working and saving normally as Bill's wife, without having to be the physical or the primary financial provider of his attendant care. I wanted to pay for our living expenses and contribute towards Bill's care costs but not be burdened by them.

I wanted to be Bill's wife, not his attendant nor his ongoing primary source of income for his very expensive attendant care. We knew that our marriage would not survive if I was either or both of these.

Bill's work pinning the federal and state levels of government against each other resulted in a two program solution being suggested to get us what we wanted and needed for our marriage. The solutions involved Bill having access to the Medicaid Waiver program and I being enrolled in the Spousal Impoverishment program. (fig. 2 Nebraska Spousal Impoverishment) The only problem was that the Spousal Impoverishment Program was created to respond to the financial needs of senior couples, and we were not old.

Fitting us as a younger couple into this program felt like we were jamming a round peg in a square hole. But we were determined to make it work. And this meeting was our attempt to figure out how we were going to get me into the Spousal Improverishment program, as a person with a lower middle class income.

Before this meeting with the state, Bill explained the history of the Spousal Impoverishment program to me. After I heard it, I was able to understand why we needed it, what the program needed from me and what I needed to do to get into it.

The program was set up to help elderly couples financially as they aged and one of them became sick and needed to move into a nursing facility. When one elderly person in a couple who had some assets needed nursing home care, the "community" spouse of that person (the one staying at the couple's home in the community) was becoming "impoverished" by the nursing home industry, in order to pay for the care of the sick spouse.

Sadly, the nursing home industry could demand that the spouse at home sell everything to pay for the care of the sick spouse including the family home, car and money for basic living expenses, before the state would start to pay for the care of the ill spouse. This would leave nothing for the at-home spouse to live on. At-home spouses were going from a comfortable lifestyle to becoming destitute in order to pay for their sick spouse's nursing home care.

In response to this problem among older middle class couples, the US federal government created a program that would allow the sick spouse to access Medicaid services to pay for their nursing home care, in exchange for the couple giving the Medicaid system the remainder of their assets, but only beyond a preset amount. The government would not touch the family home or car because the spouse living outside of the nursing home would need them. And, if the at-home spouse did not have enough to pay for basics like food, the government would support them financially so that they would not become "impoverished." This program allowed the "community" spouse to have the dignity of being able to stay in the family home while the sick spouse had the care they needed for as long as they lived.

Bill and I didn't fit into this middle class senior demographic. We were at the beginning of our earning lives and we wanted to be able to earn money like everyone else, partly to help to pay for a reasonable amount of Bill's care, such as what one would pay for a medical insurance premium. Unlike older people who are living off their assets, at the time of applying for the program, I was at a stage in my life where I was accumulating my savings for my life's needs such as a house and retirement. And Bill because of his need for the Medicaid program had already been living in poverty.

But re-writing the program for younger people would take years of work by federal and state regulators. Because the federal government believed that this program could be workable for us, they told the Nebraska state government to 'let us in' to this program.

So we had to make it work. It was our only option except for the back-up plan which was not yet passed and was just that, a back–up plan.

On the positive side, once I got into this program I would be financially "home free." Since older people were not expected to accumulate wealth after entering the program, the government would not be concerned about my future assets. In fact, the government's concern was that I have enough income to live and they would check in with me to make sure that I had at least the preset amount available to meet my basic needs.

Bill and I relished the sweet irony of our situation.

This program set up to help one older spouse die with dignity in a nursing home while keeping the well spouse supported in the community, was now being used to give us a chance at a life together as young people, both living in the community.

We were truly pioneers, trying out something new on the frontier.

And I praised God for giving Bill the courage and ability to push for a workable solution, between the Feds and the state of Nebraska.

Nevertheless, now, sitting before the bureaucrat, I was squirming. Even though I knew it was the bureaucrat's job to go through my financial papers and that we had asked for it, I couldn't help feeling like some greedy stranger was trying to find ways to take my money from me, in the name of the state. It was my first experience of having "Big Brother" "pry" into my personal affairs. I was feeling violated.

The bureaucrat, in a calm manner, shared with me that she was looking for all "countable" resources.

These were what I called the "fair game" assets, ones that they would look for in making a determination of how much I was allowed to keep and how much needed to be given to the government, when we signed up for the Spousal Impoverishment program.

These included but were not limited to savings, checking or other bank accounts, stocks, bonds, time certificates, investments, cash on hand, accessible trust funds, cash value of life insurance if the face value exceeds $1500 per person, and real property, other than a home. She said that we were allowed to have one vehicle and one house. A second or third vehicle would be "countable." The bureaucrat also said that most retirement accounts could be accessed and that mine with the Nebraska Teachers would most likely be "countable."

The bureaucrat quickly calculated that the total value of my personal assets could not exceed $16,152.00 at the time of my marriage.

The sum of my Nebraska state teacher's retirement account total value, cash value of my life insurance policy, and money from my IRA account was quite a bit more than the total allowed. And, if I choose to disclose my 'out of country' Canadian accounts, I more than doubled the allowable amount. This did not include the money that sat in my bank accounts, awaiting transfer to the lending company once the house was completed.

I needed my car to get to work and to do my job so I couldn't let the state take it from me at the time of our wedding. Using our accessible van for my work was not an option for several reasons including the fact that I travelled over a thousand miles a month, the van was a gas guzzler, and it needed to last because replacing it was going to cost a lot of money.

We'll need to do some creative work to "protect" my vital assets before we get married, I thought to myself, stunned to see an actual number value of my total liquid assets at the time, and the difference between it and the number that I couldn't go above.

I need to clarify that I was not a rich person according to North American standards at the time of this meeting. I had only a middle class income and I had been merely doing as I had been taught by my parents. They encouraged me to save a little from each paycheck so that I would have money put away for a house, a rainy day and for my retirement. Following their example, I now had some savings of various kinds in various places after working for sixteen years.

But there were situations, such as the one I was in right now, where it was not such a good idea to have been financially conservative. I had to figure out how to get rid of some of my assets-at least temporarily- or the state would take them from me.

Bill and I thanked the bureaucrat for her assistance with this "dry run" and left the state building.

"Bill we need a plan." I said.

"I'm already working on it," Bill stated, and we headed for our apartment building. No doubt Bill had been doing some problem-solving during the meeting, figuring out how we might get beyond this latest hurdle, allowing me to keep as much of my hard-earned and most importantly needed either now or in the future resources.

Leaving Bill to ""work on it," I had my job to get back to, and quickly got on my way.

When I returned to Bill's place later that afternoon, I found Bill working on a letter to the Nebraska Public Employees Retirement Systems to question whether my account could be withdrawn while I was still employed by a state school agency. His logic was that the state could not demand that I leave my job to get married and if my retirement account was inaccessible while I was working, then the Spousal Impoverishment program could not get to my retirement fund. I liked Bill's logic.

Bill asked me if my IRA retirement accounts could be spent down on the house. That was another good idea. I would call and ask about that.

"These are really good solutions to protecting my assets and using them for what we need right now," I said and then added. "Bill, what should we do about my car?"

"That's easy Chris. My mom will own it for you for 6 months around the wedding."

He then rolled over to his Ability Phone and pressed the pre-programmed button to make a call to his mom. I heard Lois answer over Bill's speaker phone.

"Hi Bill. What's up?" Lois answered in her cheery voice.

"We need to protect Chris' assets from the state so that they won't take them when we get married. We need someone to own her car for 6 months or so."

"Sure. I can do that." Lois responded without hesitation.

I stood by the microphone to speak with her. "That would be great. I'll pay for the insurance and the license. We just need to move it into someone else's name for six months around the wedding."

"Tell me what I need to do." Lois said.

Bill responded. "I'll get the blue book value of the car so that you can write a letter saying that you bought the car for the blue book value, in case we need it. We'll have to get the deed transferred over to you so that you can get it plated and insured."

"How about if I give you the value of Chris' car toward the cost of something you will need for the house like a door opener? That way I have paid for the car." Lois offered.

'Great. Thanks mom," Bill said.

Thank you." I said, relieved that Lois would step in, without hesitation to help me out, allowing me to have transportation to go to work while we worked with the state to get married. What a bizarre situation this was!

'No problem." Lois responded, in a very matter of fact manner, and then hung up.

"Wow. That was easy." I said to Bill and then added, "Your mom and the rest of your family are great at helping with all the practical stuff. And she's right. We will need an electronic door opener for you at the house. Your mom figured out how to "pay" us for the car, by giving us a payment in kind. We couldn't do this without them, Bill." I had tears in my eyes for both of us.

"My family is very generous when it comes to helping me with stuff I need." Bill said and then added, "Chris, we are getting close. Mission Impossible is almost completed."

In his excitement, Bill let out his bull moose sound of sheer delight. I hugged him and laughed.

Figure 1: Nebraska Waiver Program Pamphlet

Waiver
Services For
Adults With
Disabilities

The Nebraska Department of Social Services is committed to affirmative action/equal opportunity employment.

Home and community-based waivers provide service options for persons who have care needs and experience disabilities not related to mental retardation.

NEBRASKA DEPARTMENT OF SOCIAL SERVICES

MS-PAM-4 10/89 (99104)

PURPOSE

The Aged and Disabled Medicaid Waiver is a service system based upon the belief that people with care needs should have options for receiving services. After thorough needs identification and service planning, eligible persons are offered the choice of receiving home and community-based services or entering a nursing home.

ELIGIBILITY

Adults age 64 or younger may be eligible for waiver services if they -

1. Experience a disability that is not related to mental retardation;

2. Are eligible for Medicaid (including clients who pay for a portion of their medical expenses on a "spenddown");

3. Agree to participate in needs identification and choose to accept support services;

4. Have needs which would otherwise require them to live in a nursing home; and

5. Can be safely served at home at a cost not more than Medicaid would pay for nursing home care.

SERVICES

This waiver allows Medicaid money to be used to purchase the following services that are not usually considered "medical."

* Chore Services: Includes necessary housekeeping activities, meal preparation, essential shopping, errand service, escort service, and supervision.

* Adult Day Health Care: A structured program of activities in a supervised setting out of the client's home which provides for health and social needs.

* Independence Skills Management: Training in daily living skills, home management, and use of special equipment.

* Respite Care: Temporary relief for the usual caregiver from the stress of providing continuous care.

* Transportation: To community resources identified in the service plan.

APPLICATION PROCESS

Department of Social Services case managers accept referrals from all sources. A visit is scheduled to meet with each potential client. During the interview, the case manager, a nurse, and the client determine needs and develop a service plan.

HOW TO APPLY

To request waiver services for yourself or to refer another person, call your local office of the Department of Social Services.

Sometimes the medical needs of one spouse are so great that a couple turns to Medicaid for Health care coverage for special living arrangements. If you are in this situation, you might be concerned about how Medicaid will affect your income and assets.

If Only My Spouse Needs Assistance, Do We Both Need To Apply?

No. Only your spouse needs to apply. However, we must still look at your combined resources in determining your spouse's eligibility for assistance.

You have the right to apply for yourself, but only if you want to.

Am I Allowed To Keep Some Of Our Resources?

Yes. If your spouse is in -
- a long term care facility,
- an adult family home,
- center for the developmentally disabled, or
- the home with you but is eligible for Home and Community Based Waiver Services,
- assisted living.

We allow you to keep a portion of your combined resources so that you can take care of your needs as well.

If My Spouse Is In One Of The Listed Living Arrangements, What Do We Need To Do?

If your spouse has been in any of the previously listed living arrangements for 30 consecutive days you may request an assessment of your resources from Nebraska Department of Health and Human Services office. You will be asked to provide proof of the ownership and value of your resources.

The assessment form will identify all the "countable" resources that you or your spouse own, either individually or jointly and their equity value.

The purpose of this "assessment" is to determine how much of your combined resources you will be allowed to keep and when your spouse will be Medicaid eligible. **This is not a "split" of your resources. There is no need to divide ownership now.**

Once the assessment of resources is complete, we will determine the amount of resources reserved.

How Much In Resources Am I Allowed To Keep?

You may keep one-half of the combined value of all countable resources that you and your spouse own up to the maximum protected amount OR if the total of all your combined countable resources is at or below the minimum protected amount you can keep the minimum protected amount.

For current minimum and maximum protected amounts, contact the local office, Department of Health and Human Services. (The amounts change every January.)

Countable resources include but are not limited to such resources as savings, checking or other bank accounts; stocks, bonds, certificates, investments; cash on hand; accessible trust funds; cash value of life insurance if the face value of all policies exceeds $1,500 per person; real property, other than your home.

Some resources that you own are not counted, such as your home if you continue to live in it; burial spaces, up to $3,000 for each of you if irrevocably assigned in a burial trust or burial insurance policy; household goods and personal items; a motor vehicle.

If you own resources with other people we only count the interest that you and your spouse have in that resource.

We will total only the countable resources and divide the total in half. You may reserve one-half of the total, up to the maximum amount. If the total is at or below the minimum protected amount, you may keep them all.

When Will My Spouse Actually Be Eligible For Assistance?

To determine when your spouse may become Medicaid eligible, the total of your combined resources should equal the amount you were allowed to reserve (on the assessment form) plus $4000 for your spouse. Apply for assistance at this time.

What Happens When My Spouse Applies For Assistance?

You must complete a designation of resources at the time your spouse applies for assistance. The designation of resources will list the resources owned by you and your spouse the month Medicaid eligibility begins. Your share of the resources may not exceed the reserved amount calculated during the assessment of your resources.

What Happens After We Complete The Designation Of Resources?

Once you have completed a designation of resources, we will keep it with your spouse's Medicaid case.

You and your spouse must complete any assignments or transfers of ownership so that it will be legally clear which resources now belong to you and which belong to your spouse.

Figure 2. Nebraska Spousal Impoverishment Program Pamphlet

The transfers of ownership must be completed within 90 days of the date a determination of Medicaid eligibility is made for your spouse.

What Happens If We Later Get A Resource That Wasn't Included On The Original Assessment And/Or Designation?

Any resources received at a later time in your name only will not be counted towards your spouse.

If your spouse gets resources at a later time, they can be transferred to you if the value of these resources combined with your own resources does not exceed the amount you are allowed to reserve which was calculated at the time of the assessment of your resources.

How Often May I Complete An Assessment And/Or Designation Of Resources?

You may request an assessment and/or designation of resources if your spouse has received care in one of the previously listed living arrangements for 30 consecutive days. **The assessment of resources is only completed one time.**

How Will Our Income Be Considered When My Spouse Is Medicaid Eligible?

You may keep all of your own income. If your income is not enough to meet a minimum need standard you will be allowed to keep some of your spouse's income. This will be calculated when your spouse is actually eligible for Medicaid.

What Should I Do If I Don't Agree With The Amount Of Resources Or Income I Am Allowed To Keep?

You may request an appeal hearing if you do not agree with the amount of resources or income you are allowed to keep. Your spouse must make an application for assistance in order for you to request an appeal hearing.

What Should I Do If I Have More Questions?

If you want more information contact the local office, Nebraska Department of Health and Human Services

The Nebraska Department of Health and Human Services is committed to affirmative action/equal employment opportunity and does not discriminate in delivering benefits or services.

printed on recycled paper IM-PAM-45 Rev. 3/99 (99250)
(Previous version 12/97 should be used first)

Treatment Of Assets And Income When Your Spouse Resides In A Special Living Arrangement

Nebraska Health and Human Services System

Sometimes the medical needs of one spouse are so great that a couple turns to Medicaid for Health care coverage for special living arrangements. If you are in this situation, you might be concerned about how Medicaid will affect your income and assets.

If Only My Spouse Needs Assistance, Do We Both Need To Apply?

No. Only your spouse needs to apply. However, we must still look at your combined resources in determining your spouse's eligibility for assistance.

You have the right to apply for yourself, but only if you want to.

Am I Allowed To Keep Some Of Our Resources?

Yes. If your spouse is in -
- a long term care facility,
- an adult family home,
- center for the developmentally disabled, or
- the home with you but is eligible for Home and Community Based Waiver Services,
- assisted living.

We allow you to keep a portion of your combined resources so that you can take care of your needs as well.

If My Spouse Is In One Of The Listed Living Arrangements, What Do We Need To Do?

If your spouse has been in any of the previously listed living arrangements for 30 consecutive days you may request an assessment of your resources from Nebraska Department of Health and Human Services office. You will be asked to provide proof of the ownership and value of your resources.

The assessment form will identify all the "countable" resources that you or your spouse own, either individually or jointly and their equity value.

The purpose of this "assessment" is to determine how much of your combined resources you will be allowed to keep and when your spouse will be Medicaid eligible. **This is not a "split" of your resources. There is no need to divide ownership now.**

Once the assessment of resources is complete, we will determine the amount of resources reserved.

How Much In Resources Am I Allowed To Keep?

You may keep one-half of the combined value of all countable resources that you and your spouse own up to the maximum protected amount OR if the total of all your combined countable resources is at or below the minimum protected amount you can keep the minimum protected amount.

For current minimum and maximum protected amounts, contact the local office, Department of Health and Human Services. (The amounts change every January.)

Countable resources include but are not limited to such resources as savings, checking or other bank accounts; stocks, bonds, certificates, investments; cash on hand; accessible trust funds; cash value of life insurance if the face value of all policies exceeds $1,500 per person; real property, other than your home.

Some resources that you own are not counted, such as your home if you continue to live in it; burial spaces, up to $3,000 for each of you if irrevocably assigned in a burial trust or burial insurance policy; household goods and personal items; a motor vehicle.

If you own resources with other people we only count the interest that you and your spouse have in that resource.

We will total only the countable resources and divide the total in half. You may reserve one-half of the total, up to the maximum amount. If the total is at or below the minimum protected amount, you may keep them all.

When Will My Spouse Actually Be Eligible For Assistance?

To determine when your spouse may become Medicaid eligible, the total of your combined resources should equal the amount you were allowed to reserve (on the assessment form) plus $4000 for your spouse. Apply for assistance at this time.

What Happens When My Spouse Applies For Assistance?

You must complete a designation of resources at the time your spouse applies for assistance. The designation of resources will list the resources owned by you and your spouse the month Medicaid eligibility begins. Your share of the resources may not exceed the reserved amount calculated during the assessment of your resources.

What Happens After We Complete The Designation Of Resources?

Once you have completed a designation of resources, we will keep it with your spouse's Medicaid case.

You and your spouse must complete any assignments or transfers of ownership so that it will be legally clear which resources now belong to you and which belong to your spouse.

CHAPTER 54

(Bill's Voice)
"God Help!"

Severe pain on my left side told me that I had broken some ribs. Blood from a cut over my left eye was dripping down my face.

"Please call Chris. Here's her cell number. Tell her I really need her to come." I told the police officer using my Liberator™. I was in big trouble and I desperately needed help.

"God help! And please get Chris here!" I prayed, knowing that the Holy Spirit intercedes when we don't have words.

The police officer immediately called Chris and then told me that she was on her way.

I had been crossing the street in the crosswalk, a block from my apartment, when suddenly, I found myself being pushed sideways by a vehicle down the street I was trying to cross. When my wheelchair and me stopped thirty feet down the road, I found myself leaning to the left side of my wheelchair in pain.

A police officer, having been called to the scene by the driver, had dragged me and my power wheelchair weighing approximately 300 pounds to the side of the road because my head controlled driving mechanism on my chair was broken and so I couldn't drive myself. It had been hard work for the officer, because he didn't know how to take my chair out of gear and he hadn't asked me and then waited for me to tell him how to do it.

He took my statement and that of the driver who had hit me. I was given the information about the driver's insurance. She had what is called high risk insurance, in other words, she had been a reckless driver.

I was trying hard not to panic. I calmed myself by thinking about how God had helped Chris and me to get this far. Surely He wouldn't let us down now.

If God could help us to find our way through the government mazes of Immigration and Naturalization Service, Health and Human Service, and help us to build a house, surely He could help us to figure our way out of this mess! I rationalized to myself.

I thought a lot about Chris to keep my mind from racing. She would soon be here and then with God's help, Chris and I would figure out what to do.

My lunch time aide came running towards to me. I was never so delighted to see him.

"Bill what happened?" Tom asked.

"Accident" was all I could manage to say with my Liberator™.

Then I saw Chris running towards us.

Thank you God, here she is, I thought to myself. The police officer talked to Chris and then left me in her capable hands.

"Oh Bill you're bleeding! Are you OK?" she asked me, looking very distressed.

I shook my head no. I was too upset to talk and I felt like crying. We needed to get me to the hospital.

Taking charge of the situation, Chris then looked to my aide and said, "Hi Tom, I'm glad you're here. We really need your help. We're going to have to push Bill up to his apartment. Then we'll transfer him to his manual chair and take him to the hospital. Will you follow me over to the hospital in case we need your help there too?"

"Sure. Whatever," Tom replied, as Chris took my chair out of gear so that Tom could push me to my apartment.

Thank you God! Chris was problem-solving! I needed her to do the thinking for me. The proverbial rug had been pulled from under me. My sky was falling and I was trying not to act like Chicken Little.

I was putting all my energy into trying not to think about the fact that the timing of this accident couldn't have been any worse! Chris had closed on our house the previous week and she was moving in two days.

In two days Chris would be fifteen blocks from me; when I really needed her to be two floors below me!

Oh God how could this happen now? We were planning to get married in the spring. What will happen to our wedding plans? I asked God, getting way ahead of myself in my fear and frustration.

Deliberately bringing myself back to the immediate circumstances, I thought about what had happened during the accident. When my wheelchair stopped suddenly, after being pushing sideways down the street by the car, my ribs had hit the back and side of the chair really hard and had really hurt. I knew that at least one of my ribs was most likely broken.

When my ribs cracked, there went my support system as well. I knew that I didn't have the supports in place to deal with having broken ribs. This hurt just as much as the rib pain. My hard-fought-for support system consisted of four attendant care visits per day, but only one helper per visit. It worked as long as I was healthy. But now I wasn't.

Because I was usually able to stand with 'balance help' from the attendant, I could be pivoted between my chair, bed, and bathroom fixtures. However, I had to push hard from my toes to the top of my head in order to be able to stand. This would be much like the physical exertion of stretching the entire body upwards hard and fast for someone without cerebral palsy.

But with cracked ribs, I knew that I would no longer be able to move this way. Doing this extreme forced action on my broken ribs would re-tear them.

I was plunged back to a place I had been many times before in my life; trapped by an inflexible system that could not meet my needs when my circumstances changed, without causing great hardship to the ones I loved. I was living in the able-bodied world, having a normal relationship with Chris, but also living dangerously close to abusing her or having to move to a nursing facility if I needed more care. The reality of all this caused me great anguish.

I needed wiggle room in my support system and I hadn't achieved that yet.

This seemingly small accident would require that I ask someone to help my attendants to keep me safe during each transfer until I healed. I could not ask my aging parents or brothers who had families and lived in other communities.

I would have to ask Chris. The thought of doing this to Chris hurt more than the rib pain.

I was very angry because my power wheelchair -functionally my legs - were also broken. I knew that I would be weeks without it. The state would be crazy to pay to replace my expensive head control system, after some reckless driver had broken it. And I would have to fight with the insurance company of the person who hit me to get the money to pay for my power wheelchair to be fixed.

I had always joked about TV commercials that advertised accident lawyers. Imitating the voices of the lawyers on these commercials using my Liberator™ was great fun. And now, ironically, I needed one. My joke wasn't so funny anymore.

Soon Chris and I were on our way to the hospital, with my attendant following us. At least for this trip to the hospital, unlike my trip after falling down the stairs by the city-county building, I wouldn't lose my ability to communicate. Chris would make sure that I was heard.

Chris explained to the hospital intake person what had happened. Once admitted and in Emergency, someone looked at my eye and said that I needed sutures just above my eyelid. Chris held my head still so that it wouldn't move involuntarily as it often did, while they injected me with anesthetic and took a needle and thread to stitch me back together. Looking at her smiling at me helped to take my mind off what the doctor was doing.

The doctor said that I was lucky. If the headgear had moved a quarter of an inch closer it would have poked my eye.

The radiology technicians took some pictures of my ribs to confirm that I had fractures on the 10th and 11th ribs and possibly the

12th. Then the doctor confirmed what I already knew, "Don't pull on those ribs. They'll need time to heal."

Chris responded by echoing what I had been worrying about, "This means two people transfers for several weeks Bill. You can't have people pulling on your ribs."

With pain meds that I didn't want to take because they would make me drowsy and even less in control of my life, we went back to my place to begin to figure out how to deal with this mess.

I thought of my youngest brother Bob, a lawyer in Oklahoma who would gladly help me but he was two states away. I called him anyway and told him what had happened.

I loved Bob's brotherly response. "It would be fun to take on this reckless driver. I'd love to roll you into a courtroom in your crappy manual wheelchair Bill. I'd get you at least a million. I can't do the main work for you from here. You'll have to get a lawyer in Nebraska. Have your lawyer talk with me Bill and I'll see what I can do to help, if anything."

Bob confirmed what I knew. I needed some local help.

"God I need a local lawyer!" I prayed fervently.

One of our church friends Karen, a lawyer, immediately came to mind. I called her. Knowing that I wouldn't be able to pay her well for her time and skill, she graciously agreed to do it without pay.

Praise God for church family who are willing to use their gifts to serve each other! I thought with gratitude.

She quickly gathered all the information to see if she could help me to settle out of court. It took a lot for her to track down the reckless driver's high risk insurance company.

In the meantime I started a list of the financial compensation for pain and suffering that I would want from the driver's insurance company. The hardship costs grew by the hour due to my anger and frustration at being without my legs, having constant pain in my ribs, and needing Chris to take time off of her work to help me.

Chris asked her employer if she could take time off without pay but her work let her use some sick time to be available to help me with transfers. Even though I wasn't yet a family member, her work was gracious in letting her use some sick time to help me for a few days. I felt grateful for their understanding but frustrated by the circumstances.

We both prayed about Chris' move. She needed to be around to help me but she also needed to get moved out of her apartment. We knew we needed help.

"God help!" I prayed again, groaning with pain from my ribs and also feeling hurt from the accident in my heart, mind, soul and spirit.

The answer came to both Chris and me. "Put out the word that you both need help."

We asked anyone we could think of if they would be willing to give up an hour or so to get Chris' stuff over to the house so that she could get moved out of her apartment. Unpacking would have to wait until sometime in the future.

We wanted a few movers. God brought us the marines.

Sixteen volunteers consisting of my family, our church family, friends and some of Chris' work colleagues took over and got the job done!

Chris stayed at her apartment to direct the marine traffic. After everything had been loaded and taken over to the house and Chris had checked out of her apartment, she stopped by to see how I was doing, and then went over to the new house.

Filled with excitement, she came back to tell me all that the marines had done.

"Bill. It's wonderful! The entire house is setup. Our movers have cleaned every room and set up everything. All the moving boxes are out for the garbage service to pick them up. Everything is put away in every room! I can go over there tonight and just go to bed, Bill. It's amazing. I have literally no more moving to do. I can be here to help you whenever you need me here." Chris said with tears in her eyes.

"God is encouraging us to stay the course, Chris." I responded and then added. "We're going to make it. I'll send everyone who helped today a personalized thank you card from both of us. It's the least I can do."

CHAPTER 55

(Bill's Voice)

Gifts of Love

Insult to injury was no longer just an idiom I had learned in school. I was living it. The gross insensitivity, insolence, and contemptuous rudeness of the reckless driver's high-risk insurance company were driving me crazy.

They refused to answer letters and faxes sent to them by my pro-bono church friend lawyer Karen, in her attempts to work out my claim with them. I was grateful for her willingness to share her time and talents in the name of Christ, but this was taking up too much of both. You could only ask so much of a volunteer, even if she was a sister in Christ.

Adding even more insult to my injury of being hit by the Sports Utility Vehicle, I lost use of my power wheelchair --that is my legs. I was not even able move around my apartment. Accustomed to being able to go for a walk to do some work, run errands for Chris or me, or just to get some air, I was experiencing a bad case of cabin fever and getting more frustrated by the day.

Leon's company who maintained my power wheelchair would not order the expensive parts, now totaling over $8000 that they needed in order to repair my chair, until they were assured that they would be paid by the reckless driver's insurance company. I could sympathize with Leon but that didn't help me get back to being able to move around by myself.

To make matters even worse, my only back-up chair was my old uncomfortable sling-type manual wheelchair. Literally hanging in this chair because it lacked support for my bottom and back, I ached all the time. I was praying that my ribs were healing, despite sitting without much support.

The seventh of November arrived, exactly a month since the date of my accident, and I was getting nowhere. It was time to up the campaign against the reckless driver's insurance company to get my claim settled.

It was also time to give Karen a break and sick my brother Bob, a lawyer in Oklahoma, on this company. I couldn't pay Bob for his time but I counted on the fact that he might have a vested interest in going after this company for me. After all, I was one of his big brothers.

I called Bob and told him what I needed.

"I'm sore from sitting in this old hunk of junk. I need my power wheelchair fixed yesterday and Leon won't fix it until he knows the money is coming. Go after the insurance company for me Bob and get Leon his money, please."

"Sure. Have Karen send me everything and I'll take it from here. I would still love to have the chance to roll you into a courtroom and get you a million bucks, Bill." Bob said with delight in his voice, obviously thinking about how pitiful I looked in my old manual wheelchair. Then he added seriously, "But I can't do that because I'm not in Nebraska. Let's get this thing settled if that's what you want."

"I just want to get on with my life. I need my legs back." I lamented to Bob.

"Sure Bill. I'll threaten them with further costs if they don't start paying up." Bob replied with determination in his voice. I was glad to hear that he was going to start a threat campaign. Nothing else had worked.

My brother's gifts of love were in the form of a constant barrage of threatening faxes and letters to the insurance company, demanding that they get my claim settled soon. It worked. The money started rolling in.

Thanks to my little brother Bob, the insult to my injury began to be lifted from my injury, or so I thought.

Leon got the assurance he needed that he would be paid. He went ahead and ordered the expensive parts. Chris was able to easily convince me to use some of the settlement money to order a new comfortable customized manual wheelchair for me. I could not bear the thought of the pain that I would endure if I had to spend another day sitting in that old manual wheelchair. And Chris could no longer live with the thought of me not having an adequate supportive back-up manual wheelchair system for times when my power wheelchair was out of commission.

By Valentine's Day 1999, thanks to Bob I had my legs back. And we were on our way to getting me a new custom-made supportive manual wheelchair, to use whenever my power wheelchair was getting fixed at Leon's shop.

Chris and I were seemingly back on track and moving forward with our lives. My ribs were feeling better too. I could now push myself to standing without pain, and I was back to doing fine with my regular support system.

The church newsletter had said that there was to be a church family Valentine's dinner at a local favorite Italian restaurant. Chris and I decided that it would be fun to go along and celebrate the occasion with our fellow congregants.

On the day that we went to the restaurant, I couldn't help but think about my own disabilities and of the story of the man in the Bible who was lowered into the building to see Jesus. This story is told in the Bible in the book of Luke.

Luke 5:17-19 (New International Version of the Bible) says: "One day as he was teaching, Pharisees and teachers of the law, who had come from every village of Galilee and from Judea and Jerusalem, were sitting there. And the power of the Lord was present for him to heal the sick. Some men came carrying a paralytic [the preferred term would be *a man who had paralysis*, since he was not his disability] on a mat and tried to take him into the house to lay him before Jesus. When they could not find a way to do this because of the crowd, they went up on the roof and lowered him on his mat through the tiles into the middle of the crowd, right in front of Jesus."

Jesus, of course, being God himself, healed the man of paralysis.

I could not imagine what that would have been like for the man in the story who could now walk. What did he say? How did he feel?

Over the years, I experienced a lot of inner conflict and turmoil whenever I thought about how I might respond, should Jesus ask me if I wanted to be healed. Jesus didn't force his power to heal on people. He, being God who honored freedom of choice for the individual, would give me the dignity of asking me first. And I honestly didn't know how I would respond.

God had given me a precious gift of being able to accept my disability and so on most days I didn't think that I would want it to be taken away. It was not only all that I knew; it shaped who I grew to be, both good and bad. And I'm not sure that I would really like myself without it. I believed that I was able to lobby well on behalf of people with disabilities because God had given me this incredible gift.

Furthermore, as a disability rights advocate I had come to believe that disability is a natural part of the human condition. It does and will always happen. I had written extensively that the biggest problem for people with disabilities is societal attitudes, and not the physical, sensory, or intellectual limitations caused by someone's disability. So if I believed that people with disabilities could and should live a fulfilling life with their disabilities, why would I want to be healed of mine?

But I do admit, there were many days when I would gladly have begged Jesus to give me the capacity to speak! It was continually frustrating for me to talk at a maximum of eight words a minute in a culture that speaks at 180! I simply couldn't compete with "talkies", those people who have natural speech. It got especially difficult when I was working on a community board or testifying to the state legislature. At these times I was always pressed for time and had to do a lot of editing in my head to use my speaking time wisely.

On many occasions, I would complain to Chris in private that I wished that I could talk. She always patiently heard me out.

But she would also remind me of how God –ironically-- used my inability to speak, as a way of emphasizing what needed to be said, on behalf of those who couldn't speak for themselves. Chris would remind me that it was stunning to see someone who couldn't walk, talk or use his hands speaking so intelligently, poignantly and often humorously, as one of the voiceless and on behalf of the silent and oppressed people with disabilities, thanks to the technology of the Liberator™. She would say that I was exhibit "A" for Bible passages which say that God's power is displayed best through weakness.

I did understand Chris' point of view, and I appreciated her affirmation of how God was using me in my lobbying efforts. However, when I was both physically and mentally exhausted from working hard to say what needed to be said in as few words as possible, I would have gladly told Jesus, that yes I would love to be able to speak!

I also learned from my accident with the reckless driver that my disability acceptance gift from God did not necessarily include any additional or acquired disabilities. When I got hit by the SUV my life changed in an instant; my broken ribs gave me what is known as an acquired disability, on top of the disability that I had from birth. What I considered to be a normal level of functioning for me was greatly impacted by that careless accident.

I was not happy and able to accept the functional deterioration brought on by my broken ribs and the hassles it caused for both Chris and me. I would gladly have had Jesus heal my ribs on the spot, right at the scene of the accident!

Meanwhile back to the man in the story from the Bible who experienced paralysis, we Americans overlook another kind of healing that probably happened. I wonder what the man was feeling when his friends told him that they were going to take him to Jesus because they had heard that He could heal people. My hunch is that-as he listened to his friends- he felt a real sense of belonging, sadly, a rare experience for many people with disabilities, even today.

His friends didn't have any guarantee that Jesus would heal the man but they took him anyway. Their love for him, demonstrated by their action of carrying him to Jesus, would have in itself, given the man some powerful spiritual healing, regardless of whether or not Jesus did heal the man of his physical paralysis.

I experienced the same kind of spiritual healing that night at the local Italian restaurant.

Chris and I had eaten at this restaurant in the past; I remembered that I had easily rolled in the restaurant's first floor accessible level to enjoy my time and food with Chris. So we assumed that we could go and easily join the group.

When we arrived for the church supper, we found out that the church group, due to its large size, was going to have its get-together downstairs in the party room. But neither Chris and I nor the church party planners had thought about checking for wheelchair accessibility to this event.

Chris and I were used to this happening, even in a post-ADA world, so we tried to make alternative plans. We decided that we would just enjoy ourselves upstairs and ask that some of the party food be brought to us by the restaurant staff. We wouldn't get to join in the fun downstairs but we would set our minds to enjoying ourselves anyway.

Then, suddenly, to our amazement, seven men from our church came up and offered to carry both my power wheelchair and me downstairs where the party was.

"But Bill and his wheelchair together weigh approximately 300 pounds!" Chris protested, stunned that a bunch of men would even think of such a thing.

"That's fine. We'll take Bill down and then we'll take his chair," one of the men offered and the rest agreed with smiles and nods of affirmation.

All I could say was, "What a gift of love!"

One of the men grinned and replied, "It's Valentine's Day Bill, so it's a day for gifts of love."

I drove carefully to the edge of the stairs and turned off my wheelchair. Looking down I saw many steep stairs, far more than the ones I tumbled down at the city-county building. I thought the guys must be crazy to offer to do this. Getting me downstairs was one thing. Bringing me back up was going to be really difficult when they no longer had gravity to assist them.

"OK Bill, so how do we carry you safely down?" one of them asked, anxious to get going.

"Two person carry, arms and legs," I responded and then Chris helped organize the guys to begin to get me out of my wheelchair so that they could ever so carefully carry me down the steep long stairs.

After I was at the bottom and sitting on a chair with Chris balancing me so I wouldn't fall off, the guys carried my approximately two hundred pound power wheelchair down the stairs, like it was just a regular chair. They then helped Chris to get me back in it.

The whole thing had taken only ten minutes. All the men were so skilled and gentle that my wheelchair and I were no worse for wear. I felt better, in fact.

I remembered when I wasn't allowed into an accessible restaurant because the manager thought my presence would upset the other customers. Now people were putting great effort into getting me into an inaccessible place to eat with people who wanted me to eat with them.

That was justice that only God could plan and execute! In a very real sense, taking me to the body of Christ, which was eating in the basement of the restaurant, had the same healing power for me that the men taking the man in the Bible to Jesus had.

After the delicious meal we were treated to beautiful music by some musicians who were members of our church. When they sang Love Lifted Me, I looked at Chris. We chuckled silently because that night the Love of God and the Love of a few Godly men had indeed lifted me!

CHAPTER 56

(Bill and Chris' Voices)

Wrapping Up Our Business with the State

In late May of 1999, after eight long years of hearing government officials say that it would never work, we *finally* got our back-up plan at the state when the newly elected Governor of the state of Nebraska Mike Johanns signed Nebraska legislative bill LB594. We could now use either the Spousal Impoverishment Program with the Medicaid Waiver slot or use this LB549 option.

No longer could a state senator tell Chris that she had to pay for all of Bill's attendant and medical care, should we marry, forcing us to live in poverty in order to qualify for the funding for Bill's care. We now had two possible options to cover the high costs of Bill's attendant and medical care, while maintaining a modest lifestyle, and allowing one of us to be employed and thus contributing toward the costs of Bill's care through our taxes.

More importantly, government attitudes toward people with disabilities were changing because of the incessant educational and lobbying efforts of people like Bill. The significance of the paradigm shift in attitude of government officials represented by this new piece of legislation cannot be understated. People with disabilities, viewed as a financial burden to the states, by their own efforts over several decades of lobbying, through this and other similar kinds of legislation around the country, were now beginning to be viewed by government officials in many states as potential taxpayers!

Bill, who had studied human rights movements at college, believed that such a momentous change; occurring in just a fifty year time period in American history represented the fastest moving human rights movement ever. People, many of whom could not physically move without assistance of others or technology, had managed to move governments and the impact on their own lives was momentous. A group of people, who had literally been hid away in back rooms of homes some fifty years ago, now had real possibilities created through legislation such as LB549, and other similar laws being put forth in other states, to become tax payers, and have families of their own! Bill was overflowing with disability pride!

For us, one short but unbelievably significant section of legislative bill (LB549) tucked in the middle of this 136 page document, presented the real possibility that Bill could be employed, while paying a pre-set percentage of his income to Medicaid, like an insurance plan, to cover the cost of his attendant and medical care, without also having to pay the usual out-of-pocket costs typically associated with medical insurance such as co-pays.

Having to choose between having a job and medical care, for people like Bill, as a single person, was now removed. This was nothing short of monumental for him and for many other Americans with disabilities alive and yet to be born.

LB549 was introduced by Health and Human Services Chairman Senator Byars. It was a slightly modified version of Senator Wesely's 1998 legislative bill that had not passed (LB 1098). The new LB549 was the same as the earlier LB1098, except that this new version reduced the total amount of income that the individual could earn, from 500% of the poverty level to 250%, so as to present less possible financial burden to the state by excluding richer participants.

If we chose to use this Buy-In legislation as a couple, our total family income allowed would be severely limited to 250% of the poverty level. But it was still a significant and hard-fought-for toe hold into the world of employment for Bill, even if he was married, while still maintaining his attendant and medical care.

For us LB549 also represented dignity. In the future, we would have the option of deciding who would be the bread winner, just like any other American family. After all, we both were college educated and Bill could write as well as any journalist. He had not sought a full time job before, simply because he would have lost his attendant care. Now we were free to think about the possibility of Bill seeking to use his skills in the job-sector.

With our LB594 back-up plan in place, we were now ready to plan our wedding.

Our first concern was that we would have to set up a stressful meeting with the state to get Chris into the Spousal Impoverishment program either right before or right after our church wedding. And we needed to get Bill signed up for he Medicaid Wavier Program. We decided that doing the state paperwork after our church wedding would be kind of like going to a graduation ceremony before taking all the finals or getting a Ph.D. without first defending a thesis. Our dissertation thesis primarily involved getting Chris on this program, as the first middle-aged person to do so, with some comfortable financial assets.

The state paperwork meeting, aka our dissertation, was set for October 5, 1999, five days before our church wedding Oct 10, 1999.

But, in order to do the state paperwork meeting, we would have to be legally married. We were in a catch-22 situation.

Call it crazy, but we set up two weddings. First, we planned a legal procedure that we called our state paperwork wedding and then, after the paperwork was done, we had our real marriage in the sight of God.

Our state paperwork wedding was low-keyed; so low-keyed that we had our ceremony in our pastor's driveway. Sadly, Pastor Lee had fractured his knee in a fall a month earlier and couldn't bend it enough to get into a car. And, if he could have gotten into his car, the morphine in his system would have prevented him from driving anyway. Because his house was inaccessible, we settled for a wedding in his driveway, of all places.

The ceremony was totally unlike us as thoughtful individuals, in a God-centered courtship. Fast and furious, it was nothing short of ridiculous. A wham-bang-thank-you ma'am affair, we didn't have music and we didn't dress up for the event. But, it was symbolic of our desire to not give the State any more than it already had already taken from us.

With a tongue in cheek attitude about what was to come next, Bill selected literally one line of scripture for this, our state wedding, Psalm 23:5, "You prepare a table before me in the presence of my enemies." (NIV) Laughing to ourselves, we had discussed the notion that we were probably the first and the last couple who would use such a scripture at their wedding. However, given that we were going to head straight over to the state office from this "ceremony" to fill out our state paperwork, this scripture seemed most appropriate.

Pastor Lee hobbled down his front steps to meet us in his driveway. He looked tired but smiled none-the-less, through the haze of his pain meds.

Bill's friend Mark showed up to be the Best Man at this non-event event. However, since Chris' matron of honor was from Canada, and couldn't be with us until the church wedding, our friend, Marlene from the League of Human Dignity, stood in for this, our state wedding.

Marlene was also designated as our "Baptist Gofer" because Lee asked her to get a folding table inside his house and then to set it up for him in his driveway.

"Bill knows just how bad I am with even the simplest of assistive technology, so asking me to do anything technical is really an act of faith," Marlene said, jokingly as she set up a small table she had brought out of the house, helping us to set up for this farce of a ceremony on the asphalt surface of the driveway.

Then, after the makeshift "altar" was in place, Lee asked the essential questions, "Do you Bill take Chris to be your wife? Do you Chris agree to take Bill to be your husband?" All that he needed was a yes from each of us.

No vows, no blessing or pastoral prayers. Just a simple question to each of us and reciting of the prayerful and crazy scripture that Bill had selected. And we were done.

We looked at each other and grinned. This was nothing short of hysterical! And it was everything we weren't. It was the quintessential drive-thru wedding!

Then Pastor Lee signed our civil license. We kept the ceremonial license until Sunday so that Sharon, Chris' matron of honor, could sign it.

Pastor Lee, concerned about the impact of his pain medication on his mental capacities, proofread our legal marriage license about five times to make sure it was accurate.

As we were wrapping things up, a group of joggers ran by us.

"Your recessional," Mark said and smiled. Too funny!

With the "service" and "recessional" complete, off we went to the Lincoln office of State Welfare to prove beyond a shadow of a doubt that Bill was poor so that he could get on the Medicaid Waiver program, and that Chris had all her ducks in a row to get into the Spousal Impoverishment Program.

"Congratulations on being married," Bill's assigned social worker said as we arrived at the state office, a bit too chipper for this nerve-wracking occasion. And then, presumably well-meaning but unfortunately, she added, "How do you like married life so far?"

"We are not married in our eyes, and we are certainly not married in God's eyes," Bill said gruffly, anxious to get the state paperwork out of the way.

Meanwhile, Chris was just trying to hold herself together, until this state stuff was complete and we were in the "clear". She was trying not to think about the implications for both of us should this plan not work, because of some unforeseen detail that we had missed. The financial responsibility for her would be immense, and living in poverty, in order to obtain necessary services for Bill, was a very scary prospect. She kept telling herself that she and Bill and God had done all the hard work to get to this point. And that God would not let us down now. The doors would open for our lives together- it was far beyond time for them to crack wide open.

Then, much to the surprise of the social worker, our marines started to land one by one. We watched her eyes get bigger and bigger, as the room started to fill with all the people whom we had asked to come to this meeting to make sure that it went off without any problems.

Clearly from her tone, the social worker saw this as a simple paper work event. And she had not expected us to bring reinforcements.

But she wasn't sitting on our side of the table, where our future together was on the line. We were not going to let *anything* get in the way of our marriage.

Shirley and Donna from the Nebraska Advocacy Services, the Disability Rights Center of Nebraska came first. They were our legal team, a lawyer and a legal assistant. Their jobs were to make sure the worker understood and followed all the state rules and to get copies of every scrap of paper that the worker had us sign.

They were followed by Don, Chris' boss. He came in case the worker had any questions about Chris' retirement money. At a previous meeting a State worker had told us that Chris' retirement money was accessible and could be used as a "countable resource", meaning that the state could take it, upon entry into the program to pay for Bill's care needs. Bill investigated and found that Chris would have to quit her job for six months before she could get that money. Since Chris was not quitting her job, it was not accessible to us, and therefore it could not be taken from her by the state.

Then came Martha from the church. She was in charge of prayer to invite the Holy Spirit to this unholy meeting. We wanted Jesus to be present in the room and guide through His Spirit. But, with us, full of nervous energy, we thought it wise to invite the matriarch of the church to provide prayer support for us.

And, of course, Marlene had come to be our expert on Medicaid rules.

To an outsider it might have looked as if we were ganging up on the social worker, but we didn't see it that way. We saw ourselves as helping the worker by sharing our knowledge and research.

Other people go to these types of meetings alone and unprepared. We would never be in that boat. We were prepared and had enveloped ourselves in support, from both our church and disability rights communities.

The social worker led us to a large office table, big enough to accommodate our group. We smiled as we remembered our "wedding" scripture of the day. Our prayer had been answered. God had prepared a fine table for us to do our paperwork in the presence of our "enemy".

And with a table to wrap up our business with the state, the paperwork meeting began. Bill was moved over to the Medicaid Waiver Program, officially via its realms of paperwork.

And, when the social worker totaled Chris' assets, they were far below the cutoff point. The social worker then had us sign the paperwork for the Spousal Impoverishment Program. Chris was in!

Shirley, ever the lawyer, asked for a copy for her files. We knew we needed her there to remember to do so.

And, just like that, in less than a half hour, we were done.

And everyone present applauded loudly. We wondered if such a celebration had ever happened at the state office building before.

The meeting felt anti-climatic. After so many years of working on all the details, it was a non-event. None of our team was needed to answer questions. The process had run as smooth as silk.

Every i had been dotted and t had been crossed. This is what the result of years of hard work looked like. Doors swinging wide open. God smiling down on us.

A bit bewildered, very exhausted and immensely relieved, we left the building.

Chris, just legally married had to rush off to get back to work. So much for a quick get away to a romantic location.

And Bill headed home to get some more things done for our real church wedding on Sunday.

As we hurried off, even though we were now legally married, we didn't feel like it - at all.

Our drive-by wedding and state meeting had been about securing the practical programs needed for our marriage. Although He had supported and equipped us, in so many ways over the years of work involved to get to the table at the state building, the purpose of all that had transpired today had not been one of worshipping God and inviting Him into our marriage.

Our real wedding would happen on Sunday, when God would show up with our families and friends to celebrate with us, and to bless and honor our sacred union.

May 25, 1999-
Approved by the Govern
Emergency Clause attach
May 28, 1999 LB 594

LB 594

LEGISLATURE OF NEBRASKA

NINETY-SIXTH LEGISLATURE

FIRST SESSION

LEGISLATIVE BILL 594

FINAL READING

Introduced by Health and Human Services Committee:
Jensen, 20, Chairperson; Byars, 30; Dierks, 40;
Price, 26; Suttle, 10; Thompson, 14; Tyson, 19

Read first time January 19, 1999

Committee: Health and Human Services

A BILL

1   FOR AN ACT relating to health and human services; to amend sections
2   42-371, 43-101, 43-102, 43-104, 43-104.01, 43-104.03 to
3   43-104.05, 43-104.11, 43-104.12, 43-104.22, 43-107,
4   43-109, 43-402, 43-1409, 43-2606, 43-2610, 43-2615,
5   43-2616, 43-2620, 43-3301, 43-3303, 43-3314, 43-3318,
6   43-3326, 43-3327, 71-1,132.09, 71-1,132.11, 71-1,132.20,
7   71-1,132.21, 71-1,132.27, 71-1,147, 71-1,147.09,
8   71-1,147.10, 71-1,147.33, 71-1,147.34, 71-2407, 71-2417,
9   71-7803, and 75-302 to 75-303.02, Reissue Revised
10   Statutes of Nebraska, sections 28-405, 28-406, 28-414,
11   28-728, 68-1020, 71-1,132.13, 71-1,132.30, 71-1,132.37,
12   71-1,142, 71-1774, 71-1909, 71-1910, 71-1911, 71-1913,
13   71-1913.01, 71-1913.02, 71-1915, 71-1917, 71-5830.01,
14   71-8228, 71-8231, 71-8236, 71-8243, 81-502, and 81-2602,
15   Revised Statutes Supplement, 1998, section 28-415,
                            -1-

Security Act, as amended;

(b) Who have income at or below one hundred eighty-five percent of the Office of Management and Budget poverty line, as allowed under Title XIX and Title XXI of the federal Social Security Act, as amended, without regard to resources, including all children under nineteen years of age and pregnant women as allowed under 42 U.S.C. 1396a, as amended, and section 2110 of the federal Social Security Act, as amended. Children described in this subdivision shall remain eligible for a twelve-month period of time from the date of eligibility prior to redetermination of eligibility; or

(c) Who are medically needy caretaker relatives as allowed under section 1905(a)(ii) of the federal Social Security Act, as amended, and who have children with allocated income as follows:

(i) At or below one hundred fifty percent of the Office of Management and Budget poverty line with eligible children one year of age or younger;

(ii) At or below one hundred thirty-three percent of the Office of Management and Budget poverty line with eligible children over one year of age and under six years of age; or

(iii) At or below one hundred percent of the Office of Management and Budget poverty line with eligible children six years of age or more and under fifteen years of age.

(3) As allowed pursuant to 42 U.S.C. 1396a(a)(10)(A)(ii), medical assistance shall be paid on behalf of disabled persons as defined in section 68-1005 who are in families whose net income is less than two hundred fifty percent of the Office of Management and

-73-

CHAPTER 57

Mission Impossible Accomplished!

On October 10, 1999, a miracle happened in the First Baptist Church on 14th "K" Streets. We were married, and God attended the wedding. He had to. He was the Center.

While most couples complain about planning a wedding, we relished the task. After ten years of advocating with the State and Federal bureaucracy, to put in place what we knew that we needed for our marriage to last, planning a wedding seemed like child's play.

The first problem that we had to address was that it didn't seem right to have all our family and friends come, some from far-away places such as Canada, to see us get married, stay for dinner and then leave. So we organized a get -together for family and close friends on the day before the wedding at Eugene T. Mahoney State Park. The park overlooks the picturesque valley of the Platte River near Ashland, Nebraska. Managed by the Nebraska Game and Parks Commission, this premier 700-acre park is open year-round. Its location on I-80 between Lincoln and Omaha made it an ideal spot for a gathering of our family and friends.

For those people who wanted to see our new home we had an open house the evening before complete with a buffet-style lasagna dinner for those who needed to be fed. And for our family and intimate friends we had a dinner at the church on the evening of the wedding. Our guests would be well-fed even if they didn't like the wedding.

But only the Grinch and Ebenezer Scrooge wouldn't have liked our wedding. We wanted the wedding to focus on God and on His awesome power because we knew that without His help, we wouldn't have made it to the altar.

"I've been waiting a long time for this service! We're going to have a great celebration today!" Pastor Lee proclaimed with a booming voice and a broad smile from the front of our filled church, rallying the congregation. He then added, "We are here today to celebrate two people who love each other so much that they would do so much to make their covenant a reality!" Pastor Lee continued to enjoy himself as he welcomed our wedding guests, both those present and those who were listening on the phone from Canada. He then prepared everyone for our unique processional.

We didn't want the traditional processional. We wanted a celebratory parade, and Martha, the most creative woman of the church joyfully helped us to create it. Sandy, our music director, had helped to organize the musicians, select the music and the worship leaders who would summon all of us to give praise to God through song.

Moving like a crowd in a parade, surrounded by children of all ages, we processed together down the center aisle and up onto the large platform at the front of the church. Rather than hide Bill's visible disability including his assistive technology, our goal was to celebrate it as part of our joyful parade! Some children wore headbands that Martha had fashioned to look like Bill's headstick with one and two sparkly balls dangling out in front and from the tops of their heads. Disability Pride was welcome at our wedding and we were proud of it! Other children were given decorative wands to shake as they processed with us to the sounds of celebratory Christian praise music, sung by the praise team and accompanied by piano, guitar and drums. What a fun and worshipful parade we were!

As we approached the narrow ramp leading up onto the platform, Bill's older brother Jim suddenly appeared to help Chris to make sure that Bill safely navigated the narrow ramps with his power wheelchair. As his big brother, Jim was still ready to give Bill some help at just the right moment.

Up on the platform with the crowd of children and the praise team, we expressed our appreciation and love for God through music.

The ceremony opened with the children's choir and the praise band surrounding us and our bridal party to sing three praise songs: "This is the Day," "I Will Celebrate" and "The Family Prayer Song." Looking out to the congregation, all on the platform led the congregation in the singing of these simple praise songs, accompanied by clapping, swaying and waving of the decorative wands and fancy headsticks. Filled with absolute delight and joy, we relished having all of our favorite people, smiling back at us as they joined in our songs of celebration.

Pastor Lee then gave the invocation in which he described a Christian marriage as, "A covenant of faith and trust between of a man and a woman, established within a shared commitment to the covenant faith in Jesus Christ, the Lord." He added, "Therefore, it requires an openness of life and thought, a freedom from doubt and suspicion and a commitment to speak the truth in love as (each member of the couple), grows up in Christ, who is the head of the Church." And, Pastor Lee went on to say that a Christian marriage is a covenant of hope that endures all things.

Then, two people, one from each of the two communities that had been instrumental in supporting us to get to this day, (Lori, a friend and a member of our church and Marlene, a friend and the director of the Lincoln League of Human Dignity's Independent Living Center) took turns reciting sections of the Scripture reading, Psalm 66, from the New International Bible. Although a little long, this scripture was very meaningful for us because God had taken us through some tough times to get to this special day. To us it was well worth the time to hear all of it.

1   Shout with joy to God, all the earth!

2   Sing the glory of his name;
      Make his praise glorious!

3   Say to God, "How awesome are your deeds!
      So great is your power
      that your enemies cringe before you.

4   All the earth bows down to you;
      they sing praise to you,
      they sing praise to your name."

5   Come and see what God has done,

how awesome his works in man's behalf!

6 He turned the sea into dry land,
  they passed through the waters on foot—
  come, let us rejoice in him.

7 He rules forever by his power,
  his eyes watch the nations—
  let not the rebellious rise up against him.

8 Praise our God, O peoples,
  let the sound of his praise be heard;

9 he has preserved our lives
  and kept our feet from slipping.

10 For you, O God, tested us;
   you refined us like silver.

11 You brought us into prison
   and laid burdens on our backs.

12 You let men ride over our heads;
   we went through fire and water,
   but you brought us to a place of abundance.

13 I will come to your temple with burnt offerings
   and fulfill my vows to you—

14 vows my lips promised and my mouth spoke
   when I was in trouble.

15 I will sacrifice fat animals to you
   and an offering of rams;
   I will offer bulls and goats.

16 Come and listen, all you who fear God;
   let me tell you what he has done for me.

17 I cried out to him with my mouth;
   his praise was on my tongue.

18 If I had cherished sin in my heart,
   the Lord would not have listened;

19 but God has surely listened
   and heard my voice in prayer.

20 Praise be to God,
   who has not rejected my prayer
   or withheld his love from me!

Pastor Lee began his meditation by quoting Romans 8:28, "And we know that in all things God works for the good of those who love him, who have been called according to his purpose." And then he added with delight and celebration, "Only the Power of God could make this day possible!"

A special letter of greeting and celebration from Pastor Howard was read to us. We were both most happy to hear Pastor Howard's words of love and encouragement.

Pastor Lee then shared his own thoughts with us. He celebrated our willingness to do all the work that was required to get us to this day over the course of ten years. He celebrated our moral victory of waiting until marriage to live together in the fullness of marriage. And he gave witness to the capacity that we had between us, that is, to communicate without words. Pastor Lee declared this as a special gift from God.

It was fascinating to hear Pastor Lee's reflection about what had come so natural to us- the ability to communicate with each other. Chris thought that our communication worked because Bill edited everything before he used his Touch Talker™ and later Liberator™ to communicate. Bill thought that communication worked because Chris was God's answer to his prayers.

After Lee's meditation we thanked each of our parents. Bill humorously thanked his parents for all they had done in raising him to become the person now, at the altar. To ease the tension of this profound moment Bill added a humorous and off the wall thanks to his Mom for typing his term papers, saying that she was better than a word processor, in that she gave him a perfect copy every time. Everyone laughed with Bill at his crazy sense of humor! And it helped to reduce some of the emotional overwhelm that we were all feeling.

We had so many people to thank that we thought it would be fun to create a slide show. Playing "Testify to Love (Psalm 151)" performed by Wynonna Judd, we displayed pictures of people who had supported us plus pictures of us doing fun things during our two weeks short of 11-year courtship.

Our time of sharing our vows and promises, unlike our quick driveway wedding, was most meaningful and profound. It was also delightfully humorous.

Pastor Lee started by asking Bill if he agreed to honor Chris as his wife. Instantaneously Bill hit the "yes" button on his Liberator™, and Pastor Lee responded, with, "Not so fast Bill. We aren't done yet!" The church was filled with laughter at Bill's eagerness to respond to complete this real wedding. When Pastor Lee had completed the promise, he then cued Bill that it was now time to respond. Bill again, very quickly said, "Yes."

Bill had preprogrammed his vows into his communication device. Loudly, boldly and clearly he vowed to take Chris as his wife, to love, honor and cherish her until death. After this Bill had added a phrase that he had adamantly requested to be added, "However, I look forward to meeting you on the other side, if it's God's will."

Chris, equally as clearly, but not quite as loudly repeated the exact same vows to "love, honor and cherish Bill until death do us part", and then added the phrase that Bill had requested, "However, I look forward to meeting you on the other side, if it's God's will."

With a declaration that we were married, Pastor Lee said that we could kiss. After we kissed, Bill let out a delightful giggle and all present laughed. Such a precious moment, shared with so many who loved us.

And then, with our ceremony complete, having made our vows and promises to each other, and having exchanged our rings, we faced the congregation and Pastor Lee announced, "By the Authority granted to me by the State of Nebraska, I introduce to you, as husband and wife, Bill Rush and Chris Robinson."

We both held back the tears that were ready to flow, while all those present clapped and cheered.

The praise band belted out the Theme from "Mission: Impossible", our personalized recessional and they made it sound great! We started our way down the ramp and up the main aisle and out the back door of the church.

The Mission Impossible theme was played to celebrate the completion of our 6-part mission. We had 1) succeeded in getting an exception to the application of the state regulations for adults with disabilities to get married when the cost of care exceeds the cap, 2) succeeded in accessing the Spousal Impoverishment program to protect Chris' resources, 3) succeeded in being a part of the creation of a back-up program LB 594 in order to protect our marriage should the waiver exemption be removed by state senators, succumbing to the pressure to be seen as being fiscally conservative. This was based on our real experience of the threat of institutionalization for Bill back in 1993 4) obtained Chris' green card 5) bought a van with a wheelchair lift and 6) build a power wheelchair accessible house. Our mission impossible was accomplished!

Sometimes over that long two weeks short of 11 years journey together, it did seem as if we were on an 'impossible' mission. However, with God, perseverance and hard teamwork nothing is impossible!

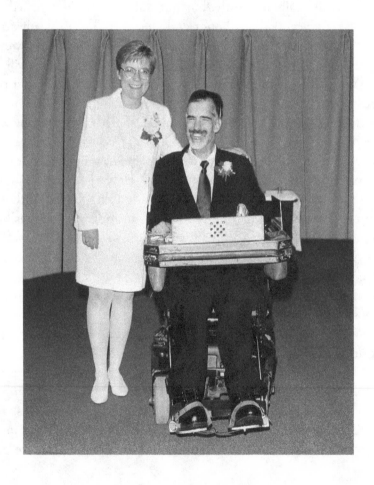

CHAPTER 58

(Bill and Chris' Voices)

Love and Grace and 14,000 Men

"Where's your admittance wrist band? You can't get in without one!" the female security guard said gruffly to Chris when we reached the entrance to Kemper Arena in Kansas City, Missouri.

"I can't have one because I'm not a guy." Chris protested with irritation and then added, "I'm my husband's attendant for this event. He's quite ill and needs my help."

By saying this Chris was admitting to doing the complete opposite of everything that we had fought for during the eleven years leading up to the wedding. All our work with the state was to ensure that Chris would not be Bill's attendant. But, for the sake of getting Bill into this special event with a group of guys from our church, she would gladly announce to anyone that she was here to provide for his personal care needs.

"Well you just can't get in without it," said the woman, issuing her final judgment on the matter.

Chris wasn't getting anywhere with this woman. Bill, who could have handled this verbal conflict with ease, was not well enough to duke it out with her. It was time for one of the church marines to land.

Bob, one of our leaders stepped in to help. He said firmly, "She's here to care for Bill. She has to come with us."

"OK," said the woman and immediately let us in. Bob's authoritative male voice, at this all male event, was Chris' ticket to go inside. Chris plus five guys from the church entered the stadium quickly before the woman gatekeeper changed her mind.

Once inside, we followed the guys from our church who had arrived at the stadium before us. They led us to the VIP level and into a skybox.

"How did you manage to get this place for us?" Chris asked Mike with delight and excitement.

"We told one of the coordinators of the event that we needed a place for one of our guys to be able to lie down and he brought us here. He was very courteous and considerate. We are VIP's for this event, thanks to Bill!" Mike exclaimed, smiling at Bill.

Bill smiled back at Mike, happy that at least his horrendously painful situation was bringing some joy to others. He did not want to be a burden; he wanted to be one of the guys on this trip and he hoped this treat would offset the help that Chris would need from the guys to move him as needed from his wheelchair to the floor to rest and then back up again.

Since Bob was Chris' ticket in and out, she thought that she had better take him to make one more trip to our van to get a large foam mattress for Bill to lie on. Looking nonchalant like they did this all the time, Bob and Chris carried a large piece of foam, the size of a single mattress, into the stadium. Bob smiled sweetly at the stern female security guard to get Chris past security a second time, while the woman looked at them stunned. With the foam piece in place on the floor so that Bill could watch the event coverage on a wall-mounted TV, the church guys helped Chris to get Bill comfortably settled.

Chris and the rest of the guys then made themselves feel at home in the skybox. With plenty of room to move about and sit or stand, the skybox was a great place to hang out for this stadium event. Suddenly a stadium worker knocked on the door to give us complimentary soft drinks and water. Wow! We really were VIPs!

The program began with praise music. Tears started to stream down Chris' face as she, the only woman in the Kemper Arena heard the glorious rich reverberating deep voices of 14,000 men at this Promise Keepers event.

This must be what heaven is like, Chris thought to herself. *The men are worshipping with all of their hearts and the sound is so beautiful!*

Never before had Chris or Bill heard Christian men, notoriously muted during the singing of praise songs and hymns in North American churches, sing out so strongly and boldly. The arena filled with rich heartfelt baritone and bass voices singing along with the all-male Promise Keepers praise band. Using a variety of instruments to reflect the emotional tone of each song, the praise band played organ music, rock style screeching guitars, loud drums or soft piano.

This Promise Keepers event entitled "The Challenge" would provide music and good teaching to usher in the Holy Spirit and challenge the men to lead a God-centered rather than self-centered life, a life lived in brotherhood rather than isolation, and a life of service to others to share Jesus Christ rather than a self-serving life.

Bill lay still, watching and listening to the chorus of praise.

A flood of emotions and thoughts were pulsing through both Chris' and Bill's hearts and minds. We were desperately in need of love and grace and we were finding it in the company of 14,000 men.

It was September 2003 and we had been through an unexpected and tragic journey for the previous three years, starting horrifically just six months after our triumphant and celebratory wedding. We were devastated and decimated from this unexpected and cruel turn of events.

Six months into our marriage we noticed that Bill's body was quickly losing the capacity to do the things that it could easily do in the past. For example we noticed that Bill was losing his ability sit in his power chair without falling over to one side or collapse forward onto his wheelchair tray. He was having great difficulty standing by himself and his control of his bladder was suddenly gone, and, he had increasing pain in his side and back.

The medical community had great difficulty giving us explanations or support for far too long, partly we believed, because of an outdated notion still prevalent in medicine that people with disabilities die young.

It took twenty-one months to find a specialist who could diagnose what was causing all these changes and problems in Bill's body, and that was only thanks to a doctor friend from our church who gave us a recommendation of a specialist to see.

A neurosurgeon diagnosed Bill with high-grade cervical stenosis or dangerous narrowing of the spinal column in the neck at three spinal cord levels. He scheduled him for emergency surgery in August of 2003, to remove bones that were impinging on his spinal cord. The neurosurgeon, without knowledge of Bill's accident, estimated that the damage began around the time when Bill was hit by the reckless driver.

Bill's neck had been X-rayed in April of 1999 after another but much less significant incident in his power wheelchair. The testing had shown some narrowing in his neck, but he had not been referred to a neurosurgeon because the radiologist did not think it was warranted. We will never know what, if anything, the neurosurgeon could have done if he had seen Bill at the time of the 2nd incident, or if he had followed Bill from the date of the car accident.

This diagnosis did give us at least one cause for Bill's significant and sudden decline and a subsequent surgery date. But the surgery had not eased Bill's pain. In fact the pain was increasing for him.

Bill was two years post-surgical treatment when we arrived at Promise Keepers. His spinal cord, released from its strangulation caused by the caving in of bone structure around it, was still trying to rewire itself. Pain and abnormal sensations were both expected consequences of this surgery that had to be endured for an indefinite period of time if the spinal cord was going to heal itself. However, two years post-surgery the pain was not letting up and the spine did not appear to be able to repair itself.

Both of us were deeply and profoundly hurt by what was happening to Bill. Feelings of anger and helplessness felt like physical pain in the chest. In our emotional pain we were asking so many questions of God. *What was happening to Bill's body? Why would this be happening now? Had we not worked long and hard to get here? Did we not deserve some time to just enjoy our marriage? Why couldn't the medical community seem to help us? God, where are you?*

From the bottom of the pit of our lives, there was nowhere to look but up. We both prayed for direction for what to do about Bill's body and for mercy and grace to help us to draw closer to God so that we wouldn't run away from God in our despair and depression.

Linda, a trained nurse and a Christian, was a gift from God brought into our home to minister to us in our pain and suffering. She became one of Bill's attendants who worked with us through the triumph of the wedding and down into the pit of despair as we helplessly watched Bill fall apart.

Arriving at our house she would say, "Hi Job! No! I mean Bill, No I mean Job, Oh well- it's the same thing isn't it!?"

And then we would all laugh together, often through tears, realizing that she was using humor to minister to us by comparing Bill to Job in the Bible who had also been suddenly and tragically struck down. Job, in the end, never got answers from God as to why his tragedy had happened to him, but he did get his health back and a new life. We did not know how or if God would work out our tragic situation.

Our church family slowly but certainly rose to the occasion, bringing us the good news of the hope of Jesus Christ when ours was depleted to the point of being gone. Martha, the friend from church who had come to pray at our state wedding meeting started to schedule lunches out with Chris to feed her not only food but also fellowship. A women's Bible study gave Chris gift certificates for massages.

The men stepped up to support Bill by organizing a Bible study around his bed at home on a couple of Saturday mornings each month. They also helped us to go to this Promise Keepers event.

When Chris had asked Bob, our church's coordinator for the Promise Keepers trip if it would be possible take Bill he had said, "Sure. Chris. Let's take him. He's one of the guys. Tell us how we can help."

And Chris, by being able to witness the demonstration of love to Bill through the actions of ordinary Christian men ended up being equally blessed.

Plus it was just downright fascinating for Chris to get to be a part of this Christian men's event. Some feminist groups had stated that these Promise Keepers events encouraged the oppression of women by demanding that men take back their biblical mandate to be the "head of their families." Chris was privileged to be able to get a chance to see first-hand what promises the men were asked to keep.

After the initial time of glorious praise singing was over, Joe White, the first speaker, dressed in a boxer's outfit, ran through the crowd of men on the floor of the stadium and up onto the stage while the thousands of men present cheered mightily. Mesmerized, both Chris and Bill watched as this man, while giving an emotive and instructive monolog began the hard physical work of building three crosses on the stage.

Chiseling, nailing, tying and then lifting the first cross to the left of center, with sweat pouring down his face, Joe spoke, in the voice of the man crucified on the left of Jesus. This self-made, independent, rebellious man, declared himself to be a fighter to the end. He taunted Jesus by asking him "Why if you are indeed the Son of God, don't you save Yourself?"

Sweating and panting Joe moved to do the hard labor of building the second cross to the right side of the center and to speak in the voice of the man on the right side of Jesus. This man was fearful of God, seeking his mercy, grace and love. He admitted that he had never known who his father was, had never known love, had been angry and had sinned, with the result that he made a mess of his life, despite his best efforts. This man in recognizing how wretched he was, asked, "Jesus, could you, would you, remember me when you come into Your kingdom?" Joe then lifted this second cross. The stadium full of men, were silent.

Putting a crown of thorns on his head to represent Jesus, Joe continued to sweat and pound as he built a third cross, the one in the center, while echoing the words of Jesus to describe Jesus' ministry, "I have come to pay the debt for all of them.' When the cross was made, Joe lifted the it, and holding it against his shoulder as Jesus would have when he started to carry his own cross, uttered the words of Jesus, "Father, forgive these men for they know not what they are doing. Father, why have you forsaken me?" And then "It is finished."

With the three crosses standing upright behind him, Joe continued his comparative description of the lifestyles and responses to Jesus of the two thieves. He then added descriptions of other men in the Bible and of men today, describing the differences between men past and present who truly sought after Jesus vs. those who chose to go their own way. Over and over he asked the essential question to this group of men, "See men, when it comes right down to it, the only thing that really matters is which side of the cross are you on?" meaning, which man are you right now?

After Joe was finished speaking, there was an altar call, asking men who were not believers in Christ to come forward and repent of their sins and give their lives to Christ. Chris and Bill watched, stunned as hundreds of men poured onto the floor of the stadium. Chris gasped in amazement as the evening ended with men prostate on the ground praying before the cross in the middle, the cross representing Jesus who died for their sins. Many who were on the wrong side of the cross had moved over that evening to the right side, perhaps even some of the guys in our skybox.

Ministry inside and outside our VIP skybox continued on the second day of the event. Whenever Chris would need to lift Bill from his wheelchair to the floor, one of our church guys would offer to help. And because we were VIPs, unlike the rest of the men who had to get in line-ups and pay for lunch at the concessions, we had free lunches delivered to our skybox.

Keenly watching and listening to the messages that were delivered to the men, Chris picked up on a consistent theme. These men were being challenged to love their wives and children like Christ loved the church.

So much so that, later in the day, men were asked to come forward if they wanted to recommit their lives to their families, to come "clean" of things that were happening in their homes that were not God-honoring. Chris expected only a few men to come forward. But they came, in droves, from the balconies and the floor of the auditorium down the aisles to the front. Chris was weeping again, delighted that all these guys would step up to get prayer and support for the sake of so many women and children.

Chris' heart cried out to God, *Praise God for this event leading men to Jesus. It was not, as the feminist's had portrayed, a place to make men more dominating. No, this was a place to make men submissive to God and more willing to serve their families. May the wives of these guys be receptive and welcoming of the changes that they would see in their husbands, when they returned home.*

When we left the conference at the end of the second day, one of our church guys offered to drive our vehicle back to Lincoln. Chris and Bill spent the driving reflecting on this event and how it had ministered to us.

Our pain and suffering had not changed. Bill was still in excruciating pain. All our dreams for our marriage were crushed.

But the presence of God in the midst of 14,000 men including the men from our church who demonstrated their love for us with actions, reminded us that we were very much loved by God, even as we drove home to continue to live out the tragedy of Bill's sudden and horrific decline.

CHAPTER 60

(Bill and Chris' Voices)
How NOT to do Self-Advocacy

"$^%$^$^$&^% What do you mean Bill can't have an attendant while in a rehab facility?!" Chris swore into the phone at the state worker.

Having somehow managed to survive being up round the clock for over four years, only catching naps when Bill would fall asleep in total exhaustion, while still managing to hold down a job for three of the last four years, and having lived in hospitals to stay with Bill for the last 6 months, Chris was beyond exhausted. She was at the end of her otherwise long fuse, both physically and emotionally. She was blowing and it wasn't pretty.

Chris continued to holler at the state worker on the phone from Bill's room at the Madonna Rehabilitation Center in Lincoln. "No I can't leave him to go home and get any sleep! He's in pain and needs help 24 hours a day. No, the nursing staff can't help him. They are too busy. I have to move him sometimes every 5 minutes! He needs to move again. I have to go!" Chris said abruptly and hung up.

This was definitely not one of Chris' finer moments. She prayed that Bill was too zoned out on pain meds to have heard her. Bill would have been horrified to hear Chris' palpable anger toward the government bureaucrat. The first rule of advocacy was always to stay assertive and not become aggressive. If you were either too passive or too aggressive you had lost.

This regrettable telephone conversation had been about Chris advocating to get some help so that she could get a little sleep, in the midst of Bill's horrific medical situation. And Chris, exhausted by an ordeal that had gone on for four years without relief, had nothing left to do self-advocacy well.

Chris pondered what had just happened. *How did Bill manage to stay for the most part civil in his advocacy over decades of his life? Advocacy must happen when you are at your point of greatest of need, and when you have the least energy to put into it. Bill has depths of resources both energy and intellect beyond that of most people and definitely beyond mine. I know he doesn't want to be acknowledged because it sets him up as 'better than others'. He's not better, he is very human... but his gift has been refined well through adversity...*

But, Chris' shamefully foul 'squeaky wheel' did manage to get some grease. It would take a few months for the slow government engines to eventually get us some help, but it would come.

Deena, a God-selected helper, came along side to walk this road with us, thanks to Marlene at the League of Human Dignity who went to bat for us at the state to fund an attendant through the regular Medicaid system, that was now also paying for Bill's costly hospital care.

The torture of being on this noisy ventilator unit at Madonna was probably the final straw that set off Chris, who was highly sensitive to sound anyway. Obnoxious alarms that were continuously going off and staying on, outside the patient rooms in this cramped unit to tell the nurses that someone needed help prevented both Chris and Bill from getting even a nap. Sleep deprivation and alarm sound torture in addition to Bill's excruciating pain were making us crazy. And Bill was feeling uncontrollably anxious that he would be left in this institution.

We had to get out.

Continuing in her role as an obnoxious advocate, Chris demanded that she see the respiratory therapist and make plans to discharge Bill to home. Jen, the respiratory therapist was equally as nonplussed by Chris' aggressive behavior as the state worker had been. At least this time, Chris could pride herself on the fact that she didn't use foul language.

Her demandingness, a trait needed in this situation, but not a character trait that she usually exhibited, got things moving quickly. We needed a home ventilator unit to be prescribed so that we could get out of this God-forsaken place. Chris managed to get it and the doctor's orders we needed to get Bill out, within 24 hours.

With Bill's portable ventilator unit under his manual wheelchair, we left just like we had entered the facility, with our church family and Bill's mom's support. Like a parade, this group had helped us to move Bill's foam mattress and all of his technology and equipment back to our home. What a sight we were!

Having spent half of 2004 living in the hospital, treating Bill's intractable pneumonia, with Bill in the hospital bed and Chris lying on the floor, we just wanted to be home. But our stay back in our own home would be short lived.

Bill's body was tanking once again. His breathing was slowing as his lungs were filling with fluid and he was having difficulty staying alert. If we didn't get to the hospital soon, Bill would die.

But he didn't want to go back to the hospital. Chris wasn't sure that Bill was ready to die; he just didn't want the horrific hospital pneumonia treatment again. The powerful super drugs would take away the pneumonia but would cause him great abdominal pain and horrendous diarrhea.

In crisis Chris called Dr. Paulus our family physician, at his home number. Our gentle physician had given Chris both his home and cell number. He had said to call him when we needed him and now we needed him more than ever.

"Bill's oxygen levels are falling. He needs to get to the hospital. He doesn't want to go and I don't think he's ready to stay at home to die. Please talk to him and help him to make a decision," Chris asked of Dr. Paulus.

"Bill, you don't have great choices, as you know. If you stay home I will get you whatever narcotics you need to be comfortable. The sky's the limit. But you know that you will die. If you are not ready then we will have to do the hospital round again. Which is it going to be Bill?" Dr. Paulus asked with his kind but firm voice.

Because Bill was too sick to use his Liberator™, he was now using very slight head nods to indicate yes, while Chris recited the letters of the alphabet. Slowly Bill responded, "h-o-s-p-i-t-a-l" and we moved once again, back into the ICU.

We were in a catch 22 with no way out. Bill's excruciating pain required increasing doses of narcotics but the narcotics were leading to repeated recurrences of pneumonia.

CHAPTER 60

(Bill and Chris' Voices)
Finding a Way When There is No Way

"Bill, what did you think of the pastoral candidate we brought in to see you?" two members of the church's pastoral search team asked.

Probably one of the most unusual experiences ever for any potential pastor of a church, the search team had brought the candidate into the Intensive Care Unit to get Bill's highly valued opinion regarding how he saw the match between this individual and the needs of our church.

Using subtle eye movements to indicate which of the letters that Chris was saying needed to be included in his message Bill spelled out, "No. There are concerns." And then he listed a couple of them. The team, having obtained what they wanted that is, Bill's insightful comments, left him, now exhausted, to get some rest.

Chris, fascinated by this interview, and amazed that Bill could be so cogent with so many narcotics in his system, also wondered if it could have been one of the reasons why Bill was still alive and continuing the struggle in his catch 22 situation between pain and pneumonia. Perhaps the church *had* needed some straight talk from Bill around this potential pastor.

Still being very much a part of our church family even though we were at the hospital and unable to attend church worship, a parade of church people, in addition to Bill's mom who spent much time each day with us, brought the hope of Christ, food for Chris and their fellowship to us in our long term stay room in the ICU. Pastor Don, the interim pastor paid us a visit almost every day. A couple of church women sacrificed their night of sleep to be with Bill so that Chris could go home and sleep. With this pastoral interview our church brought us the latest church business too.

However, being surrounded by more typical ICU patients who either moved quickly to a medical unit after surgery or in some cases moved on to heaven because they died, we wondered why we were the only ones who were staying indefinitely in the ICU. With Bill too sick to go home or to another medical unit there was no way that we could leave the ICU. We were trapped.

Some of the physician staff didn't like the fact that we were taking up residence in the ICU either. During the early morning rounds each Monday morning Chris would be asked why we were still taking up residence in the ICU by the new hospitalist doctor who was starting a week's shift. Chris' consistent answer was that Bill was still working through his health problems and that she was not going to make the decisions for him.

Most physicians had great difficulty understanding that the man in the bed, non-verbal and looking drugged was cogent and capable of making his own decisions. Chris had to keep contending with the unbelieving looks and comments of the new doctors (each Monday morning starting their weekly shift) who didn't understand that Bill was still as intelligent as ever. Some physicians in a round-about way would suggest that Chris make a decision on Bill's behalf to go home on hospice.

After one particularly difficult Monday morning session when the hospitalist was particularly blunt, Chris called Dr. Paulus and asked him to please make a visit to the hospital. He came as soon as he was able.

"Dr. Paulus, some of the physician staff are saying that Bill is costing the system too much money. They want me to push Bill to go home to die and I won't do it. Is the hospital going under financially because we live here?" Chris asked, feeling most upset because dignity for Bill in making his own healthcare decisions was not something that Chris was going to take from him.

"Chris, don't worry about the cost. This hospital will survive just fine even if Bill's cost are now are about a half million dollars. What Medicaid doesn't pay, they will make up from other peoples' insurance. It all works out in the end. It's going to take as long as it takes Chris. That's OK." Dr. Paulus said giving Chris the assurance that she needed to just walk this road with Bill for as long as it would take.

Abiding with God until whatever was supposed to happen was our only answer.

Our personal financial concerns were also a serious reality during this time of abiding. We could only trust God with our mortgage and with Chris' job that she had been unable to do all summer. We were so grateful that Chris' employer stepped up to offer her use of the United States Family and Medical Leave Act of 1993 to access three months of non-paid leave to care for Bill in the hospital. With this in place, we could abide through the summer and into the fall of 2004, with Chris' job security intact and ready for her return to work in November.

Abiding plus Chris' hissy fit a few months earlier had brought Deena, a capable caring woman to be Chris' fill to give her a little respite. Deena quickly learned how to help Bill to communicate and how to help him to move in our attempts to support him around his persistent pain. Knowing that Bill had what he needed and valued the most that is the power of communication, Chris could go home and get a nap for a few hours in the afternoon before facing another long night of cat naps at most on the hard couch in Bill's ICU room.

The hospital responded to Chris' insistency that all should be tried to help Bill with his catch 22, and that Bill must be make his up his own mind, by bringing in their options of last resort.

An osteopathic doctor with eastern medicine training was brought in to teach Chris how to use acupuncture on Bill's head to treat his pain. A psychologist was brought in to work on pain management by accessing certain brain wave-lengths through specific sounds waves that Bill listened to through a headset. Unfortunately, none of these less commonly used approaches were effective in reducing Bill's pain, but at least Chris and Bill could say that they had tried all that was available.

And then the last of the last resorts was approached. A pharmacist came to talk with Chris and Bill about using a specific combination of pharmaceuticals to support pain relief. The goal was to support Bill's body with a specific concoction of drugs to allow him to live with his pain and not continue to have bouts of pneumonia.

The theory was that, if Bill needed narcotics that were very physically addicting, to at best dull his pain, perhaps Methadone, a synthetic narcotic with less issues of dependence than regular opioids could be substituted. Methadone, at a lesser dosage would hopefully not have the same side effect of slowing Bill's breathing that was leading to his recurrent pneumonia. At the same time Bill's body would be supported with a concoction of other things to fight the pain, such as antidepressants, thought to be able to support pain tolerance by increasing the level of serotonin in his body.

A physical detox would be a necessary part of moving Bill from his highly addictive narcotics over to Methadone. Ironically Bill had been saying that the regular narcotics barely touch the surface of his intractable nerve pain anyway. We would need to return to the rehab center to do the detox. Chris was insistent that we not go back to that noxious ventilator unit and we didn't.

Bill, realizing that this was the last of the options available to get him out of his catch 22 was game to try it. Chris, with at least some idea of what the physical detoxification of the body from narcotics could look like was completely terrified. But she knew that we had run out of options and that the time of waiting with God was over. It was time to make the next move.

Federal Register, Vol. 58, No. 106, June 4, 1993.
Family and Medical Leave Act of 1993.

Federal Register / Vol. 58, No. 106 / Friday, June 4, 1993 / Rules and Regulations   31839

Appendix C to Part 825--Notice to Employees of Rights Under FMLA

YOUR RIGHTS
under the
FAMILY AND MEDICAL LEAVE ACT OF 1993

FMLA requires covered employers to provide up to 12 weeks of unpaid, job-protected leave to "eligible" employees for certain family and medical reasons. Employees are eligible if they have worked for a covered employer for at least one year, and for 1,250 hours over the previous 12 months, and if there are at least 50 employees within 75 miles.

REASONS FOR TAKING LEAVE: Unpaid leave must be granted for any of the following reasons:

- to care for the employee's child after birth, or placement for adoption or foster care;
- to care for the employee's spouse, son or daughter, or parent, who has a serious health condition; or
- for a serious health condition that makes the employee unable to perform the employee's job.

At the employee's or employer's option, certain kinds of paid leave may be substituted for unpaid leave.

ADVANCE NOTICE AND MEDICAL CERTIFICATION: The employee may be required to provide advance leave notice and medical certification. Taking of leave may he denied if requirements are not met.

- The employee ordinarily must provide 30 days advance notice when the leave is "foreseeable."
- An employer may require medical certification to support a request for leave because of a serious health condition, and may require second or third opinions (at the employer's expense) and a fitness for duty report to return to work.

JOB BENEFITS AND PROTECTION:

- For the duration of FMLA leave, the employer must maintain the employee's health coverage under any "group health plan."
- Upon return from FMLA leave, most employees must be restored to their original or equivalent positions with equivalent pay, benefits, and other employment terms.
- The use of FMLA leave cannot result in the loss of any employment benefit that accrued prior to the start of an employee's leave.

UNLAWFUL ACTS BY EMPLOYERS: FMLA makes it unlawful for any employer to:

- interfere with, restrain, or deny the exercise of any right provided under FMLA;
- discharge or discriminate against any person for opposing any practice made unlawful by FMLA or for involvement in any proceeding under or relating to FMLA.

CHAPTER 61

(Chris and Bill's Voices)

Going Home to Go Home

"Your husband needs you to be strong so that he can let go," one of the wise and caring nurses said to Chris as she wandered the halls of the rehab facility in the middle of the night.

The nurse then added, "You are unusual, you know that don't you? Most spouses bail when it gets this bad. Bill is hanging in because he doesn't want to leave you. You are going to have to help him to let go and die. You will do it. You love him too much not to."

"I know, I know." Chris responded through tears, realizing that this sage nurse was correct. Bill would not be able to go home to die without Chris' strength behind him. The tables had turned and Bill now needed Chris' strength. Chris would give him her all. Love would not let her do otherwise.

The government system had been rallying and preparing for Bill to go home on hospice. Marlene, our self-appointed Waiver case worker had been in regular contact with Chris during the horrific detox, keeping her up to date on what was happening at the state end. During one conversation she reported that state officials had told her that she was to give Chris whatever she needed because it was for Bill Rush.

Dr. Paulus also came to visit us and would also call Chris to check in. During one telephone conversation, he again reassured Chris that if Bill were to go home, "The sky's the limit Chris. I'll get Bill all the narcotics he needs to be comfortable." Then he would add, "I'm praying for both of you. Call me anytime, I mean *anytime* you need anything."

Pastor Don, a two-time retired but working again interim pastor from our church continued to drop by almost daily.

Chris continued to report to Marlene, Dr. Paulus and Pastor Don that Bill was not ready yet.

Then the day finally came.

"Dr. Paulus, Bill is ready to go home." Chris said in tears on the phone.

It had been every bit as horrific to detox Bill off his regular morphine and onto Methadone as Chris had imagined -and then some. To watch Bill writhe in the pain of detox on top of his intractable neurological pain was more excruciating than Chris could have imagined.

Chris had hung in with Bill because to not try was not an option. Bill had to know that he had tried everything possible to get himself out of his catch 22 situation. And this was the last option, worthy of a full and complete trial.

Bill, now detoxified from regular morphine and with the power of the pharmaceutical concoction that was supposed to aide him in living with his pain, had been up in his wheelchair doing some exercises. The super concoction made his body look vibrant and healthy on the outside. Ironically, he looked better than he had looked in a long time.

Chris asked the question that needed to be asked, "Bill how's your pain?" and then started counting from 1 to 10, using the medical pain scale with the lowest indicating no pain and the highest excruciating pain, to get a sense of Bill's pain in that moment.

Bill indicated 10 and then spelled out, "I can't live like this."

"We're finished Bill. There is nothing else. You have tried everything. Are you ready to go home?" Chris asked, choking back the tears.

"Yes," Bill answered.

"Bill you are breaking new ground again." Chris explained. "We will have hospice care in combination with the Waiver to get regular nursing. Dr. Paulus says that you are in charge. He will work with you to get you whatever meds you need."

It was the day before our fifth anniversary, and four and a half years since the ordeal with the pain had started. Bill had finished his fight.

The next day Lori, a friend from church who had been a constant source of help, came with a bouquet of red roses for Chris that Bill had asked her to go and get.

The anniversary card attached to the flowers said, "Fragile is a rose like me. Beautiful is a rose like you. Love your husband Bill." Our love had never tasted so bitter sweet.

With Chris staying strong for Bill, she worked with the "system" to take Bill home to 'go home to heaven.'

Arriving at our house via medical transport, Bill was rolled into the living room and transferred over to his hospital style bed by the medics.

With a broad smile on his face, Bill indicated that he was absolutely delighted by the warm welcome he found at our home. Martha, a constant church friend throughout our ordeal, had come to decorate the house with "Welcome Home" banners and balloons. Chris' parents, there to be of help to Chris, had positioned all of Bill's awards and pictures at a height where he could see them from his vantage point of lying in his hospital bed.

In the coming days and weeks, an unending parade of people would come through the doors of our home to celebrate Bill's time of coming home to 'go home'. They came to celebrate our love and Bill's life.

Real hope for life after death through Christ, was brought in the door by Jesus-with-skin, the hands and feet of His people, was the balm that we desperately needed for our deep sorrow. Our families, friends, our Christian Community and the Disability Rights community brought it into our home by the truckload.

CHAPTER 62

(Chris' Voice)
Dying Well

"Bill thank you for your friendship. We love you." I heard people saying, in a spirit of gratitude and love.

I was coming downstairs after taking a much needed catnap to find a spirit of joy and celebration, laughter and fun surrounding Bill in the middle of our living room where he was lying on his hospital bed. Many people from our church were there celebrating Bill's life with him and sharing what felt like palpable hope, in the midst of such profound despair. I wondered if this group of Brothers and Sisters were even the slightest bit aware that they had brought with their presence right into your home, the hope of eternity with Christ beyond this pain and sorrow.

After this latest group of people left, I checked in with Bill to see how he was doing with all the visitors.

"Are you doing OK with all these people being around you Bill?" I asked.

"Wonderful. Thank you." Bill spelled out as I recited the letters of the alphabet.

He later added, "Amazed that people want to come to see me."

I was amazed too. Not because I didn't think that Bill hadn't impacted many people's lives. I just didn't know how many people would willingly be around someone who would die soon. But many from both our church and disability rights communities and our families and friends took me up on my invitation that they come and celebrate Bill's life with him.

People came in pairs and small groups and as individuals to visit Bill, talking with him about his life and what he had meant to them. Some came to read a poem, play an instrument or read scripture to him. Bill's friends Mark and Anne came and Bill was visibly delighted to have them with him. Deanne, who had come to the hospital to visit Bill, called on occasion to talk with him now that he was home. Marlene from the League of Human Dignity and Tim from Nebraska Advocacy Services came and spent some time with Bill too. Other people in the disability rights community rolled into our accessible home to visit with Bill.

Our church friend Lori continued the task that she had begun while she had stayed with Bill in the hospital when she came to provide some respite for me. Together Lori and Bill would painstakingly review the chapters that Bill wanted included in this book, his next book. While proofreading his work, Lori would read Bill's chapters out loud, often inadvertently enticing the nursing staff to stop and listen to Bill's clear word pictures. Bill also enjoyed hearing Lori read his favorite books about John F. Kennedy out loud. Thinking was an enjoyable distraction from his pain and Lori provided much for Bill's bright mind to continue to chew on.

Bill's brothers came to challenge him to a game of chess, just as they had done in the past. One brother would play against Bill with at least one of the others 'coaching'. I was never sure who was ganging up on whom. And Bill's Mom would come every couple of days too. My folks, acting as den parents, took the role of welcoming people to our home and making sure that I was fed.

Each day I would print off the newest emails and read them to Bill. Two hundred and fifty email messages had arrived in response to my email invitation that people show their love to Bill by sending him a note before he became sedated by his pain meds.

Taking charge of his dying just as he had done for his living, Bill had asked for a meeting with Dr. Paulus and Pastor Don. He wanted to talk about a plan for increasing his narcotic pain meds as well as his own funeral. Learning that he would have about a two week life expectancy after the addictive narcotics were started, Bill set the date when he would start to increase his medications. He allowed himself a couple of weeks to do his good-byes well before that date.

His way. His body. His life. Rush's Rule until the end. That was my Bill.

And so, too quickly it seemed, the celebrations of Bill's life with him were over and the narcotics were increased according to Bill's own preset timetable. With the arrival of hospice, the reality of death and the impending separation between us set in.

One night, Barb, one of the home health nurses paid for by Bill's Wavier exemption program so that I could get some sleep, woke me up to say that Bill was distraught and that she couldn't figure out what to do. Jumping out of bed, I found Bill visibly upset and wide awake.

"Cosmic joke," Bill spelled out. I knew exactly what he meant. We had worked so hard to create a life that we never got and he was suggesting that some evil force had had its way and won at our expense. He was hurting terribly from the injustice of our situation.

"I feel like that too." I responded in anguish.

"Can't leave you," he then spelled out and started to sob.

Crying with him, I crawled into his hospital bed as far as I could get into it and held him until the sobbing stopped and he fell back into his opium stupor.

Bill continued to work through his own unique worries and concerns and wrap up loose ends. Fortunately, with a large variety of people involved in Bill's life, each of whom had different skills and abilities that they were willing to share, we would be able to help Bill to die well…

One day, Bill was insistent that he sit up in his wheelchair to be able to get his computer to print out something.

If Bill were to write about it, I'm sure that he would say that it took more work to move him from bed to chair on this day than it normally takes to move the Shuttle on the launch pad in Florida.

With the help of four people consisting of the respiratory therapist Jen, (who was gracious enough to forgive me for my rudeness at the rehab center and was now helping us when we needed her anytime day or night), Deena, and a paid nurse, it took us forty-five minutes to get Bill up into his wheelchair and sitting at his computer. It took all of us to figure out how to support his now very weak body, while moving him around with his ventilator and all of its tubing.

After pushing his headstick down around his forehead, I supported Bill's neck to keep his head upright. Turning the computer on, I looked to Bill for his indication of where his file might be stored on his hard drive. It took about fifteen minutes for us to find the specific file that Bill was looking for, partly because Bill needed so much help to use his headstick.

Opening the folder we saw a list of the files he had created to be considered for this book. He wanted to print all of these chapters so as to help those of us who would be left to complete his second book. After inspecting what the printer had spit out to make sure that his file list was complete, Bill then lowered his head and his headstick fell in his lap. This grueling physical task was finished.

And so was Bill on this earth.

Carefully the team of four helped to get Bill back out of his wheelchair and into the hospital bed. Exhausted, Bill was asleep within minutes.

With tears in my eyes, I looked to my parents who had been watching Bill's determination to do what he did with amazement, from the kitchen. They too had tears in their eyes. We all knew that was the last time Bill would be out of bed.

On another day, Bill was concerned that he be able to vote in the upcoming general election. When a friend arrived to visit, Bill asked her to please go and get him an absentee ballot, help him to fill it in and then return it to the elections office. The friend was delighted to help. Bill was relieved to have done his civic duty, especially because this was the presidential election.

In addition to his daily drop in, Pastor Don was also summoned a few times when Bill was struggling to come to terms with being separated from me in heaven, and how that could possibly be a good thing.

On one occasion Bill was wrestling with the theological concept that there is no marriage in heaven. He was afraid of feeling alone without me, as he had been for years before he met me. I didn't know how to comfort him. So I called Pastor Don.

Always the available pastor when someone was in genuine need, Pastor Don came right away to bring his particular gifts of wisdom and caring to help guide Bill's thinking. Pastor Don was able to gently assure Bill that he would have knowledge of me in heaven and that our love would continue there in a form only known in heaven.

Another time Bill was distressed because he didn't know what to do with his wedding ring. Bill was genuinely distraught because he didn't know how to think about this issue and he needed to know that he had wrapped up this concern. Once again, not knowing how to help him, I called Pastor Don. He came right over to help alleviate Bill's distress.

"Bill there is nothing written in the Bible about what to do with your wedding ring. You are free to choose." Pastor Don reflected honestly to Bill, wisely giving him the freedom of thought that he needed to make his own decision.

Bill carefully and slowly spelled, "People would have to break every bone in my body to get it off me while I am alive so I'm not going to take it off after I'm dead."

"Bill, I think that God would be just fine with that answer." Pastor Don said with great wisdom and compassion.

Bill, relieved that he could keep his wedding ring on his body after he died, was able to settle yet again. And with Bill feeling better, I could then settle too.

CHAPTER 63

(Chris' Voice)

A Voice from Above

"I'm so sorry for bothering you in the middle of the night Dr. Paulus. Bill is in lots of pain and we need his morphine and valium dosages increased again. The pharmacist needs new orders and I need to know how much to push into his pic line to help him get more comfortable."

"Push the same dosage of each every ten minutes until you notice Bill getting more comfortable and then increase the dosage of each by a quarter of the quantity he is currently getting. I'll call in the dosage changes. Call me again if you need anything." Dr. Paulus responded sounding awfully awake for it being three o'clock in the morning.

With the orders called into the 24-hour pharmacy, I was able to pump more into Bill's veins and more shopping bags of morphine and Valium would arrive via courier in the morning.

I had been trying to stay on top of Bill's pain levels for nine weeks. But the pain kept getting away from me. I was grateful for Dr. Paulus, who was true to his word. He said that the sky was the limit and we were getting pretty close to it, so much so, that the pharmacists continued to ask for clarification of the dosages because they had never seen anyone before Bill, have such a high dosage of morphine and Valium.

At one point, Bill, who was still unbelievably cogent, spelled out to me. "I have to carry my cross to the end."

With frustration I responded, "Bill you have carried your cross far enough. The drugs can carry you the rest of the way. We'll just get more."

God, I don't want to lose him but I need you to release Bill from his pain! I cried out silently.

Two weeks of hospice became nine weeks.

And with my Family Medical Leave Act time running out, I had to return to work in the middle of Bill's time of hospice. I was anxious about leaving him. But knowing that I was leaving Bill in capable hands at home, I forced myself out the door and to begin to get back into work again.

After a week back at work, I received a call from Dr. Paulus who was at my home. He wanted me to come home. The ventilator was no longer supporting Bill and he wanted me to come to be with Bill while it was removed.

Concerned for my safety when driving myself home, my co-workers asked me whom I should call to come and get me. I told them to call Sandy, the music director from my church.

Delivered safely home by Sandy, I found Dr. Paulus and Jen, the respiratory therapist, standing around Bill's bed. They showed me how the ventilator was no longer supporting Bill's breathing.

Hearing my voice, Bill awoke.

Dr. Paulus explained what was happening to Bill and asked for his permission to remove the ventilator. Bill agreed. I stroked Bill's arm and smiled at him while this now seemingly permanent part of Bill's technology was rolled out the door. We thought the end was near.

But Bill had seven false alarms before he died.

It was a bittersweet and excruciating time for me. I had more time with Bill than expected. But the longer he lived, the more his body deteriorated. It was horrifying beyond anything that I could have imagined. We couldn't stay on top of his growing deep gangrenous pressure sores, increasing pneumonia secretions and excruciating pain.

Dr. Paulus became a key source of support to me both as a physician and a Christian. I kept asking him why Bill was still here. I was so hurt to see Bill in so much pain with a body that was ripping apart.

Dr. Paulus prayed for my peace and never tried to give me an answer. He just listened to my cries for release for Bill into a new body. He recited Bible scriptures about the new body that Bill would receive in heaven to bolster my spirit. I didn't think that I could stand by and watch this a minute longer.

People volunteered their time to be extra hands to help with the difficult task of taking care of his dying body while continuing to acknowledge and support his still alert mind and spirit. I needed their presence to support me and bolster my faith when I was afraid that God had forgotten Bill.

Amanda, a former young aide for Bill who lived close by offered to come and help me when I took care of Bill alone for eight hours without nursing care. She helped to turn Bill and clean the sore areas so that I didn't have to look at them.

On the last time she was there to help me with Bill, she said, "I'll see you next week Bill."

Aware that the end was near responded with my help to say the letters of the alphabet, Bill wanted to say "No" to Amanda. This was followed by, "Thank you."

"Goodbye Bill. Thank you for letting me get to know you." Amanda responded with the maturity of one much older than her years.

Bill knew that his time was short. I asked his family to come to visit with him one more time. They surrounded a now sedated Bill who briefly opened his eyes to see who was there and then was asleep again. He was getting close and he knew it.

Knowing that Bill wanted to see Mark one more time, I called him to come as quickly as he could. Mark was on an airplane flying back from California and came to the house as soon as he landed.

After these visits Bill's body appeared to be calmer and he gave in more easily to the medications. The pain was finally controlled enough and Bill's was fading.

The day finally came. The nurse woke me up before dawn, saying, "Chris it's getting close. Bill has very little time now."

I sat with Bill and stroked his hair talking to him, while his body struggled horribly to the end.

I prayed that he would be feeling some peace inside rather than the agony of death that his body was experiencing.

Suddenly the agony was over, his body was quiet and I heard his last exhale.

Within seconds of Bill's death, I felt hands pressing down on my shoulders, and heard a male voice right above my head saying excitedly and adamantly, "I'm OK! I'm OK!"

It had to be Bill. I thought. The strength of the personality was undeniably him. He was communicating to me from the 'other side'.

Plus there was so much in his message. By pushing on my shoulders in a way that he never could do when he was alive because of his cerebral palsy, Bill was telling me that he had a new body and that he was OK with being in an able-body. God had found a way to reconcile Bill's pride in his disability with the notion of getting a new body after he died.

And the excitement in his voice told me that God had also dealt with Bill's fears of being separated from me.

In the presence of God, Bill was truly OK and he needed to let me know so that I would be comforted.

Bill it's you! Of course you would be the one to break the barrier of death if anyone could! After all you spent your lifetime breaking down doors here on earth!

And then he was gone.

Sobbing the depth of my grief, I was feeling the full impact of realizing that Bill was gone from me.

But, I was also so happy and relieved to know that my incredible Bill had told me that he was now enjoying himself in his new body in the presence of God! Bill was finally home!! Praise God!

Epilogue

(Chris' Voice)

State of Nebraska Honors William L. Rush

It was February 14, 2005, my first Valentine's Day without Bill. With grief feeling like it was suffocating me, I had somehow managed to force myself to make it through my workday. I returned to my far too quiet and lonely home to find a message on my answering machine from Marlene at the League.

"Chris, I have a package for you from Senator Byars. Can you come by to pick it up?"

Curious to see what the state senator had left for me, I went over right away to get my package.

"You know that Senator Byars had called and asked if he could eulogize Bill at his funeral, don't you?" Marlene asked me.

"No. I didn't know that anyone had asked to do a Eulogy." I responded and then added, "I assumed that everyone knew that Bill had planned his funeral around the concept of Servant Leadership, as describe in Martin Luther King's Drum Major Instinct sermon. Because Bill wanted a focus on serving Christ, by serving others, he didn't want to be eulogized." I responded.

"Well, here's something from the Senator for you." Marlene then said and handed me a large envelope.

Not sure of how I would respond, I decided to take the envelope home where I could be alone to open it. I found an official note care from Senator Byars with a picture of the Nebraska Unicameral

Legislature on the front. There was also a folder containing some official legislative-looking pieces of paper.

Opening the note card first, I found a hand written message from Senator Byars. It said,

> Chris,
>
> Bill was a special person and a special friend and I hope this in a small way draws the respect and love that I had for him and his unbelievable courage!
> God bless Bill.
> God bless you Chris,
>
> Dennis Byars.

In the folder I found a true and correct copy of Legislative Resolution 33, passed by the Legislature of Nebraska on the 9th of February, 2005, and signed by both the president and clerk of the legislature. It stated:

Introduced by Byars,

WHEREAS, William Rush was a quadriplegic because of cerebral palsy which required him to be confined to a wheelchair but did not confine his accomplishments; and

WHEREAS, in 1984 William Rush was the first quadriplegic to graduate with honors from the University of Nebraska-Lincoln, graduating from the college of Journalism; and

WHEREAS, William Rush used voice synthesis technology which allowed him to have voice and speak up for people with disabilities; and

WHEREAS, by using a stick attached to a helmet he wore and typing each letter, he wrote his autobiography, Journey Out of Silence, which was published in 1986; and

WHEREAS, William Rush was a writer and an advocate for people with disabilities at the local level by writing op-ed (Opinion-Editorial) pieces in the Omaha World Herald, Lincoln Journal, and the Lincoln Star, and testifying before Congress about the American with Disabilities Act., and

WHEREAS, William Rush married Christine Robinson, who saw the man and the possibilities; and

WHEREAS, the state has been fortunate to have an advocate of William Rush's caliber defending the rights of, and being the voice for, so many disabled individuals; and

WHEREAS, William Rush died at the age of forty-nine succumbing to pneumonia but not to his disability;

NOW, THEREFORE, BE IT RESOLVED BY THE MEMBERS OF THE NINETY-NINTH LEGISLATURE OF NEBRASKA, FIRST SESSION:

1. That the Legislature extends its sympathies to William Rush's wife, Christine Robinson
2. That a copy of the resolution be sent to Christine Robinson

Tears of grief, love, joy and gratitude rolled down my face as I read and re-read the card and the legislative resolution honoring Bill. The state of Nebraska had sent me a sympathy card on Valentine's Day, a card that expressed recognition of Bill's character and gratitude for his work on behalf of people with disabilities. It also recognized my ability to see who Bill really was, and the profound love that we had for each other.

It was also big enough to be a declaration of Bill's love for me.

Yeah, I thought, *If Bill would write to the President of the United States of America, to try to figure out how to marry me, my advocate in heaven would have no problem petitioning God Himself for this special Valentine's Day message for me! Oh my amazing Bill!*

NINETY-NINTH LEGISLATURE

FIRST SESSION

LEGISLATIVE RESOLUTION 33

Introduced by Byars, 30

WHEREAS, William Rush was a quadriplegic because of cerebral palsy which required him to be confined to a wheelchair but did not confine his accomplishments; and

WHEREAS, in 1983 William Rush was the first quadriplegic to graduate with honors from the University of Nebraska-Lincoln, graduating from the College of Journalism; and

WHEREAS, William Rush used a voice synthesis technology which allowed him to have a voice and speak up for people with disabilities; and

WHEREAS, by using a stick attached to a helmet he wore and typing each letter, he wrote his autobiography, Journey Out of Silence, which was published in 1986; and

WHEREAS, William Rush was a writer and an advocate for people with disabilities at the local level by writing op-ed pieces in the Omaha World-Herald, Lincoln Journal, and the Lincoln Star, and testifying before Congress about the Americans with Disabilities Act; and

WHEREAS, William Rush married Christine Robinson, who saw the man and the possibilities; and

WHEREAS, the state has been fortunate to have an advocate of William Rush's caliber defending the rights of, and being the

LR 33   LR 33

voice for, so many disabled individuals; and

   WHEREAS, William Rush died at the age of forty-nine after
succumbing to pneumonia but not to his disability.

   NOW, THEREFORE, BE IT RESOLVED BY THE MEMBERS OF THE
NINETY-NINTH LEGISLATURE OF NEBRASKA, FIRST SESSION:

   1. That the Legislature extends its sympathies to William
Rush's wife, Christine Robinson.

   2. That a copy of this resolution be sent to Christine
Robinson.

PRESIDENT OF THE LEGISLATURE

   I, Patrick J. O'Donnell, hereby certify that the foregoing is
a true and correct copy of Legislative Resolution 33, which was passed
by the Legislature of Nebraska in the Ninety-Ninth Legislature, First
Session, on the ....9th.... day of February 2005.

CLERK OF THE LEGISLATURE

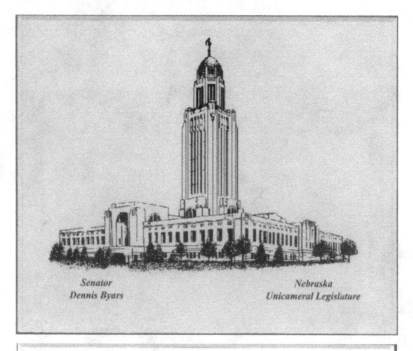

Senator
Dennis Byars

Nebraska
Unicameral Legislature

Chris,

Bill was a special person & a special friend and I hope this in a small way shows the respect & love that I had for him and his unbelievable courage!

Dennis Byars

God Bless Bill

God Bless you Chris

Bibliography

Arends, Carolyn. *Wrestling with Angels*. Eugene: Harvest House, 2000.

Bays, Matt. *Finding God in The Ruins How God Redeems Pai*n. Colorado Springs: Cook, 2016.

Bouman, Mark. With D. R. Jacobsen, *the tank man's son A Memoir.* Carol Stream (IL): Tyndale House, 2015.

Chan, Francis and Lisa Chan. *You and Me Forever Marriage in Light of Eternity.* San Francisco: Claire Love, 2014.

Eiesland, Nancy. The Disabled God: Toward a Liberatory Theology of Disability. Nashville: Abingdon, 1995.

Eldredege, John. *Beautiful Outlaw Experiencing The Playful, Disruptive, Extravagant Personality of Jesus.* New York: FaithWords, 2011.

Elliot, Elisabeth. *A Path Through Suffering Discovering The Relationship Between God's Mercy and Our Pain.* Ann Arbor: Servant, 1990.

Gertzen, Jason. "Citizens Gather to Fight Cuts." *Omaha World Herald*, March 4, 1993.

Goff, Bob. Love Does Discover A Secretly Incredible Life in an Ordinary World. Nashville: Nelson, 2012.

Hockenberry, John. *A Memoir War Zones, Wheelchairs, and Declarations of Independence.* New York: Hyperion, 1995.

Jensen, Margaret. A Nail in a Sure Place. San Bernardino: Here's Life, 1989.

Kidd, Sue Monk. *When the Heart Waits.* San Francisco: Harper Collins, 1990.

Lawrence, Brother. *The Practice of the Presence of God.* Uhrichsville, (OH), Barbour, 2004.

Lewis, C. S. *A Grief Observed.* New York: HarperCollins, 1961.

Lewis, C.S. *The Problem of Pain.* New York: HarperCollins, 1996.

Longmore, Paul. *Why I burned by Book and Other Essays on Disability.* Philadelphia: Temple, 2003.

Meyer, Joyce. *The Everyday Life Bible. (AMP)* New York: Faith Words, 2006.

Morrison, Suzanne. "Meeting of The Minds." *The Hamilton Spectator* Hamilton, Ontario April 1, 1989.

Nolan, Christopher. *Under the Eye of The Clock.* New York: St Martin's, 1987.

Nouwen, Henri. With Timothy Jones. *Turn My Mourning Into Dancing Finding Hope in Hard Times.* Nashville: Thomas Nelson, 2001.

O'Connor, Elizabeth. *Cry Pain, Cry Hope Thresholds to Purpose.* Waco: Word, 1987.

Peterson, Eugene. *The Message The Bible in Contemporary Language.* Colorado Springs: Navpress, 2003.

Reynolds, Thomas E. *Vulnerable Communion A Theology of Disability and Hospitality.* Grand Rapids: Brazos, 2008.

Rush, Bill. "ADAPT." *Nebraska Rehabilitation and Community Newsletter,* Vocational Rehabilitation, Nebraska Department of Education, September 1995.

Rush, Bill. "A Perfect "Roll" Model." *Nebraska Rehabilitation and Community Newsletter,* Vocational Rehabilitation Nebraska Department of Education, December 1994.

Rush, Bill. "A Personal Spiritual Journey Testimony." *First Baptist Church Tower,* Vol 3, Issue 26 (1996)

Rush, Bill. "Belonging and Compliments: Both are Necessary" *Nebraska Rehabilitation and Community Newsletter,* Vocational Rehabilitation, Nebraska Department of Education, October 1995.

Rush, Bill. "First Baptist Lincoln Gets A Very Special Thank You!" *The Messenger- American Baptist Churches of Nebraska,* Summer 1991: 7

Rush, Bill. "the perfect memory." *Prentke Romich Inc. Current Expressions Newsletter* (Summer 1992)

Rush, Bill. "On the Road-Finally." *Nebraska Rehabilitation and Community Newsletter,* Vocational Rehabilitation, Nebraska Department of Education, July/August 1996.

Rush, William. "ADAPT-Empowerment NOT Terrorism." *Nebraska Rehabilitation and Community Newsletter*, Vocational Rehabilitation, Nebraska Department of Education, December 1994.

Rush, William. "A Model To the Community." *Christian Single* November 1992: 32-33.

Rush, William. "Adding Insult to Injury." *RN*, September 1991: 21-25.

Rush, William. "Dalton's Legacy." *In Beneath the Surface Creative Expressions of Augmented Communicators* International Society of Augmentative and Alternative Communication, edited by Sarah Blackstone, ISAAC Series: Vol 2, 2000.

Rush, William. "Harvesters with Disabilities: A Journey Testimony." Journal of Religion, Disability & Health, Vol. 7 (4) 2003.

Rush, William. "Invisible Healing The Personal Testimony of a Quadriplegic." *Presbyterian Survey*, March 1994. 18-20.

Rush, William. "It's Time to Deliver on Promises to Americans with Disabilities." *Lincoln Journal Star* Lincoln Nebraska (April 27, 1996).

Rush, William. *Journey Out of Silence.* 2nd Edition, Lulu.com, 2008.

Rush, William. "Liberating Myself." In *Speaking Up and Spelling It Out,* edited by Melanie Fried-Oken and Hank Bersani, Jr, 148-152. Baltimore: Brookes, 2000.

Rush, William. "My Turn to Speak." *Communication Outlook*, Vol 13 Number 3: 19. (1992).

Rush, William. "The Making of a Square Hole." *On the Level Newsletter of the League of Human Dignity Lincoln Nebraska*, November/December 1999.

Rush, William. *Write with Dignity.* Gilbert M and Martha H. Hitchcock Center Publication, School of Journalism, University of Nebraska Lincoln. 1983.

Shaw, Luci. *The Crime of Living Cautiously Hearing God's Call to Adventure.* Downers Grove (IL): Intervarsity, 2005.

Sittser, Gerald. *A Grace Disguised: Expanded Edition.* Grand Rapids: Zondervan, 2004.

Stoddard, Martha. "Proposal Could Prevent Medicaid Loss." *Lincoln Journal Star* Lincoln Nebraska, Jan 12, 1998

Thomas, Gary. *Sacred Marriage What if God Designed Marriage to Make Us Holy More than to make Us Happy?* Grand Rapids: Zondervan, 2000.

Thompson, Francis. "The Hound of Heaven" in *The Works of Francis Thompson.* Ann Arbor: University Press, 1913.

Watterson, Kathryn. *Not By the Sword.* New York: Simon and Schuster Inc., 1995.

Zola, Irving. Missing Pieces: *A Chronicle of Living with a Disability.* Philadelphia: Temple, 1982.

Mustafa, Nujeen. and Christine Lamb. *Nujeen.* New York: Collins, 2016.

Reeve, Christopher. *Nothing Is Impossible Reflections on a New Life.* New York: Random House, 2002.

Shapiro, Joseph. *No Pity People with Disabilities Forging a New Civil Rights Movement.* New York: Random House, 1993.

Vujicic, Nick. With Kanae Vujicic. *Love Without Limits A Remarkable Story of True Love Conquering All.* Colorado Springs: WaterBrook, 2014.

Watterson, Kathryn. *Not by the Sword, New York: Simon and Schuster, 1995.*

Yancey, Philip. *Disappointment with God Three questions no one asks aloud. *Grand Rapids: Zondervan, *1988.*

Yancey, Philip. *Prayer Does It Make Any Difference?* Grand Rapids: Zondervan, 2006.

Yancey, Philip. *Where Is God When It Hurts? A Comforting, Healing Guide for Coping with Hard Times.* Grand Rapids: Zondervan, 1990.

Zola, Irving. *Missing Pieces: A Chronicle of Living With a Disability.* Philadelphia: Temple, 1982.

Zondervan Bible Publishers. *The Holy Bible New International Version.* Grand Rapids: Zondervan, 1990.

Zondervan Bible Publishers. *Women of Faith Study Bible.* Grand Rapids: Zondervan, 2001.

About the Authors

William (Bill) L. Rush (1955-2004) was an accomplished Nebraskan journalist and disability rights advocate and the author of *Journey Out of Silence* (available through Amazon online). He was a beloved husband, son and brother, and also a recognized church and community leader. Bill was a self-declared "recreational level" chess player, who enjoyed competing in local tournaments and in the Cornhusker State Games. Many of the chapters included in this memoir are taken from a compilation of writings that William Rush had earmarked for inclusion in this, his second book.

Christine (Chris) Robinson is the widow of William L. Rush and an emerging writer through this memoir. She is an occupational therapist and psychotherapist who owns and works for The Canadian Self-Reg Clinic Inc. Christine currently lives nestled into the trails of the Niagara Escarpment in Ontario, Canada. She appreciates time with her family, friends, and her church and local chorister communities. Often you will find her walking or cycling on the local trails, while also deepening her relationship with God. When she is able, she can also be found reconnecting with the people and places, still important to her, in Nebraska.